INTERNATIONAL TEXTBOOKS IN ART EDUCATION

Italo L. de Francesco, Consulting Editor

Design
a search for essentials

An Australian stone churinga with tribal symbol. (Courtesy of the University Museum of the University of Pennsylvania, Philadelphia, Pa.)

Design
a search for essentials

ELIZABETH ADAMS HURWITZ
Professor, Art Education
Kutztown State College

INTERNATIONAL TEXTBOOK COMPANY • SCRANTON, PENNSYLVANIA

Second Printing, June, 1967

 Printed in the United States of America. Designed by Angelo D. Rinaldi. Library of Congress Catalog Card Number: 64–14429.

TO MY GRANDFATHER
AND GOOD COMPANION
WARREN PERRY ADAMS

For now we see through a glass, darkly; but then face to face: now I know in part; but then shall I know even as also I am known.

I Corinthians XIII, 12

Editor's Preface

It is unusual for editor and author to have been professionally related over a long period of time. That is precisely the case in this instance—a condition which has permitted candid, thorough, and occasionally severe criticism of a manuscript from minimal outline to completed work ready for publication.

The author, a gifted painter and a talented teacher, is a meticulous draughtsman whether the medium be the brush, the word, or an idea. Deeply perceptive, highly sensitive, and always logical to a fault, she turns these gifts to a text which can only inspire to quality performance.

The mind perceives, the eye envisions, and the hand executes, in coordinated sequence, what the the emotions, the intellect, and the intuitive powers reveal. Thus design, be it decorative or structural, is at once expressive and disciplined. Nature is the source of man's inspiration for all he creates. From the most primitive and unspoiled motif to the sophisticated expression of the cultivated artist, earth, sea and sky, vegetation, animal life and human form—all these become sources of design if one but observes with minute care and deep respect.

Color, in its myriad moods and modes, adds dimension to the art of seeing. As decoration, symbol, or allegory, albeit as a scientific phenomenon, color is intrinsic in nature and enhances and gives life to art.

Thus, the author, in unique fashion, presents elements and principles which are historic and fundamental, yet fluid at the hand of the creative designer who seeks to express his own time and mood.

This then is a sound, inspiring and lucidly written text for students and teachers whose search goes beyond formula, but for an avenue leading to understanding and originality.

I. L. DE FRANCESCO

Acknowledgments

I am indebted to Dr. Italo de Francesco, President of Kutztown State College, not only for the opportunity to write and publish this textbook but also for his faith in its value to students and teachers of art. Without this kind of encouragement I should have hesitated to add another to the increasing number of books on the important subject of design.

Photographs of art and other objects in their collections were supplied by the University Museum of the University of Pennsylvania, Philadelphia; by the Stovall Museum of Science and History of the University of Oklahoma, Norman, Oklahoma; by the Reading Art Museum, Reading, Pennsylvania; and by the American Museum of Natural History, New York. The Eastman Kodak Company of Rochester, New York, granted permission to use diagrams from their published booklet, *Color as Seen and Photographed*. The Munsell Color Company, Inc., Baltimore, Maryland, provided charts of the Munsell system of color notation and I am appreciative of the help and suggestions of Mr. W. H. Hale of their organization. For photographs of nature, of her students' crafts, and of her own pottery I am indebted to Josephine Krum of Linden Hall School for Girls, Lititz, Pa.; to John Stolz for his furniture designs; to Eugene Bowman, Ephrata, Pa., for assistance in preparing photographic material and for his unusual close-up studies; to Mrs. Harriet Nichols for preparation of the manuscript.

The designs of a number of students of the Kutztown State College are shown and identified. I am indebted not only to them but also to members of the teaching staff under whose direction the work was done: Mrs. Rose Marie Sloat, Miss Mary Grace Wible, Dr. Horace Heilman, Dr. Harold Mantz, Mr. Howard Collins, Mr. John Grossman, and Mr. John Sawyer, who also did the excellent photography of these works.

To the anonymous, but nevertheless identifiable, individual craftsmen who designed and executed long ago the weaving, masks, tools and utensils, the baskets and ceremonial pottery, the sculpture, toys and illustrations I am also sincerely grateful, for these typify that rich and ancient heritage of design in which all may share.

Contents

Introduction

Man's idea of what is beautiful is inevitably derived from nature's forms. In nature what holds together will live; what is weak or disused will die. A part of nature himself, man knows this from the inner feeling of health in the strong, working parts of his own body. "Wholesome" is a useful and concrete word for this concept. What stays whole will survive, and this is true in art as well as in nature. When man creates a form of his own, he cannot escape the need for the same wholeness. Each part of the new form he is creating must belong to the whole. The whole must gather the separate impacts of the parts, be they many or few. The whole thing must convey one meaning whether it be done in an hour or a lifetime.

A work of art, unlike a child or a grain of wheat, is not born; it is made. Part by part, out of materials which already have their physical being in that other, more comprehensive order of life, man shapes and uses rather than creates. What he may create, if one may say this without sacrilege, is meaning. Somewhere in the dim past of his life on this earth it became of supreme importance to him to convey this meaning to the minds of others.

Impulsive gestures, the core of all of man's experience, led him to start on the long road of art. The gestures of his hands were the beginnings of language. Impulsive sounds became words and music. With movement of his flexible and erect body, he found a way to communicate his pride and love, his fear and exaltation in the dance. And with that same beautifully coordinated body he learned to shape the insensate material about him to his needs. What he formed "in the elder days of art" was inevitably formed, subconsciously right. With eyes and hands long used to the sight and touch of living things, he instinctively reproduced their sureness of proportion, their basic strength and flexibility, and their rhythmic growth.

We are not close to living, natural forms today. Our lives have become filled with man's own imperfect products. Books about design would not need to be written were it not that we lack that intimacy with the physical phenomena of life which we once had. Our need to reach the minds of others is as impelling as was primitive man's, perhaps even more so. Tradition has given us a language of words, sounds, movements, forms, and colors which we may, even must, learn by rote if we are to communicate at all in the society of man. To master even this language would fill a lifetime. Nevertheless, since we are human, we must communicate not by writ and rote, but out of the individual experience of our lives and by whatever means and ineffectual skills we have.

It is for all, for children, for maturing students, and for others who feel this need, that this book is written. It contains few long words and few ideas, if any, which are not drawn from life, from physical, concrete reality. If this book does no more than reveal the world of living design about us, it will have fulfilled some of its purpose. If it persuades some to think as well as to feel, something will be gained for the serious student. If it serves to show that to design is natural and inevitable, that no child is too young to seek its essentials or anyone too old in the ways of art to relearn them at the original source, it will satisfy the humble hopes of the author.

ELIZABETH ADAMS HURWITZ

Design
a search for essentials

Why We Strive to Create

I

Sun prominence, Mount Wilson Observatory. (Courtesy of the American Museum of Natural History, New York, N. Y.)

[Art is] an ever-living question, asked of the visible world by the visual sense.

CONRAD FIEDLER
Uber den Ursprung der künstlerischen Thätigkeit, 1887

Ferns fan out on a wooded roadside to reach the light.

THE PERVADING SENSE OF ORDER

There is one most important and profound concept which man has formed in his long struggle to understand the universe of which he is a part. This is the conviction that, at its core, there is an eternal plan of immense proportion and grandeur. It is from this conception of order in all living things that the arts of man have stemmed.

If one can find a place where the earth has been undisturbed, there the rocks and soil obey only the forces of wind, water, and gravity. There is a profusion of plants, insects, birds, and animals almost beyond the mind of man to count. Yet this scene is not one of confusion. Rather, one is conscious of a natural order which results from the necessities of physical existence. Some rocks have been where they are for a long time and will remain for centuries to come. Some, because of their makeup, will crumble and fall. Stronger plant forms will push aside the weaker ones. Animate creatures will live and die. The wind and rain will inevitably be followed by summer's heat, and that, too, will give way to the icy stillness of winter.

We are, at first, likely to be lost in the infinite number and variety of the things we see. Somewhat like an infant, we see a world of colors, shapes, forms, and textures in an indistinguishable blur. However, when we grow accustomed to being alone and take time to observe more carefully, we begin to see each form as a complete design in itself, suited exactly to its function as a part of nature.

A rock seems to be held together by its very hardness. A tree has sufficient strength to cling firmly to the rocky soil and yet is pliant enough to yield to the wind. Even the most delicate grasses are so constructed that they will bend to the pressure of our feet but rebound when we have walked on. Each form in nature has a central core of strength from which its more fragile parts seem to spring. Indeed, the very parts of parts—the grains of wheat in the spike, the tentative tender buds of leaves, the inmost delicate centers of flower stamens

A hardy young mullen weathers the winter.

and pistils—are alike in one respect. They are held together in a structure so protectively firm that only the most wanton handling can destroy them. To live and complete their physical being, this wholeness must withstand the natural stresses of life.

In the mountains, large rocks jut out from the surrounding earth in an uncompromising angularity. This angle vaguely repeats itself in a distant ridge, of which the mountain under our feet proves to be a part. A river in the valley has cut through the rocks and revealed the inner structure of the mountains, partially composed of layer upon layer of softer rock of varying colors and thicknesses. Conforming to the core of the ridge and yet obeying its own rhythmic pattern, it is very much like the mud along the banks of a small stream in spring flood. In fact, it once was soft mud and was pressed and changed into stone by chemical reactions deep within the earth. In places it has been heaved upward in a mighty sweep, yielding to forces within the earth which lifted the core rocks into great mountains. A highway has sliced deftly through the rounded hills but tunneled through or discreetly skirted the angular ones. Blasting has only served to break these rocks into tremendous smooth facets which pick up the light of the sun in early morning and late afternoon as a cut jewel does in the mounting of a ring.

If we have ever come upon the bones of some wild creature, we may have noticed that its skeleton, too, has a wholeness about it. Although the separate bones have long felt the cleansing action of wind, rain, and sun, they still fit together. The skeleton is a more beautiful piece of engineering design than one might find in any of man's efforts at locomotion. These bones are, in fact, designs for flying, for running, for fighting, and for protection of the animal in all the natural dangers of its precarious life. How completely do the skull and the pelvic bones encase the vital but perishable parts of a moving creature! Perhaps our eyes have chanced upon a snail with his shell. So defenseless is this soft creature that it may hardly be said to have a skeleton, yet its shell is so designed that it can roll up tightly and safely within itself.

Bones are the structural design of the animate creature.

Serpentine shale on the face of the Blue Ridge.

But we need not find a primeval spot. We may sense the same ordered profusion on the walks of a well-kept garden or in a well-cultivated corn field. Only when the animate and inanimate forms of nature are not permitted their natural existence, being forced by the hand of man or by the elements to perform feats unsuited to their physical structure, do we have an uneasy sense of incompleteness or confusion. Content, we let our eyes be filled and our hands touch at will, our ears be open to the sounds of wind in trees or water on rocks. We have a sense of well-being just to be a part of it. This is an experience everyone should have, and often.

Now, all who love the world of nature and respond as creatures of nature themselves may experience these things and go their way refreshed. But an artist, especially, needs to know how to lay his senses open to the beauty and to the inevitable rightness of the forms in nature.

WHO IS AN ARTIST?

The word "artist" here and throughout this book means any person who works with both love and skill to make useful, meaningful, and beautiful things. To work with love means to work with continuous devotion and personal involvement in the doing. To work with skill means that a high degree of achievement and a unique quality of personal expression are recognizable in the result. The word "artist" is quite properly applied to a child and also to a primitive craftsman, provided they work with the highest degree of personal expression and skill of which they are capable. It may also include those who do many kinds of work not usually called art, such as cooking, gardening, homemaking, and teaching. It may but does not necessarily include the professional, such as the pianist, the dancer, the novelist, the landscape or portrait painter, the architect, potter, and industrial designer.

It is from an understanding of nature's forms and of his own existence as a part of nature that man has learned to give the work of his hands an enduring beauty. He does not create in the sense that the universe was created. Compared with the designs of nature any artist's most expressive forms must fade into weak and inadequate gestures. Nor does he duplicate, imitate, or attempt to compete with the Creator's purpose. Instead, he tries to understand and to use materials in harmony with their own natural character. In the same way, he tries to make use of his own powers as they were intended in the plan of nature to be used.

INSIGHT

What happens when we open our senses to a profound experience of nature is entirely personal. Subconsciously, while we stopped to listen, look, and touch, we were growing in power to understand ourselves. Perhaps we can identify some of the moments when this was happening. When we first saw the skeleton, we probably were not very scientific, nor were we immediately ready to accept it as a beautiful thing. We could not help feeling first that this had once been a living creature. We could almost feel it panting, see it curl up to protect itself and extend its claws to fight for life. The twisted tree may have reminded us of the way we turn about in the force of a storm. We, too, sprawled in the sun and huddled in the rain. Perhaps we dropped a lump of clay in the very path where ants of a colony were working. We could not help but sympathize with their confusion until they found a detour.

In some way we were *imagining ourselves within* the life of these things of nature. We cannot be sure just how much the other sensate beings of the earth can do this. If we watch an animal when it discovers another of its kind no longer living, we recognize some of our own reactions to the skeleton. We can see the involuntary surprise and sudden stiffened alertness, somewhat like fascination and like fear. We watch its futile search for movement and response. We see it draw away not in aversion, but in acceptance of the fact of death. Nor can we be sure that animals share with us the ability to learn from experiences other than their own. It seems that man is more highly sensitive to other forms of nature and their needs. He is gifted with *insight,* the ability to see within. We do know that this peculiarly human development of mind and spirit gives us some of our richest experiences of wholeness. We feel at one with nature and with ourselves. Insight is the reservoir of experiences from which man draws his power to create and also the common sense to make his creations of value.

Redwing's nest left untouched by the harvesters.

THE URGE TO HELP THINGS GROW, TO CONSERVE AND PROTECT

Along our way we caught a glimpse of green things under a heavy mass of dead leaves. We stooped and carefully freed the shoots. In our garden we may discover that one branch of a fruit tree is scarring another by rubbing against it. We wisely prune the less vigorous branch, permitting the other to grow. We remove rocks which make insecure footing near the place we live. We encourage the plants and living creatures we enjoy the most to thrive near us. We teach some animals to work and live with us. Ourselves not the strongest nor the longest-lived of creatures, we see to the protection of those from which we can obtain food and material for clothing. In doing this sometimes we learn as much as we teach. Last year's fledgling orioles seem to know exactly how to make a nest, a construction of grasses, twigs, down, and leaves on swaying branches far enough above the ground for safety. We toss a few raveled rags on the ground for them to intertwine with other thin, tough fibers. They often carry the rags to the tree but leave them unused to dangle in a nearby crotch. *Instinct,* the power to deal with physical needs which is inborn, is guiding their choice of materials and ways of building. Man no longer builds by instinct, but he has learned much from those who do.

The cat will be having her kittens soon. We prepare a soft, clean bed for her in a sunny spot; then one morning we hear the unmistakable piercing voice of her young from a dark corner in the barn. If we move them to the box, she will soon carry them back. Our insight this time is obviously at fault. We have meddled in a task which she is especially equipped to do. Nevertheless, she struts a little with pride; she will even leave them while we linger to handle and admire. She has become accustomed to our way with animal-kind. She understands and trusts us.

Mother cat with a problem.

In these acts we have felt a reassuring sense of their value to us. Living things have responded. The branch we cut will form a protective scar tissue. We shall enjoy the restored symmetry of the tree and later the full perfection of its fruit to eat. We have learned to respect the way animals and birds work to solve their own problems. We now recognize that when we tamper with their growth, transplant them from their natural soil, pen them in enclosures they would not have chosen by instinct, provide them with foods unlike those they find themselves, we have given them new problems with which they may or may not be able to cope. We are now responsible for understanding their needs. They must adjust to us, but we also must respond to them.

We need them and they need us, and not only for physical needs. We know that the very touch of our hands, our presence in their stalls, the sound of our voices becomes a part of their lives and ours. We remember the remark of a very old lady whose house plants are always in bloom. "You have to talk to them," said she. We are not sure how to talk to a geranium, but we reserve our skepticism.

Mutual dependence and affection are the source of insight.

Young herds are bred with care and intelligence.

Man still weaves his own roof in southeastern Asia. (Courtesy of the University Museum of the University of Pennsylvania, Philadelphia, Pa.)

It is true that we do not need a geranium. We cannot eat it, wear it, or make a house of it. But the very act of cultivating it for its beautiful foliage and flower and for the tang of its odor has made us realize that we need it and many other things for a different reason. We need the presence of natural beauty.

We have discovered that "man cannot live by bread alone." We are more content (contained within) and cognizant (knowing) of our own being when our place to live is in order, our bodily needs are foreseen, and our relations with other living creatures are assured. Our minds and spirits are then free to enjoy as well as to use the world about us. We do not know that man is alone in having this urge to improve his surroundings. We cannot tell whether or not other creatures of nature are open to the sensation of beauty aside from usefulness. But we can be quite sure that all of these needs are very urgent in us and that we are unusually sensitive to them. They have impelled man to do many things over and above solving his physical problems of finding food, shelter, and clothing and moving about to keep his growing family alive. All of the arts man has devised to make living more comfortable and satisfying have arisen from this basic desire.

Man's increasing insight into the nature of other living forms has made it possible for him to transcend his physical needs. Out of his understanding of the instinctive ways of living among other creatures stemmed most of man's dramatic arts. He imitated bird and beast in their ways of fighting and hunting, and often he invoked their courage and pride by wearing their borrowed plumage, talons, and teeth. He clothed himself in their skins to strike terror in his enemies and masked his pallor under their manes. It is no wonder that the first crude attempts to give form to the gods in wood and stone bear the aspect of wild beasts. It was a long age before man had the temerity to carve a god with the face of a man. Both sculpture and painting began in the time when man accepted himself as a part of animate creation, and long before he thought of himself as its master.

An Alaskan helmet of wood, leather, and hair. (Courtesy of the University Museum of the University of Pennsylvania, Philadelphia, Pa.)

Garden wall of adobe brick and the cacti of the desert.

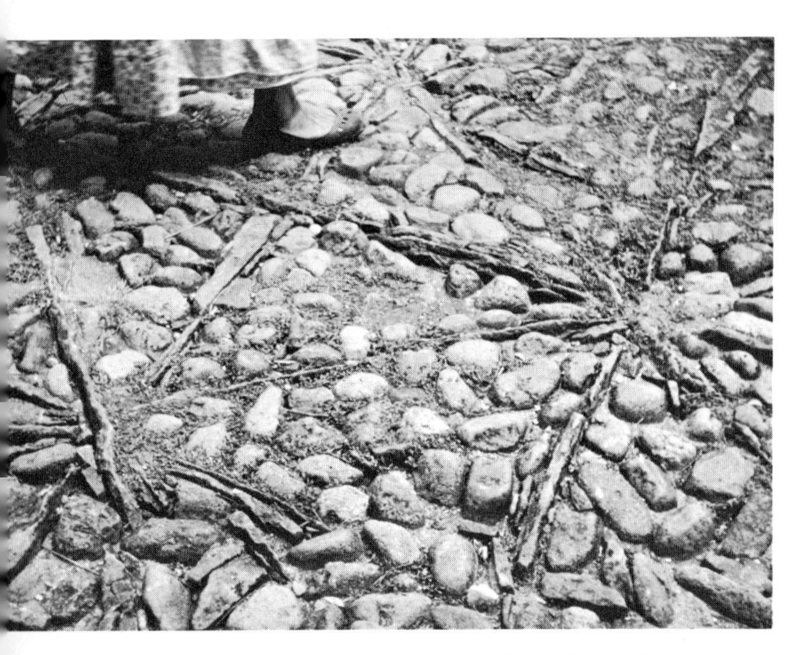

Pavement of pebbles in San Miguel d'Allende, Mexico.

A buffalo robe tells the story of the war of the plains. (Courtesy of the University Museum of the University of Pennsylvania, Philadelphia, Pa.)

THE URGE TO COMMUNICATE AND TO SHARE EXPERIENCE

We could not live without contact with other human beings. Not only do we have actual physical need to cling together for protection; the sound of others' voices, the touch of their hands, the expressions in their faces, the feeling of working together are vital to us. Children and even grown men and women become something less than human if they are deprived of these things. All our experiences would be meaningless without them. A baby's whimper on awaking will rise to a hearty wail when his mother comes near him. He will cling to her when both are in danger and be quiet at her touch. They respond to each other. Her irritation will make him cross, and her smile will teach him to be happy. Children spend many of their waking hours quarreling or competing with each other for the attention of their parents. They tease and irritate each other endlessly, domineering over the younger and weaker ones. However, a sudden attack from the outside or a calamity within the family will find them defending a staunch united front. They have a sure sense of interdependence. Only when some unnatural circumstances have made it difficult for each to communicate with the others can this sense of belonging fail to develop. So impelling is this urge to communicate that a child born both blind and deaf will resort to screaming tantrums, striking at persons within reach in an effort to make contact. Other children in the same family will try to hear for the deaf, see for the blind. They find a way to help him to be one of them. Human experiences must be shared, or they will have no human value.

This urge and power to communicate is not exclusively human. Birds in flight will turn at the direction of a leader. Crows set a sentry in a high tree and rise to his cawing signal of danger. When fire starts in the forest, the news of danger has been spread in the animal world. A steady stream of wild creatures are running not to catch and kill each other, but to outrun their common disaster. We may watch, if we do not disturb them, how animals and birds woo their mates. They also educate their young not only in foraging and defensive skills but also in proper respect for their elders and natural leaders. They give man, too, warning of common danger, and they do accept human aid when they are in trouble. Whether they communicate is hardly in doubt. The puzzle is, how do they do it?

Man has given to this urge to *communicate* the major part of his time and effort. His success has been remarkable though not complete. In making himself understood by others of his kind he has attained considerable skill. To communicate, he invented *languages,* using gestures, sounds, and drawings or symbols, and giving them particular meanings mutually acceptable to other human beings. One can make physical wants and intentions known in any part of the world by gestures of the hands or body. Man has invented words for most of the actual objects, actions, and aspects of the physical world. Pictures or graphic symbols convey some ideas even more clearly than gestures or words.

Drawing probably originated in impulsive gesture, and in some ways it has remained essentially that. When we try, however, to make clear some of the experiences which stir us more deeply, we find difficulty. Yet these are the very things which we have the strongest urge to share. To communicate them, man has perfected innumerable combinations of gestures, words, sounds, and graphic markings. After infancy, children spend almost all their time and adults a great deal of their time practicing them. Some gestures, words, and symbols are understood by almost all peoples. Others are quite impossible to translate from one group of people to another. Nevertheless, it is from these forms of language (gestures, sound, and words) that many of the visual arts of man have developed. Writing, lettering, illustration, advertising, chart- and map-making are familiar visual art forms which originated in simple communication. Recognizable symbols are seen on articles of daily use, in architecture, in sculpture, in painting. In the dance and on the stage are also evidences of the need for visual communication in the more abstract arts.

An Australian stone churinga with tribal symbol. (Courtesy of the University Museum of the University of Pennsylvania, Philadelphia, Pa.)

We share with all human beings who have ever lived on the earth these three urges: first, to understand nature; second, to adjust ourselves to it and to use it to make life more satisfying; and third, to communicate our feelings and purposes to other living beings. Fourth, we have learned to combine our efforts with others, for together we can often reach solutions which would have been impossible alone. This applies to more than the physical needs of man. He plays, works, sings, dances, and worships with others because of an impelling urge to share himself. All four of these urges are concerned with being like others and being liked or accepted by them. Because the arts which sprang from these basic urges are understood by almost everyone, they make us conscious of the likeness or wholeness of the human race. Some of the important arts which have developed very highly because they are performed by people of many different skills working together are town and city planning, architecture, symphonic music and opera, and drama.

THE URGE TO BELONG

There is another, fifth, urge in man. This is the desire to belong, to identify himself, to feel that he is an important part of an important whole. To understand it, one must study the few primitive societies of man now living on the earth. Almost all tribes we know have some communal organization, some forms of communication, and some graphic symbols, devices, or decorative patterns which distinguish them from other tribes. Membership in a tribe is jealously guarded. We do not know whether the mark of an individual man's identity or the tribal markings were the first to be inscribed on the bodies and on the possessions of primitive man. But one might almost feel that a single person in a primitive society does not really exist except as a member of the tribe.

Peruvian implements and utensils of wood suggest that forms persist though symbols change. (Courtesy of the University Museum of the University of Pennsylvania, Philadelphia, Pa.)

Man has been called the tool-using animal. Tools may have been the first things marked as a symbol of ownership. For instance, a piece of obsidian (natural glass) has a good cutting edge for slashing tangled vines, peeling the bark of a tree, and skinning an animal. Because a man found it useful, he might place a mark on it, even make a pouch and sling it from his wrist or neck. He might use this mark on all that belonged to him and his family. Owning and being skillful with a good tool would give the man considerably more power and prestige than others. Possibly the mark of a good craftsman eventually became the mark of the tribe.

A ceremonial paddle from the Austral Islands, its form developed from centuries of use. (Courtesy of the University Museum of the University of Pennsylvania, Philadelphia, Pa.)

Intricate geometric detail characterizes the decoration. (Courtesy of the University Museum of the University of Pennsylvania, Philadelphia, Pa.)

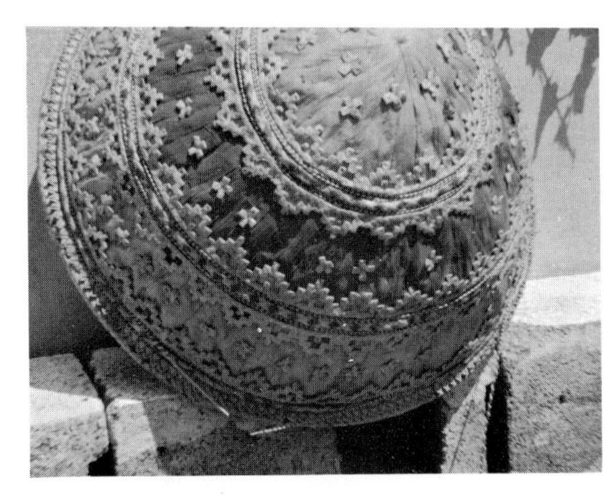

Food basket from the Philippine Islands.

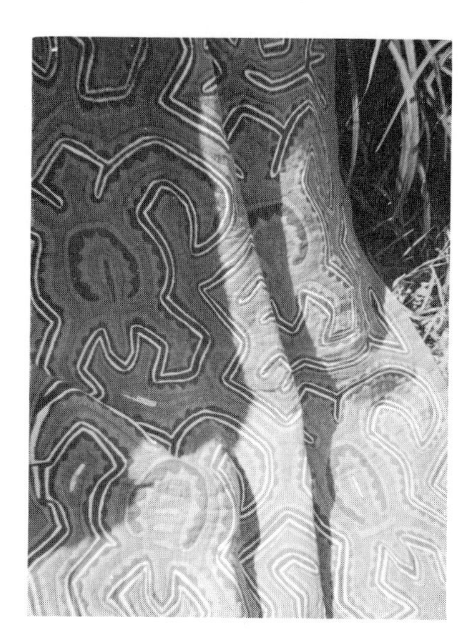

Abstract symbols of man fill this appliqué made in Ecuador.

OWNERSHIP AND IDENTIFICATION

Museums are full of tools which man has invented, and these collections show the change from primitive societies to the complex one in which we now live. We keep the tools and the objects made with them (such as weapons, pottery, weaving, baskets) not only because they are useful historically but because many of them are beautiful as well. The marks of ownership on tools and utensils also give us clues to the life of the people who made them, for they became a part of the communication system of the society in which they were made. The marks can still be read if we can discover the meanings, but oftentimes the meanings have been forgotten even by the people who still live in the same tribal groups in which the objects were made. As with other kinds of communication, we can easily translate the symbols or designs which represent things in nature such as birds, animals, plants, water, or the sun. But those which are more complex (or so simple that they are not identifiable) have no meaning for us, though they may be very beautiful. Nevertheless, they did serve originally as a means of distinguishing one tribe from another, and they identified the individual craftsman as a member of that tribe. Objects and tools of this kind are often called folk arts. The folk arts of each society of man show unique and definable differences from the folk arts of other societies. We recognize, for instance, a Navajo blanket, an Egyptian costume, a Persian miniature painting, or a Spanish sword by its *structural design* (the way it is made) and by its *decorative* design (the way it is enriched by symbols, colors, and tool marking).

Knitted bag from Solala in Guatemala.

Carding and spinning wool for rugs at the Instituto de San Miguel d'Allende, Mexico.

Women in Guatemala weave and wear the distinctive cloth of their village.

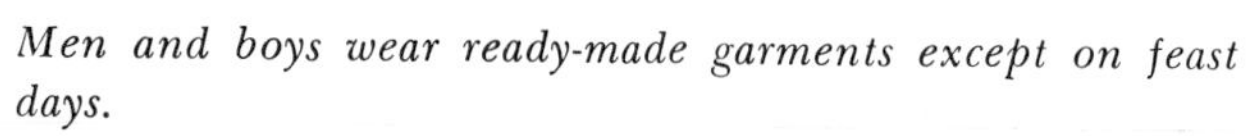

Men and boys wear ready-made garments except on feast days.

Roman Catholic saint carved by Guatemalan Indian craftsman.

FOLK ARTS

The folk arts, those which originate and are perfected within the communal life, are not separate from the practical arts, those by which natural materials are converted to suit basic needs. Nor are they separable from the language symbols man has invented. Rather, they combine these two. One might say that advertising design in modern times is a folk art. It is basically practical; for it is concerned largely with material needs. It is also a part of our communication system: it pictures, informs, and persuades us. It is full of symbols of ownership (such as trademarks and pictures recognizable to everyone), and as an art it bears the unmistakable character of our own society. We can usually distinguish, for instance, between a French poster and an American one, even without reading the captions.

Primitive folk arts are also characterized by the materials of which they are made and show a high degree of skill; for their makers were thoroughly familiar with both materials and tools. By the *style* of the symbols we know that the folk arts were made by particular groups of people at particular times in their development. Although they may not bear the signature or mark of the persons who made them, some particular pieces of pottery, carvings, some songs and legends, some buildings, some ways of dress seem to us more perfectly formed than others. The fact that these particular pieces are still intact may be further evidence, if we need it, that they were prized not only by their owners but also for trade with other people and even by looting enemies. Conquering armies often captured the artisans, scribes, and musicians and took them home as slaves. Sometimes the slaves were more highly civilized than the conquerors. These transplanted workers retained the integrity of their skills, and the actual forms of the folk arts were changed but never entirely lost. It is said that the craftsmen's influence accounts, partly, for the rapid blending of barbaric peoples with others whom they invaded. We might almost read the history of roving man by studying folk-art forms alone. They give us much knowledge about the beginnings of civilizations which still survive.

Egyptian hand maidens in procession; from a model 2100 B.C. (Courtesy of the University Museum of the University of Pennsylvania, Philadelphia, Pa.)

THE PLACE OF THE ARTIST IN PRIMITIVE SOCIETIES

In simple societies, any person who has a special skill is highly regarded. Just as one who performs certain feats of bodily prowess is much admired, so one who excels in any of the tribe's means of communication or one who makes objects of value to everyone is rewarded by the tribe with special privileges. If his work is really essential, he will be responsible for training some young members of the group in the mysteries and skills of his craft.

It comes about quite naturally, therefore, that highly skilled persons develop a sense of pride in their work. They are personally responsible to the tribe. They may make spears, tell stories, dance in ceremonies, build houses, weave cloth, or do any of the things which the tribe needs. They compete with other skillful craftsmen; therefore, they must always improve their work. As the tribe's needs broaden and change, their products must meet those changed needs, and the symbols they use must convey new meanings.

So it is that in highly developed folk arts the work of an individual sometimes is valued by the tribe for the particular qualities which he alone

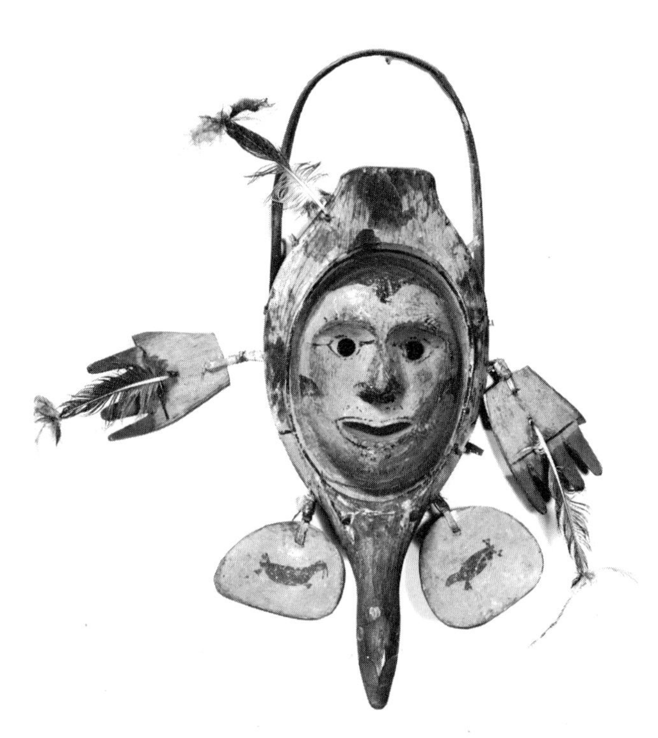

Wooden ceremonial mask from Alaskan island. (Courtesy of the University Museum of the University of Pennsylvania, Philadelphia, Pa.)

can put into it. When people are concerned with important events such as going to war, marrying, burying the dead, or selecting a chief, they call upon the most highly skilled and inventive members of each particular art. These are ceremonial activities in which the whole group is seeking some Power outside and above their own to help them. Such a ceremony will require the finest weapons for this Power to bless. The most perfectly formed vessels and utensils will hold a marriage dowry and the wedding gifts. The sheerest cloth will wrap the dead for a journey to the place of the gods. The most elaborate of houses and furnishings are necessary for the prestige of a new chief; for he represents the choice of the Supreme Being. It will be necessary for someone to make the images of the gods themselves for the tribal processions.

The singers, the dancers, the carvers, the tellers of tales, and those who pray must, for these occasions, surpass even themselves. They are responsible in a new way. They must somehow please a Being more powerful, more perceptive and more demanding of perfection than mere humans are. They must interpret His purposes to the people, for they stand between the people and the gods. Perhaps we can understand why artists traditionally have both humility and an intense pride in the importance of their work.

THE URGE FOR INDIVIDUAL EXPRESSION AND RECOGNITION

Just how and where and when a sixth urge or conviction began in man's conscious mind that he, personally, is of particular importance in the total plan of things cannot be told. The answer is lost in the countless generations of man's physical being. It has been covered over with the accumulation of things man has made, and forgotten sometimes in the urgency of fulfilling group purposes. Nevertheless, the work of his hands must always have revealed, as it does today, the personal identity of the one who made it. We have already seen how important the artist was in the communal life and how inevitably this must have led to personal pride and recognition for the individual artist.

The very existence of social groups must have begun because of the keener insight and intelligence of particular men. Group living was invented for self-protection; for by combining efforts and purposes, each man would be more likely to live than to die. Every society had to decide just what kinds of responsibilities each member would have. The group determined what each would do in return for this security and what penalties he must suffer if he did not perform his duties. The artist, too, was subject to the traditions of the group. He developed their symbols, carved their gods, faithfully transcribed their tribal lore. One may well imagine the courage it must have taken to invent new art forms, just as it took courage to voice inner convictions which were in any way different from the ideas of others, no matter how right they might seem to the unlucky possessor of a more perceptive brain. That there were men who had that kind of courage in every group we can see by the very fact that group life and arts did change. Old ways of life and old forms of art were discarded for better ones. We have seen that whole barbaric tribes have been known to learn even from a few captive artisans, musicians, and seers. It is likely that these slaves led a precarious existence, even with special privileges.

We must credit a few perceptive individuals in every society for the very fact that there is any large agreement upon the ultimate purposes of societies now existing. More than that, we must credit man with an unusual power to absorb new and better ways of living. These ways of group living are becoming more alike than they are different all over the world, now that it takes only a few hours to fly from one side of the globe to the other. The indigenous tribal and national arts (those which are developed by separate peoples for their own needs) are being replaced by the arts of industrial civilizations. Machines are supplying the products for group living, and the individual craftsman is gradually withdrawing from a futile conflict with the mass production which machines make possible. His insight into the needs and purposes of his own people will not be replaced for a long time.

THE PLACE OF THE ARTIST IN DEMOCRATIC SOCIETIES

The chief difference between societies of men now seems to lie in the conflict between the group purposes and the individual rights of each man: whether man exists for the state or the state for man. The artist, like all perceptive individuals, stands squarely in the center of this conflict. Some societies in the past have permitted a great deal of variation and deviation in the life of their members. Some religious leaders of every land have had insight and faith in the individual nature of man. They saw his individual importance in the total scheme of things. But some societies cannot accept the responsibilities of this mighty conception; for the implications are these: *If each person is of value to society because of his individual abilities, these gifts must be cultivated as highly as possible. Society must give full range to each person's life; it must not deny him the right to education, full self-expression, and complete freedom within the moral law. Nor can the individual renounce his responsibility to contribute his best toward the highest attainable good of all men.* Where this concept may lead the artist no one knows, but it has given an entirely new direction to the minds of men since the eighteenth century, a short time when one considers how long it was first voiced by the great religious leaders and philosophers of ancient times.

We do know that societies which deny the concept of the individual rights of man often resort to false promises of individual freedom and ownership of land to win their people. They have a great deal of trouble with simple people who are attached to the soil and also with the highly learned. They have even more trouble with those who follow the teachings of great religious leaders; for these persons put the responsibility for moral and spiritual decisions upon each man's conscience. Artists, who cannot work unless they trust in inner convictions of rightness in whatever they make, are difficult citizens indeed in an authoritarian state. Many religious leaders, scientists, philosophers, and artists have tried to work in parts of the world where the group purposes have been put above the rights of individual men. This is evidence of their willingness to contribute their own gifts to the betterment of all. But many of these men and women have discovered at great cost the fallacy and hypocrisy of political thought in communistic or socialistic states. The fact that these highly useful people often turn to areas of the world where primitive human beings have need of their skills is also very revealing. Oftentimes what they learn there has benefited the rest of the world. People who live close to nature have some gifts of spiritual perception, healing, artistry, and knowledge of man's own nature that we have either forgotten or never knew.

SOCIAL EXPERIMENTS

The American schools have committed themselves to the concept of the intrinsic value of each person in our total society. We insist upon each person's right to reach the fullest possible use and enjoyment of his powers. We believe that in this way we will attain thc highcst good of all. The men who first conceived of this kind of education called it a holy experiment. Certainly it has had some of the difficulties and some of the frustrations of all experiments. We find ourselves teaching with imperfect skills; for schools have traditionally insisted on uniformity rather than on individuality in thinking. We discover with dismay that human beings are not always eager to learn. Often they would rather follow traditions than think for themselves. Many would be glad to have all the benefits of education but are unwilling to contribute to the cost and labor. Some people in every society would gladly deny their personal convictions for profit or for temporary security. The worldwide implications of the concept of individual freedom itself have only begun to dawn upon us. It is going to be necessary to enlist the most perceptive individuals of every land as teachers of their own people; for the society of men is turning out to be as far-reaching as the minds of men can communicate with each other. It may be that the place of the artist in this new, larger society will be a great one; for the arts have always been a sure means of communication and artists have an intuitive respect for individuality in people. If the artist is to have this greater importance, a student of art must learn to accept a personal responsibility for his own convictions in the work which he will do. He cannot neglect to learn the nature of this world by constant study and observation. He must try to sense the important principles of all physical life, because he is a part of it. He must learn and use whatever means of communication he can to understand the life of other human beings and enlarge his own. He will have to organize his own life so that his efforts will contribute tangibly to the community, large or small, in which he works. His work, in a society which believes in individual self-fulfillment, will no longer be anonymous. It will bear his "signature." He can look forward to calling it his own. But how can he be sure it is his own?

DISCOVERING ONESELF THROUGH ART EXPERIENCES

In choosing art as our profession we have set ourselves upon the task of self-discovery, the most difficult one that human beings have yet undertaken. Many people feel that they learn a great deal about themselves when they explore their capabilities in the arts. Some make art their lifework because they find that they can fulfill their own particular gifts. Some artists teach, because they have much to give and also to receive from others. Some choose to learn, because they feel that they can at least earn their living by art skills though they claim no special gifts.

Others become interested in art, not for their own way of life, but because it helps them to understand themselves and others. Many art experiences which have proved to be of help in this important task of self-discovery are suggested in this book. Some of the skills of visual communication which have to be learned are practiced. A few of the sources from which artists have often derived inspiration are pictured. The experience of many great teachers has been drawn upon. Some of the evidences of growth in individual power of self-expression are shown in the artwork of students and of persons who are working in particular art fields.

The six urges in man which lead him to a productive and creative life are felt by everyone: to *understand* and to *use* the physical world of which we are a part, to *communicate* to others our understanding of it, to *share* the work of solving human problems, to feel the security of *belonging* to a group and, in turn, the group's belonging to us; to *find our own particular place* in the total plan of things. A few great men, such as Dr. Albert Schweitzer, have made us realize that all of the arts of man are one in purpose and that human beings are different not in kind, but in opportunity. They themselves have not been too busy to seek out the mysteries of nature, even to turn their own soil, make their own houses. They have studied the arts of man and practiced them; they have served the needy, taught the ignorant, healed the sick. They have contributed their own work to societies they lived in and given new directions to the purposes of man. They are, indeed, great individuals. They make us feel that they are like ourselves, not different in kind but greater in the degree to which they were able to fulfill all these urges. Because they lived so fully aware of their own powers and responsibilities, we can be sure that the effort toward self-discovery will be very rewarding to each of us.

THINGS TO THINK ABOUT

1. Wherever you live and work, find a place where you can be alone in nature; learn to know it well, in all weathers; go there often; watch, listen, and touch. If you cannot find such a place, then cultivate house plants, have an aquarium, care for a pet.
2. Visit a natural-history museum, a zoological park; watch, draw, discuss, and read about nature forms.
3. Watch a pair of birds build their nest, a mother animal care for her young.
4. Discuss with a musician what he hears in the woods, in a factory, on the street.
5. Make friends with a good carpenter, shoemaker, tailor. Discuss with each of them what constitutes a really good piece of his work.
6. Read some excerpts from letters by famous artists to their own friends in which they describe their work.
7. Read a description by an anthropologist about some primitive society.
8. Read about the place and work of the artist in a totalitarian society.
9. Discuss with an artist-craftsman what he feels about his work and why he does it.
10. Talk with a child about the pictures he makes; try to understand and recognize all he wanted to express.
11. If you had all the art skills at your command, what ideas would you most like to express?
12. What folk arts are a part of your own heritage of culture by virtue of your family's racial, religious, or occupational background?
13. Do any members of your family now participate in the traditional folk arts of Question 12?
14. What symbols such as crests, coats of arms, trademarks, or other designs of identification do you consider yours?

THINGS TO DO

1. Sit in a meadow or a garden and trace the outline of each different kind of leaf you can reach without getting up.
2. Gather the stalks of all the different grasses you can find along a roadside. Lay them between sheets of thin paper and run a brayer, lightly inked, across them.
3. Rub with a pencil on soft, strong paper held firmly on the surface of different kinds of rocks.
4. Make impressions in soft clay or plaster with shells, bark, seeds.
5. Make blueprints of wing forms, leaf skeletons, hairs, tendrils.
6. Gather twigs and vines and place them in a container. Revolve the container behind a translucent glass or paper, lighted from the back. Enjoy the changing silhouettes.

How We Recognize Beauty

II

Every part is disposed to unite with the whole, that it may thereby escape from its own incompleteness.

LEONARDO DA VINCI
Codex Atlantico

The trunk of the white birch tree invites the touch.

THE SEARCH FOR ESSENTIALS

All of the things which man has made for his own needs have their counterpart in the great plan of nature. He has invented no different structural principle, no way of building or moving which has not been derived from the original design. It is true that understanding of these underlying principles came slowly and often with great difficulty to the mind of man. Like us on our mountain top, all he saw at first was a profusion of forms, all he felt was awe and considerable fear. Moreover, he was not an observer only, but an actual part of it. He had a body of his own, subject to all the impact of the elements and plagued with the same needs for food, water, and air. Nor was he by any means as strong or as large as many other creatures. He had little time and plenty to do just to protect his almost defenseless body, find the wherewithal to live, bring forth his children and care for them until they could help themselves. Contemplation, philosophizing, even remembering and reasoning were luxuries he could ill afford, but it seems that of all nature he was uniquely equipped for them. How else can we conceive of this creature, man, having the courage to pit himself against the elements, to force the earth to feed, clothe, and shelter him, and to wander at will anywhere on its surface and even below and above it? Why should he presume that he should one day understand yet other and more profound principles of life? We can only know that, like all of the forms in life, he will inevitably fulfill the purpose for which he is designed.

How shall we keep these concepts within our grasp? Is it enough to spend a lazy afternoon incuriously exposing ourselves to nature's sights and sounds? Someone has said that artists are like children because they try to retain the fresh vision and impulsive curiosity of youth. They can, more than most other people, give themselves thoroughly, like a child, to any experience they have and to any work they conceive. This is true. It is the reason why being an artist is a very rewarding way to live. Not only that but the artist does, more than any other worker, depend upon the sensitivity of his body as well as his mind to accomplish his purpose. Today many of the forms which artists plan to fill our needs are not even touched by human hands between drawing board and the retail merchant's shelf. No artist can hope to create even an intelligent solution to any human need without understanding his materials by feel and physical experience of them. Much less can he hope to create a beautiful thing unless he absorbs a sense of beauty, rightness, and order from nature itself. He must return again and again to the earth, to the sea; he must explore all forms of life. He is not only seeking their external appearance but trying to understand why they appear as they do; how their essential character is expressed visually and tangibly in the master plan.

Let us, then, return to our own mountain path. The longer we remain in one place the more keenly our minds begin to compare and reorganize our first impressions. We see that there are some growth principles which occur again and again in plants, animals, rocks, and water, in fact, in all forms of nature.

Diabinese crystals, magnified one thousand times. (Photomicrograph, courtesy of Charles Pfizer & Co., Inc., New York, N. Y.)

A colony of Penicillium Chrysogenum. (Photomicrograph, courtesy of Charles Pfizer & Co., Inc., New York, N. Y.)

THE CENTRAL PRINCIPLE

The first of these principles will be seen in the forms which radiate from a *center*. Notice how pine cones flare out, how lichens spread in successive layers. Flowers open to the light and enclose within a center the stamens and pistils which will make the seed. A spider lays out a spreading wheel of struts on which to stretch his web. A microscope will reveal that organic forms are built of cells, each of which has its living nucleus and a protective mass of protoplasm within a wall. The sun itself throws out light in all directions from its hot inner core. Scientists now surmise that the very pattern of the known universe, a central scheme of great magnitude, exists also in every infinitesimal particle of matter.

Tree roots tap the reservoir of moisture deep in rocky soil. (Courtesy of the American Museum of Natural History, New York, N. Y.)

THE AXIAL PRINCIPLE

Plants which live upon dry earth are almost invariably built upon another principle, the *axial* pattern of growth. They have a single strong vertical stem which branches out above the earth to catch light and penetrates deeply into the earth to find moisture and food. This principle repeats itself in the midveins and subordinate veins of leaves, buds, and seeds. The central and the axial principles are often combined; for the branches radiate from the trunk and as many small roots fan out from the tap root.

THE GEOMETRIC PRINCIPLE

Inert forms, like rocks and minerals, seem to have a built-in geometry. Quartz will cleave, or break into facets, at one angle; diamonds at another; slate, shale, and mica into thin layers. Only with great difficulty can they be cut against their "grain." Microphotography has revealed that this is due to their individually different atomic structure. Even pebbles, worn though they are by constant tumbling in a stream bed, show their original geometric form. They will conform roughly to the crystal forms they originally were, figures of three, four, five, six or more sides.

Pebbles are gradually shaped by the spring floods.

Organic forms of sea creatures turn to rock.

Inorganic forms break, decompose, become soil, and support life.

THE SPIRAL PRINCIPLE

Shell creatures that live in water often reveal still another structure, the *spiral,* which seems to constantly expand or to curl in toward a center, not directly like a wheel but indirectly. This beautiful self-contained form has caught the imagination of artists as no other one has. It is by no means limited to shells. Young ferns push spiral heads through the weight of leaves in spring. Many trees spread their branches spirally as well as radially along the trunk in order to obtain the greatest possible amount of light.

THE VERTEBRATE PRINCIPLE

Like the trees, most of the sensate creatures which move about have a single axis, the backbone. It is composed of many small bones fitted together. A firm encasement for the brain is balanced by a flexible tail. Arms and legs, like branches and roots in plant forms, are appended from the axis. They are vestigial at certain times in the animal's life and variable in number and shape, depending upon the needs of the creature.

Almost within the reach of our hands, forms following the central principle, the axial principle, the spiral principle, and the vertebrate principle can be seen in endless combinations. Variations of these hold together the outward and visible forms of all the world. They explain that sense of wholeness (a natural and inevitable experience, since

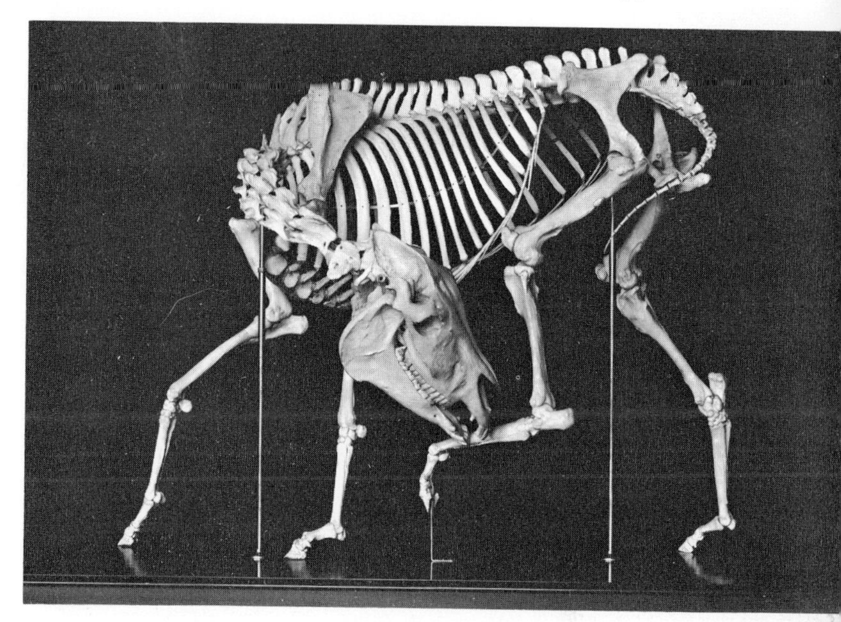

A donkey's skeleton, built for endurance and grace. (Courtesy of the American Museum of Natural History, New York, N. Y.)

our own bodies are so held) which seems to be inseparable from all the experiences which we call good. We love a pebble because we can grasp it wholly within the palm of the hand, a baby because it is so completely like ourselves. We fear things which we cannot see in their entirety. We cannot wholly accept a malformed being until we understand it. Perhaps children uproot things that grow, not so much from an urge to destroy them as to see with their own eyes how they are made. This sense of wholeness, of built-in strength, is the most important principle of man's art forms as well.

Our discoveries thus far on the mountain top have been only a part of the total experience to which we have opened our being. As time passes we begin to have a sensation of aliveness and movement all about us. No blade of grass is still; no stone seems dead, but, rather, it seems to wait. The trunks of trees seem to be thrusting out the branches, and roots seem to push into the soil. A procession of ants intent upon conserving the carcass of some larger insect go about their gruesome but orderly business of dismemberment. A hawk hovers long and suddenly darts to the edge of a thicket. The stem of elderberry we broke is overflowing with a milky life blood. Clouds roll up and rain falls. A flower closes its petals while a shower lasts and opens again to the sun. Movement is all about us. Our own heartbeats are a part of it.

Twisted tree stumps reveal the strain and stress of growth in rocky New England soil.

Lichens thrive on a fallen tree.

MOVEMENT AND GROWTH

As artists we need to know more than the structure of things. We must also try to understand how they move and have their being, how they begin and mature, fulfilling their natural purpose. We must learn how they undergo not the finality but the infinity of their last change in death; for it is clear that the end of one form in nature is but the beginning of another. The hardest rocks eventually are worn away. They are carried by wind and streams into the valleys. Plants absorb the minerals, grow and mature, and return their substance to the earth in changed form. Animals and birds consume the fruit and leaves and are returned themselves to the earth. This unending process has often been likened to a cycle, a movement which returns upon itself. To sense this wholeness of movement is much like sensing the oneness of each form we see.

INWARD AND OUTWARD MOVEMENT FROM A CENTER

In each center we find, whether it be in a whorl of leaves or in the eye of a turtle, we can feel both an inward and an outward movement. Rays of light seem to emanate from a spark and return to its burning core. It seems that for every thrust outward from the inmost growing center of a form there is a withdrawing inward. This feeling, too, has the satisfying completeness we experienced before. Indeed, knowing that our earth is a sphere, the very upthrusting movement of trees and plants and the upheaval of mountains are a part of the outward movement from its center. The falling to earth of meteors seems to prove to us the existence of an opposite, compensating pull from within. In miniature we might see this force in a bit of magnetic ore to which metal particles will cling.

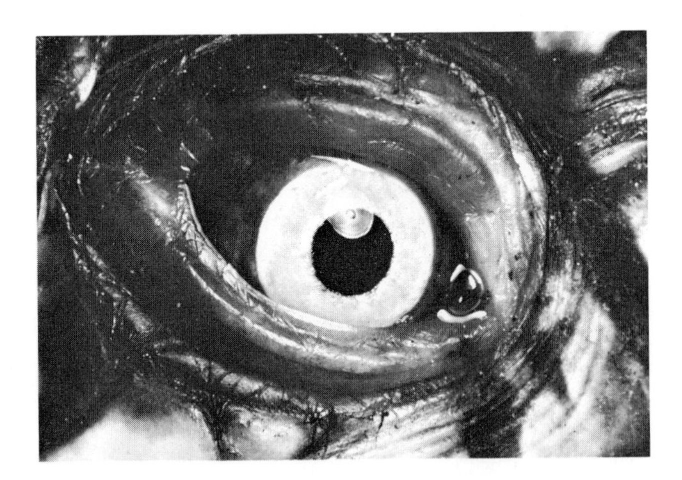

The eye of a turtle emerges from its horny rim. (Photograph by Eugene Bowman.)

Swirling water, pebbles, and expanding ice crystals have formed a pothole.

Caves formed by the tides in the Bay of Fundy.

THE PRINCIPLE OF EXPANSION AND CONTRACTION

Far from being unmoving and inert, the hills and valleys are in a constant condition of movement and change. The principle of their movement is simply described as upward and outward expansion counterbalanced by downward and inward contraction. A part of this tremendous principle, we recall, is the ebb and flow of the tide.

We shall find that the root, stem, branch, leaf, and seed patterns of each plant will prove to be variations upon an identical design. A hollow reed which supports itself by means of long columnar structures will prove to have leaves with parallel veining and a spike of seeds set into channeled pipes. It has been designed for life in a fluid environment. It will yield to the swift ebb and flow, yet stand upright until it has borne its seed. Rigidity and flexibility are both requirements of its nature.

GROWTH IS IMPLICIT IN STRUCTURE

We may learn much from watching a plant grow. Within the seed are all of the parts of the mature plant. When moisture sets the seedling free, the roots unerringly turn earthward toward the moisture and food the plant needs. The stem and leaves seek the light. Both upward and downward movement are implicit (implied or foreseen) in the plant's structure. Seen through a microscope, the root is equipped with a growing point which will penetrate the soil and find a hold in a crevice. The stem and leaf have channels through which to raise the moisture and food for the life of the plant and spongy cells to spread in the energy-creating light. In the flower are the cells which will enable the plant to produce countless identical plants of its own kind, to be returned to the earth and begin the process anew. Plants have been grown from grains and lotus seeds which have rested in Egyptian tombs for more than four thousand years. One might conceive that the forms of nature exist solely for the sake of growth and reproduction.

THE SPIRAL PRINCIPLE OF GRADUAL ASCENT AND DESCENT

So resilient are the structures of mountain pines and fruit trees that they will maneuver a footing on a rocky hillside, even though the gales sweep from all corners of the sky. Such forms are often seen twisted into a spiral. This is the principle of "yielding a little to endure a lot." Many tender forms, too weak in their own structure to rise vertically from the earth, turn themselves about in midair until they strike some upright thing. They twine around it and produce their leaves and fruit as they hang upon its strength. The bittersweet and the wistaria vines can strangle mature trees by this infinitely strong principle of spiral movement. A hawk will ride the updraft between mountain peaks in a gradually widening spiral. On winding roads animals and men carry heavy burdens to the tops of steep hillsides. It is the principle by which the limited powers of natural forms master the pull of gravity. It is not strange that the spiral symbol has come to mean aspiration in the graphic language of all peoples.

SIMPLICITY AND COMPLEXITY; ADAPTION

While the basic structures of a plant form tend to repeat themselves in all its parts, the separate parts are, after all, not identical. They vary in size and strength. They become more complex or revert to the simplest basic structure according to the function of each part. For example, the outside leaves of the dandelion plant are rugged, simple, and rigid in construction, while the inner leaves are flexible, with many serrations. Those which surround the sun-like corolla are mere points. Yet all are alike in possessing a strong midvein, and each serration occurs at the same angle from it. Another familiar instance may be seen in a seashell. Along the edges of a shell are excrescenses which at the center are mere dots on the surface. At regularly increasing intervals they emerge at the outer edge of the spiral in spiky formation. These are calculated to give any fishy marauder pause when he attacks the soft creature within. *Gradual and measurable changes in the shapes and proportions of parts seems to be the clue to adaptation in nature.* This will often appear in the arts of man as well.

A pine root finds a precarious footing in shale.

Veins part from the main stem at precise, though variable, angles.

The trefoil flower and leaves are adaptations of the same geometric pattern.

Wheat is cut and shocked when its color ripens to gold.

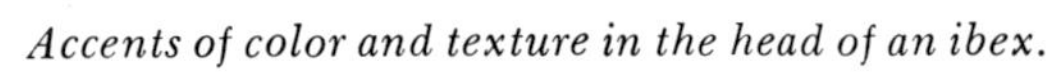

Accents of color and texture in the head of an ibex.

CRESCENDO AND CLIMAX OF COLOR

Even the color of growing forms seems to grow. Like the earth at the bottom, a rising stem will gradually change in color, sometimes to warmer, sometimes to cooler tones, even to complementary red before it reaches a climax in the flower and fruit. Each change signifies a difference in function or a phase in the growth of the living form. A farmer watches the color of his field of grain to know the right time for harvest. A blacksmith knows the moment to strike his iron and the precise heat of his forge by the crescendo of color changes. In animate nature, color changes are no less noticeable. The soft spottings of the fawn are an effective means of concealment in spring for the young animal in the forest bed. As it reaches maturity the even darkness of the upper parts of a fully grown animal and the comparative lightness of its softer under parts appear. We usually notice more color contrasts in and around the head and lesser ones at the tail, as though the color followed the smooth flow of the moving creature.

All of these movements and rhythmic changes of nature are a part of everyone's experience of the world about him. Their effect upon him becomes a part of his existence. One may be even more conscious of them when something interrupts their flow. One is very conscious of sudden stillness before a storm. Uplanders miss the mountains if they vacation at the shore, and the fisher-folk are lonesome for the pound of the surf when they travel inland. The changing look of the earth as season follows season is a part of everyone's sense of being at home.

We have discovered some of the most important principles which seem to pervade the physical world. A comprehensive plan that is capable of great variation but is perceptibly ordered and sequential not only permeates every living form but also governs every movement. So far we have been observers only, experiencing but taking no part in the drama of nature, actually understanding very little of it; for we are unaccustomed in our way of life to dealing with nature directly.

May flies and a fish fly rest on a rough-hewn plank. (Photograph by Eugene Bowman.)

Grass, fragile and yet delicately strong, grows among boulders and dry shale.

THE NATURE OF MATERIALS

The feel of the earth, planting, cultivating, and harvesting a crop were once the everyday experience of man. Each family built their own house and cared for and fed the animals, from which they spun and wove the clothing they wore. Needs of that kind today are filled by the ready-made, but much may still be learned by even the most elementary experiments with growing and building things. To build a really livable home, one must know a great deal not only about the soil but also about all the natural and the man-made materials which are to be used. We do not find or make them all ourselves but must choose intelligently from the products others have made available to us.

Not all of the materials an artist uses are natural ones. Many of the combinations which man has made of nature's materials will need to be studied carefully. The processes by which they are handled will make them unlike what they were in their natural state. Nevertheless, here, in nature, are the basic things man needs to understand. There are principles of weight, porosity, resilience, pressure, and so forth to be learned at first hand. The important thing is to gain an understanding of them, to become increasingly sensitive to them.

EXPERIMENTING WITH TOUCH

Touch, too, we can begin to experience on the mountain we climb. No longer content with the evidence of our eyes, we begin to handle the small stones and pebbles on our hillside. They vary in weight, in smoothness of texture; some feel cool, some warm, some dry, and some wet. We pick a few grasses and stems of other plants. Some are tough, some brittle. Some are firmly jointed, some are flexible. We experiment to find out which fibers will tie in a firm knot, which will wind without breaking. We pick up some fallen branches and break one from a living tree. There is a difference in strength, in weight. The sticky red clay we pressed in our palms an hour ago still retains the imprint of our lifeline, but the footprints we made in sand have begun to crumble. How dependable is the sense of touch? We begin the test with our eyes closed. We can distinguish between trees, leaves, mosses, stones, and insects by touch alone to some extent. True, we are more skillful with our eyes open. Clearly, our hands need educating!

Once drawn, a form is understood in a very personal way. (Crayon drawing by Diane Petraitis, Kutztown State College.)

THE SENSE OF HEARING

While we are about it, suppose we test our ears! Eyes closed and hands still, we hear at first indistinguishable sounds. Then we begin to identify the creaking of one limb against another, the whirr of a small winged creature, a frog's throaty chuckle from a nearby pond, a dry leaf rustling. Here are some things about movements which our eyes did not tell us. Sounds, too, seem to have distinctive patterns. We notice that the song of a bird has a completeness to it, almost as though he had something to say and said it. There is a building up, a climax, and a gradual quieting in the hum of a bumblebee. Our own breathing is a part of the throbbing, living sound around us.

DRAWING TO REMEMBER

Since we are chiefly concerned with visual and tactile experiences in preparing for an art profession, drawing and modeling are the two most important ways for an artist to fill his mind with images of living and growing forms. Take up one small leaf, turn it about. Its details are only beginning to be noticed. Pencil its outlines, trying for exactness and precision from positions where its structural parts are easy to see. Try to match its color. This form will be remembered; for it has been "experienced" in a different way. Drawing is a way of concentrating. It tends to verify the image of the visual and tactile aspects of things. An artist cannot draw too much or too often. We are not concerned at this time with making a picture of our own, we are simply trying to experience with our hands what we think we see. Now put the leaf aside and draw it again, from memory. We can remember its irregularities but not the way it holds together. Perhaps we have paid attention to the wrong things. Pick up a different leaf and try again. Try to get the important parts first. This time our drawing goes better. We can now draw it in almost any direction. We seem to know what we need to know about its structure. We find that as long as we retain certain important parts, such as the main veins and the general outer shape, in the same relation to each other, the drawn leaf still seems alive and whole.

COLLECTING, SELECTING, AND DISCARDING

Collecting is a good way for an artist to fill his mental reservoir of forms. (It comes naturally, too, to small boys.) We begin to collect certain things until our hands are full. We decide to be more selective, keeping the very finest or the most out-of-the-ordinary, or we shall try to find a perfect sequence from the tiniest to the largest. We begin to arrange and rearrange, discard some, add others. To be sure, they seem a little different when we take them away from their natural setting. Perhaps the reason why we picked them up in the first place is now not too clear. Soon we find examples of our chosen form no matter where we are. (Somewhat in the same way one recognizes a familiar theme or tune in a symphony, even though it is played by different instruments.) But an artist is not a hobbyist. Collecting can itself be a way of life, and an absorbing one. Its value to the artist lies not so much in the gathering as in the choosing, in seeing relationships of form. The artist does not tend to be possessive. He can know and understand the most priceless works of man without owning them. He can satisfy himself in studying the myriad beautiful forms of nature and be content to leave them in their natural state.

USING A CAMERA

The camera has proved to be a very useful tool for anyone who would like to develop his power to see. A minimum of study of the mechanical processes of taking pictures will suffice. Skills with the camera will improve with practice. Taking photographs from nature has many advantages and disadvantages compared with actual collecting. The student can "have" his subject and yet always see it as he did at first in its own environment. True, he cannot touch it or watch it move, but he may return to photograph it many times to record its whole life-span. He may look at the form frequently and study it in detail. He can show it to others with a minimum of projecting equipment. The camera, however, will not distinguish for him between points of view in which the form reveals its basic structure and those in which it is lost. It cannot "see around" things as we do, nor can it see within the outer structure. The pressing of the trigger does not take the place of drawing or modeling the form from life. In both drawing and modeling there is an experience of self-involvement in the actual movement of hands, eyes, and mind together which the camera cannot give. It is easy to forget what one has seen and taken with a camera. But an artist is trying to expose his mind, not a roll of film, to the visible world. The work of organizing, arranging, adding to, and discarding from the pictures is still to be done. As with actual collecting, this, too, can become an absorbing business. Should we choose this method of study, we shall have to weigh carefully its advantages and disadvantages for our own purposes. Nevertheless, let us use it for what it will contribute to our need. We have not yet begun to deal with our real purpose as artists but are still concerned with preparation. Any method which will keep us constantly exposed to nature and encourage us to study it will be of great help to us.

In our day one is perforce very close to the scientist. An artist's concern is more and more with a complexity of needs, not only with natural ones which have always been, but with others which are created by scientific experiment in our society. The demands of our age are so insistent and we are so walled away from actual contact with living and growing things that we are likely to miss some of nature's own solutions. We have been learning some of the techniques of the scientific method just in identifying, classifying, and arranging our embryo collection. They will be useful to us when we begin to realize the complexities of our own work. But the chief value of an artist's collection of natural forms lies much deeper, in an understanding of wholeness, of the perfect blending of a form and its function, or its reason for being.

Studying the complete plant form reveals its real character.

SUMMARY

We are beginning to realize that this business of understanding the world through our senses is going to take a long time. We feel fine. That sense of well-being, of being a part of the total scheme has, if anything, become more keen. But we were particularly happy when we were doing something more than just recognizing things and sorting and handling them. The struggle to draw was both rewarding and disappointing. We found that no matter how deeply involved we became in representing the true appearance of things, our results still failed in accuracy and lifelike quality. We really did not succeed in conveying anything which the real form could not convey better. Our drawing does not excite us as the real thing does. Like the birds who are said to have plucked at the paintings of grapes by the Greek artist Zeuxis, we are intrigued but still hungry. We found considerable satisfaction in the sorting and arranging and in the search itself to make our collections reasonably complete. But no matter how we organized things, there were some pieces which seemed to be valuable but did not fit into our scheme. Moreover, there were many possible organizations into which our treasures would fall if we looked at them in different relationships. If we showed them to someone else, he would be unsatisfied until he had rearranged them for himself.

We were perhaps happiest when we were experimenting with things to see what they would do in our own hands. When we were drawing, we were not only concerned with picturing the form exactly as it was; we also learned how the pencil worked, how our hands could feel the form even on flat paper. And we have a kind of affectionate regard for that sketch, with all its faults, because it is truthfully the best we could do at that moment. It represents our progress up to now with using our minds, eyes, and hands together. In our efforts to weave with grasses and reeds we eventually destroyed the material, but we could see the possibilities of making something useful with practice. It is becoming evident now that it is not enough for an artist to live in the midst of the profound plan of nature, to spend his whole life just in learning its ways by heart and mind and skill of hand, without having a real purpose. In the remaining chapters we shall try to understand what that purpose can be and how it can be fulfilled.

QUESTIONS FOR DISCUSSION

1. What useful man-made structures are based on the central principle? Why are they strong? Which basic principle is used in weighing?
2. What man-made structures derive their strength from the spiral principle? How has man used the flexible vertebrate principle in transportation?
3. Which of man's inventions have arisen from his need for very strong structures which are light in weight? What natural forms suggested solutions to this problem?
4. What effect does exposure to wind and moving water have upon rooted forms which would normally grow axially?
5. What similarity do you see between a field of grain and an expanse of water when the wind blows?
6. Why does a designer need to study the results of natural adaptation?
7. Today's designers often use materials which have been processed and finished and no longer resemble their natural state. In what ways have we made these materials more useful, more beautiful?
8. In inventing synthetic materials, does man ever learn from nature?
9. Has man's body changed as a result of the work he does? How has his power of movement affected his skeleton?
10. Is it possible that man has not yet recognized all of the basic principles in nature? What new concept of importance may be credited to our times by generations to come?

THINGS TO STUDY AT FIRST HAND

1. Gather together all the leaves, roots, flowers, fruits, and vegetables you can find which seem to radiate from a center. Draw them inside perfect circles and discover how they vary in number of parts, shapes, and proportion.
2. Draw the ice crystals which form on glass.
3. Under a microscope, study slices of vegetable and animal matter to see the tissues of living cells.
4. Loosen a weed or a tree seedling from moist soil or sand without breaking the roots. Discover for yourself the pattern above and below the ground; draw it with care on a paper which measures the total length and width of the growing plant.
5. Sink a spade into the earth in a grassy field. Study the spreading pattern of roots the cut reveals.
6. Spread a dark, soft paper under a spider web and lift it gently until the web clings to it. Study the spacing between the struts, the supporting bridges, the compact radiating center where the spider awaits his prey.
7. Gather a handful of pebbles. Fold paper or metal foil around each to try to find what geometric shape it may have been.
8. Study crystal forms in a good book on minerals. Learn to draw them geometrically and in perspective.
9. Cross a stream on stepping stones. Make a drawing of the rocks in the creek bed where the water runs fast, where it spreads out, where it undercuts a bank.
10. After a rain, study the miniature mountains, gorges, precipices, and dry river beds in a sandpile.
11. Draw in detail the debris which has collected around an undisturbed piece of driftwood on a beach or a jutting rock in a stream. Try to discover how the wind blew and the torrents ran.
12. Compare the skeletons of several animals and make diagrams showing their proportionate divisions, especially with reference to the backbone. Study the line of movement the backbone makes, its flexibility, and its strength. On several photographs of the living animal draw in the backbone and the most important other skeleton parts.
13. Find spirals in lichens, ferns, vine tendrils; look for twisted tree trunks and roots, for a miniature whirlpool in a stream. What determines their direction?
14. Metal filings on a piece of glass will help you to see the connection between radiating forms and spirals. Try moving a magnet under the glass in a variety of ways.
15. Draw many different kinds of shells. First feel for the overall shape of the solid form; then find the spiral inside it. A shell sawn in slices in either direction will also reveal inner patterns of great strength and delicacy.

Our Minds

III

Men are ruled by imagination: imagination makes them into men, capable of madness and of immense labours. We work dreaming. . . . Imagination changes the scale of everything, and makes a thousand patterns of the woof of nature, without disturbing a single thread.

George Santayana
Soliloquies in England

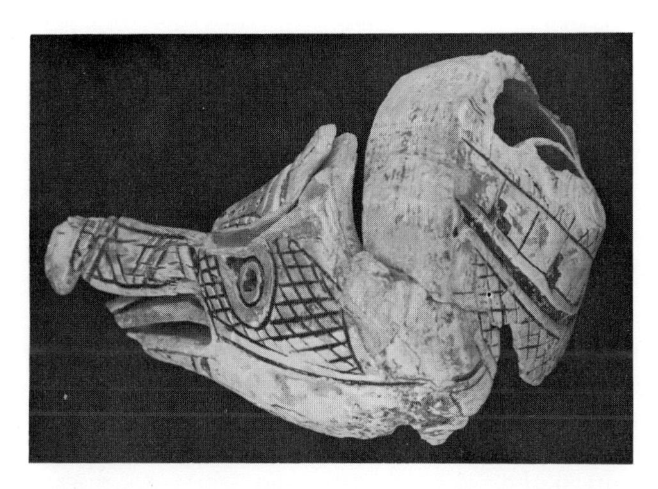

The head of an animal incised in a seashell; from the Spiro Indian mound. (Courtesy of the Stovall Museum of Science and History of the University of Oklahoma, Norman, Okla.)

PRODUCTIVE EXPERIENCE

One cannot really have a productive visual experience without presence of mind, readiness to see and learn. For this reason, in the experiences with nature we have concentrated upon how we use our senses of touch and sight. It was more important to learn how an artist keeps his senses alert than to master any processes or to have finished products. And we were very much concerned with discovering how we, individually, reacted to intimate contact with nature, to materials, and to the basic problems which an artist has. Conceiving art ideas, analyzing them, and bringing forth so-called finished results all require practice, too; just as in every other kind of thinking, reaching conclusions is the difficult but rewarding result. Probably no real artist ever feels that what he has made is finished or perfect, any more than any real scientist or philosopher feels that he has the final answer to a physical or intellectual problem for man.

First of all, what an artist makes is not nearly so important as the meaning he wishes to express by it, the real purpose he has in mind. Because he hopes that his work will be understood, used and enjoyed by others, he needs to know what is acceptable to their minds as well and what can be expressed in the visual language. And if it is true that an artist sees differently, it is because he does think differently. We must come now to some realization of what it means for an artist to interpret what he experiences and to take an imaginative "leap in the dark." Sometimes he must forego the tangible and the visible, forsake the habits of everyday thought, and follow a new path: his own. This is the artist's reason for being, his contribution to the life of others.

SENSING, REASONING, AND IMAGINING

This is a difficult kind of thinking to explain, because we are not sure just what happens in our minds to make imagination different from recognizing facts and reasoning. Perhaps we should go back to our experience on the mountain. When we sensed the world about us, we were *recognizing* facts; when we were examining their structure and noticing how they moved and changed, we were connecting facts; this last is *reasoning*. When we thought of the living animal rather than the skeleton, when we watched the ants find a way around the lump of clay, when we pruned the scarred branch, and when we tried to understand the song of the bird, we were *imagining ourselves in them*. Responding to that inner sense of well-being, we reached the conviction that it was good. Here we were taking it in as a whole, we were *perceiving* everything *in relation* to something both inside and outside ourselves. We do not know that man's is the only mind which has this faculty of imagination. We do know that man is never quite satisfied unless he is using it. This turn of mind is certainly not the exclusive possession of any particular people. Nor must we be adult before we experience it. Children use their minds in this way very readily. One cannot say that educated people have more imagination, but they may use it more readily and more productively than uneducated ones. It is no more common in men than in women, though perhaps it produces different results. Our environment does seem to have some effect on the kind of things we imagine; but being rich or poor or living in one place or traveling does not make us any more or less likely to be imaginative. This is the reason that one finds art going on in the remotest corners of the earth. We see it in children's play, in simple rural communities, in cities and colleges, among scientists, religious leaders, doctors, and lawyers, and in the homes of truck drivers and storekeepers. Prisoners, slaves, great potentates and statesmen, even the ill and insane take some part in the arts of man. It is the presence of the productive quality in whatever people do that makes imagination peculiarly human.

Usually, artists use the faculty of imagination just as other people do. They deal with common human problems. They use their keener senses and their intuitive grasp of essential relationships between things in very logical and practical ways, and they arrive at better conclusions because they do so. It is also possible for the human mind to take materials, sensations, and facts and throw them together without regard for their known nature and out of any accepted sequence, as in a dream. Our minds go about the difficult business of trying to organize these unrelated sensations and facts in a new way. Until we find a way that works, we simply have the original chaotic collection. When we do find a reasonable connection, we have a new concept; we see the components in a new relation to each other. "Brain storming" is a popular way to stimulate people's minds to make new connections in this way, rather than follow traditional ways of thinking. It has been profitably used in business and industry to find new solutions for recurring problems which seem to have no solution.

SEEING NEW RELATIONSHIPS; GENIUS

It is in finding new relationships of value to the whole human race that certain people seem to be taking that journey into space which we associate with the word "genius." The interesting thing about such people is not that they take off into space but that they eventually come back to earth with the payload. Most of us have minds filled with sensations and facts which we only think we understand. We are only too likely to discard them when they do not conform to any safe, familiar sequence, that is, when they do not make the usual kind of sense. What we do not realize is that when a real genius gets an inkling of some new concept, he must reorganize everything he knows in relation to it. His exhilarating glimpse of another facet of the total plan has to be substantiated. This is why genius has been defined as an infinite capacity for taking pains. Besides all of this, being human, the genius must put this new concept to work in the society of man. He has to find a way to show others what he conceives. Richard Guggenheimer, in *Sight and Insight,* says of this kind of thinking, "The genius invents nothing; he reveals. But his revelation cries out for receptive understanding."

It is fortunate, in a way, that we are not all geniuses, equipped with sensitivity and reasoning power to carry a large payload. And yet, of course, we each do carry some. Because our minds and hearts are perceiving individually, we see things each in his own way. Each person is a specifically designed instrument for experiencing. Moreover, we are not mechanisms; we are living reactors and are self-guided. This description of the power of the imagination of man is not meant to imply in any way that we are self-sufficient and do not need contact with the Source of power. Even the greatest scientists, artists, poets, and philosophers try to make us understand this. They seem to believe that our will to guide ourselves is itself an essential part of the plan. The main problem seems to be to get most of us off the earth. This requires some courage and a great deal of preparation, knowledge, and practice.

PLAYING AND LEARNING

Some part of imagination is play. We are not the only creatures on earth that have imagination. Watch animals play with their young. Time off for play happens on schedule as regularly as feeding. The mother draws the line between playing and teasing with a well-deserved swat, rolls her young into a helpless position and sinks her teeth just far enough to hurt a little but not too much. She takes the opportunity to attend to their bath. They forage for her milk and subside in sleep. Later they will experiment with the world outside together. They hide and find each other, attack and run away, pretend indifference and suddenly embrace.

Play is the beginning of constructive imagination.

We can see purpose in all of this. Their education is beginning; they are learning to think and to act, to live without her protection. We often say of animals that they act almost human. We do not refer to their sensory perceptions; for we are no match for them in that respect. Rather, we mean that they too can put things they know together in new combinations when need is great enough. They seem to understand what we are going to do, our intentions and feelings as well as our acts. They can think. They can put themselves in our place. They play with their minds.

We know that human children learn in the same way. One of the most important differences is that human beings take many years to reach maturity. Children who have never learned to play are very unlike others. Wars have left more than one generation of unfortunate ones. Those who try to help them find that they are fearful, resentful, subject to fitful anger and depression. They seem

A child of Lake Atitlan clutches her wooden doll.

A skilled Peruvian weaver creates an amusing toy. (Courtesy of the University Museum of the University of Pennsylvania, Philadelphia, Pa.)

to be entirely indifferent to what others want or feel. Sympathy, love, and laughter they look upon with weary distrust. A child who has come to attitudes like these before he is six is likely to act instinctively upon them all his life, even if he later finds good reason to believe otherwise. Of course, some children played, sang, and danced in spite of the devastation. Others found some dangerous playthings and invented some gruesome games. Far more children probably learned not to think or do anything unless someone told them what, when, and how. Imagination is dormant in their minds. As adults they do not try to play their part in the society of men.

Playing with our minds is the part of thinking over and above what we need just to identify things and to solve basic problems of existence. In anything that we make, we want more than pleasure to the touch and sight; we want more than evidence that it will serve a purpose. We want it to start our imagination to playing constructively. The arts of man give play, release, freedom, and expression to man's mind.

STORIES AND PLAYS

Consider what happens when we read a story or go to the theater. Soon we begin to imagine ourselves in the scenes and action (probably as the hero or heroine). We expect them to think, feel, and act as we would do. If they are good, we feel that we can be good; if they are brave, so can we be brave; if they can laugh at their own mistakes, we laugh with them, not at them. Perhaps, however, they are fantastic creatures, unlike ourselves. We know we are not like them, but we wish we could be. For a brief period of time we lose ourselves in them. If some incongruous thing happens in the story, we come back to reality with actual disappointment. If a story leaves us with some lingering feeling that we were more than ordinary people while we were reading or watching, we may even begin to act in that way in real life. This is the reason why stories and plays can have almost as much effect upon us as real experience. They make it possible to live more than our one immediate and narrow life.

Three characters from Plautus: "The Pot of Gold." (Papier-mâché by Sandra Ambrosius, Kutztown State College.)

A potter illustrates a Peruvian legend: four men rescuing a warrior on a raft. (Courtesy of the University Museum of the University of Pennsylvania, Philadelphia, Pa.)

POETRY

What happens in our minds when we read a poem? It does not contain incidents, but the author tells us how he felt about experiences he really had and we recognize them as like our own. The words may even suggest images we never connected or experienced with the idea, but in the poet's words we see them in a new form. Life will mean more to us than it ever did. We may not immediately understand the poem, but later, perhaps, it will ring true; we can live through another person, beyond our limited experience and even beyond our years.

THE DANCE

Think of a dancer. We watch an exquisitely formed and balanced human body in motion. We could not begin to approach her skill and rhythmic timing. We can only accept for the brief time that she is moving and feeling for us. She may be telling a story by her movements. She may even suggest actual forms in nature. But sometimes she does not act out reality. She gestures with great beauty and restraint, suggests great space with the freedom of her whole body. She ascends and descends, advances and recedes in a total arc of time and space, inclines her head and becomes still. She has not imitated any moving form. But we have gone through an experience of human meaning to us. Perhaps her dance suggested something like supplication, finding oneself free, struggling and overcoming, or accepting one's fate. These things were in both her mind and ours. She communicated with us, without words, by symbolic movements.

MUSIC

Music has no facts to give us. We do not see anything, unless by chance some remembered sound may suggest an image. But the music gives us a human experience, through another person. Just as we used to feel that poetry should rhyme, so we still look for completeness in the phrasing or rhythm of music. Poems and songs traditionally have certain forms, stanzas of so many verses. Great prose, too, has its resonance and accepted rhythm. These traditional movements and rhythms are always changing in music and poetry. New concepts bring forth new forms and create new traditions. For instance, we feel quite satisfied now with poems in free verse although they were ridiculed when they first appeared. We look for the inconclusive up-beat in popular songs and dance music. It gives us more feeling of being "out-of-this-world," to use an expressive phrase which is already becoming obsolete. We have to some extent accepted new forms and new symbols in all the arts because they have increased our capacity to understand human experience imaginatively, with new meanings.

A dancer's mask of basketry, from New Guinea. (Courtesy of the University Museum of the University of Pennsylvania, Philadelphia, Pa.)

THE GRAPHIC AND PLASTIC ARTS

In the visual arts today, changes in ways of expression have reached a point where there is a good deal of misunderstanding, chiefly because people do not accept the new symbols which are being used. There is a valued tradition in favor of realistic, factual representation. Between primitive times and our own century lie hundreds of years in which realistic art served the purposes of man well. No one considered himself worthy of the name painter or sculptor unless he had spent a long apprenticeship with a master draftsman. Years of such toil did not appear to hinder the impact of his work at full maturity. To be sure, we may often confuse the work of apprentices with that of the master, but one can easily see how that might happen. Part of the student's tuition at one time was worked out on the master's commissions. Should we ever have to sort out canvases in a contemporary exhibition without benefit of signatures and catalogue, could we tell student from master, distinguish between the originator of a popular style and the followers?

For the most part the masters of new ways, like Cezanne, Picasso, and Matisse, also reached their maturity through concentration on the actual appearance of real things. They seem to agree that to learn to draw was valuable, even essential. Either because of or in spite of their long practice in realism, they learned to see differently and better.

In their special way of looking at things some rather unheard-of solutions appeared to them perfectly natural but to others quite unbelievable. The Cubists, for instance, saw things geometrically, and painted them so. This is an unusual but a very logical way to see. Certainly it is not very new; for primitive artists have always used it. Nevertheless, it was hard to imagine for the art public of 1910, who had long admired a kind of sentimental realism. But sentiments which once had been satisfying were drastically unsatisfactory to the people of the early twentieth century.

It was natural and inevitable that the arts should change at that time. Some artists of the new generation painted forms in a kind of overall light. This did not seem at all believable to people accustomed to the most faithful study of everyday sunlight and shadow. The innovators said they could express more form when light was everywhere. The traditional artists said it was more artistic to be subtle and hide the forms. It seems strange to us now that the shadow painters were called realists and the form painters were called fantastic, *les fauves* (the beasts). We have come to accept this new tradition because we enjoy thoroughly understanding form. It seems to us more real than shadows.

Still others made extensive researches into primitive arts in the hope of finding some way which was basic to human understanding before any traditions were very strong. The work of children has become very interesting to mature artists for the same reason.

STYLES, MATERIALS, AND ART TRADITIONS

A very interesting conclusion came of all these experiments, not directly but indirectly. While some artists were content to deal with visible and tangible forms, a few rebellious and imaginative persons began to believe that somehow they were limited, almost enslaved, by the very appearance of recognizable things. Musicians had long since given up imitating noises, such as the wind or the song of a bird. They seemed to be able to convey much deeper feelings with other combinations of rhythms and intensities, pitch, and volume of sound. Perhaps, said the painters and sculptors, if colors, shapes, forms, and textures were organized in such a way that no one could say "this is a dish, that is a person," they, too, could be free of actual representation and could put more meaning into their work.

It was a very difficult thing to do. No matter how nonobjectively (not representationally) the artist works, people still ask, "What is it?" If the answers, "A wood sculpture, or a painting," someone wants to know, "Of what?" Partly this is because one cannot put down a color or line without giving it some shape. Certainly people show considerable sense of insecurity about some nonobjective works of art. Nevertheless they are quite happy if they do get an inkling of a recognizable form, even if they discover that the artist has meant to convey something quite different. Perhaps, too, the artist himself may have been having a little private fun when he named his work for the catalogue. Perhaps he thought a misleading title would help to set people free of facts and more likely to respond to the work as they see it. There is no doubt, of course, that some of the titles are straight-faced spoofing. We are not above enjoying it. Sometimes we suspect that the nonobjectivists take themselves a little too seriously.

No one knows whether it will ever become an accepted tradition in the visual arts to work without representing anything. Certainly in doing this we could be merely imitating rather weakly what music and dancing do naturally and with great

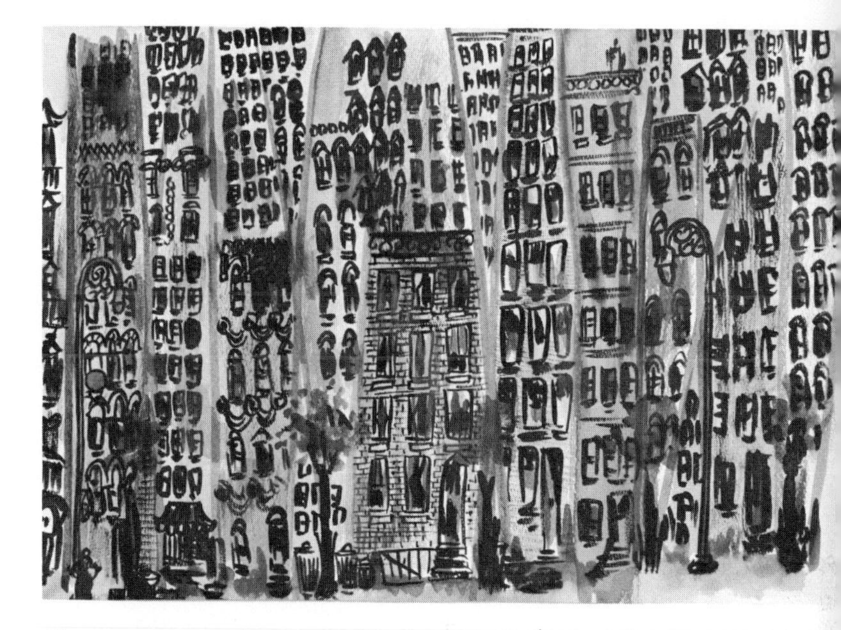

City pattern; a student's experiment with style. (Watercolor by William Ronalds, Kutztown State College.)

A Chinese potter's dog, intricate in form and highly glazed. (Courtesy of the Reading Art Museum, Reading, Pa.)

A Mexican cat of unglazed clay; its form simple and decoration skillfully controlled.

power. Before we can accept nonobjective painting and sculpture for its own sake, we must believe that it can give us human experience in a new way. Imagination only asks to be convinced that the artist has something of importance to say in his own medium and honestly.

This brings us to the second most important decision an artist must make, assuming that he does really have an idea; namely, to choose the right material for it. There is very sound reason, especially in the visual arts, behind the old saying that "seeing is believing." To satisfy our own senses and to be acceptable to the sensitivity of others, our work must be made of believable material. The materials should look as they feel, and not deceive us. Nor can we accept materials which we think will not function. For instance, in architecture, large glass doors at first seemed a precarious way to enter a building some hundreds of stories tall. Nor were we satisfied with the steel inner structure under the ornate stone and brick facades of the first skyscrapers. We knew that steel beams anchored the buildings in bedrock, but we did not believe them with our eyes. This unease of mind made it impossible for us to really respond to the beauty of the structure. Finally, architects and bridge builders frankly allowed steel to show instead of covering it up. Then we believed in its real possibilities for a new architectural form peculiarly our own.

We make other and more subtle demands of the materials we use in art. Certain materials have long been accepted as good for particular uses and occasions. People began to attach a kind of symbolic value to some. A material like gold, ivory, jade, silk, or ebony, for instance, was hard to obtain. Long and dangerous excursions and laborious refining of raw materials was necessary. Only the very wealthy or the very powerful could afford to make them into objects of use or ceremonial value. Fine craftsmanship was available only to the most important persons. This is the reason why the very names of some materials suggest to us the royal, the fabulous, the godly. Thus it is that we expect a princess to be married in jeweled satin and a priest to be robed in heavy, richly embroidered vestments. Only a golden ring of intricate workmanship is fit for the hand of a king. His throne is of solid, beautifully wrought wood or stone. Some materials were supposedly debasing and inappropriate to their use if not in their proper place. We could not accept the "idol with clay feet"; for clay was for everyday use in early tradition. Perhaps the trappings of wealth and power were, after all, not particularly functional. Even the mighty may have looked for comfort in their thrones and would have preferred to eat from dishes of earthenware instead of gold if their food could just be hot. For, given sufficient time, traditions do change. We no longer believe a king to be a god, nor even much different from common mortals. We believe ourselves to be the potential equal of anyone. We can sleep in a golden bed and bedeck ourselves with the finest of clothing and ornaments if we can afford them. We expect something else of persons of importance now. Anyone we choose to place in a position of responsibility must be like ourselves. We applaud his taste and discretion when he accepts our materials of living. He must have the common touch, own the best but not the only car of its make. He should live in the cities we build and in a home like our homes; he should study our arts and sciences and even practice them.

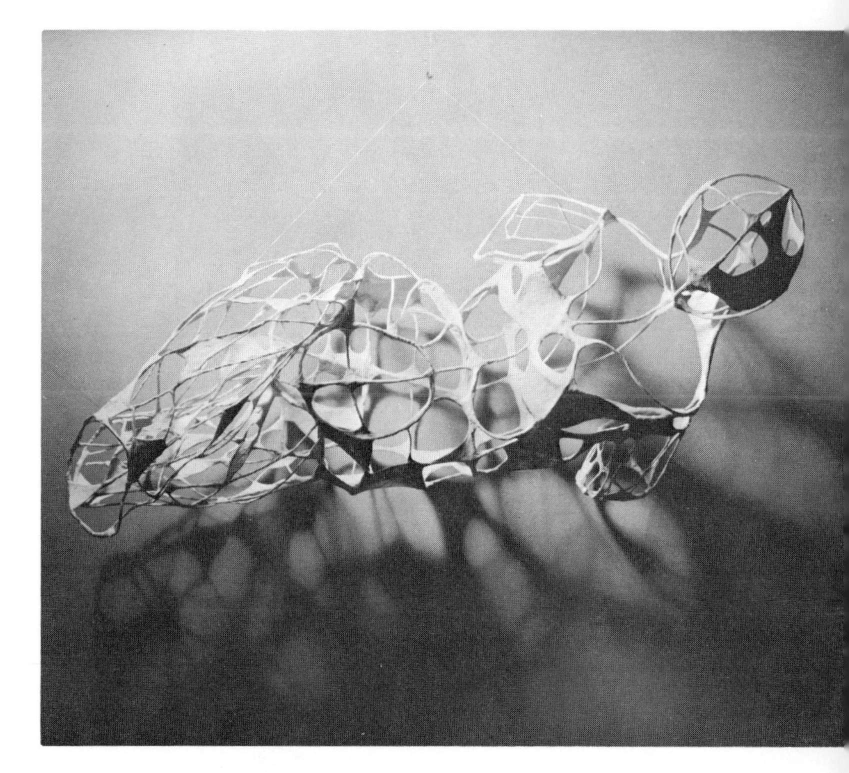

Experiment with woman's figure. (Wire and papier-mâché by Anna Diehl, Kutztown State College.)

The fact is that we have found so many new uses for natural and old materials and have invented so many new ones that we are in the midst of making new traditions. All we ask of an artist now is that he use each material that he has at hand with respect and love. He must not falsify it, destroy its intrinsic nature, or fail to bring out its very best qualities. No material is any more precious than another. None is base, lowly, or commonplace if he reveals it to us as worth his time and thought. We have learned to like chairs of metal tubing and plywood; curtains of glass fibers have proved as soft and lustrous as silk; cars of plastic, aluminum tables, and hosiery of nylon are commonplace. We still love clay, wood, metals, stone, and natural fibers for themselves, but we see no inconsistency in combining them with the man-made materials, so long as each is used frankly and beautifully.

In the representative arts we have other and different things to demand of materials. We have already pointed out that the reason why we represent things is not to compete with natural forms or to give the illusion that the real thing is there. We also have some rather definite ideas about how each medium reveals its true nature. We expect a drawing with charcoal to be full of contrast and of many gradations of tone, since this is the way charcoal works. An ink drawing is valued for its clean directness and for delicacy and precision, because the ink dries crisp and does not smudge. In oil paint we expect luminous, rich color and a certain weight or body. In transparent water color we can accept either intensity or delicacy so long as we can see through it. In hard woods and stones we look for considerable beauty on the surface. We do not demand much depth; for we recognize the resistant nature of the materials. In rough-grained materials such as sandstone and terra cotta we do not expect fine detail but hope for strong vigorous forms. We have built up a kind of tradition, too, for the kind of subject which we try to interpret in each medium. For instance, charcoal seems to us a very appropriate material for an informal portrait sketch of a man of vigor and strong, characterful features. But it is too bold for a child in a pensive mood, unless the medium is greatly limited. Pen and ink would help us to express the intricate, fragile forms in Gothic tracery. It might become unduly exacting were we to attempt the colossal Stonehenge in that medium. It would seem a pity to carve a butterfly of stone, and it would be equally incongruous to cast an elephant in glass.

Again there are certain traditional ideas about the value of each representative medium. It is considered by some people to be more noteworthy to have one's portrait done in oils than in water color or any drawing medium. Clay was at one time valued by sculptors only as a "sketching" material for developing a form which would eventually be cast in metal. Important people's portrait busts therefore were done in bronze or marble, seldom in wood or clay.

MEANING AND VISION

As has happened with other traditions, these attitudes are gradually being changed. New materials and new uses for old ones, new combinations and new methods of reproducing and preserving them are giving us more freedom of choice in materials for everything we use and enjoy.

What we ask of the artist is not that he work with materials as they always have been used. Rather, we hope that he will find new ways of seeing things through experimenting with all their possibilities. What we chiefly expect of an art work is that we shall find something new to believe. It must have new meaning to the one who made it and to others. It must give us better vision, in the larger sense of that word.

For instance, if a designer or an architect invents a new form or way of using materials, we want it to be demonstrably useful and better than we have. It should make life more adequate for us, satisfy some urge in living. If someone invents a new way to communicate with others, such as a new kind of play or music or a new way of painting, it must help us to share experiences better than the words, actions, pictures, and sounds we now have. The new art forms must be acceptable, and what they mean must be true for many, not for only a few. In the world of human relations if one group of people finds a way of living together which makes their existence richer materially or in knowledge or in power, we can believe in it only if there is room for change and growth in human experience and for sharing with others for the benefit of all men. In every creative line of work, if one person seems to see things differently and in a new way, we ask only that he will look honestly within himself and describe it for us. We know that what one human being can experience is possible to others, and therefore it can be meaningful as a part of everyone's life. The really great poets, philosophers, religious leaders, statesmen, and artists seem to have this faculty of imagination in common, so that they see far ahead of other persons in their own generation and discover new meanings for all mankind.

Imagination, like charity, begins at home, right in our own hands, eyes, and minds. In fact, we have already begun to practice it. The experience on the mountain top was as much a reasoning and imaginative one as it was a sensing one. Drawing the leaf, weaving with the grasses, arranging our collection of nature forms challenged not only our sense of order but also our ability to visualize something new and peculiarly our own. It demanded a considerable amount of imaginative judgment to choose what to take in the visible, tangible form of a photograph. We had varying success with the sketches we made. Sometimes others accept and believe in what we do, sometimes they do not. This happens even to skillful and accomplished persons.

WHAT A TEACHER CAN DO FOR YOU

Perhaps here is the place where you need to understand just what a teacher can do for you. Actually, his work begins when you feel finished. He has little to do with your instinctive and individual way of reacting to nature, or of using your hands, except to remind you to treat your tools and materials with honest respect and to work rhythmically. He cannot expect you to work in his way. No more can he expect your mind to imagine what his does. But when the thing is there, visible, he can accept it as a possible interpretation, he can try to believe in it. He can show you where it is understandable and where he loses your thought. He can suggest ways to make it more visible or tangible. He can point out inconsistencies in the way you have expressed form and used tones, colors, and textures. He can tell where you hesitated, lost your thought. And he may draw out your thought beyond the point where you stopped. He does these things because he has experience not only with his own hands, the tools, and the material but with ideas. He has respect for the idea in your mind and may even have had or seen a similar one.

ORIGINALITY

There is no need for you to struggle to be different or clever. If your idea is real to you and seems true, the way you express it will make it original. The real meaning of that word, "from the source," implies that you do not copy, imitate, or even recall any other person's expression. On the other hand, there is no reason to be dismayed if someone else seems to have hit upon what you thought was your idea. It would be a strange thing, indeed, if we did not see some similarity between our experiences and those of others. For most of us there are many more ideas where the first arose—in our imagination. We can follow any one of them. Selecting the most meaningful idea is just as important work for the mind as choosing materials, tools, and means of expression. Because you discover that your way of working is different from that of others, it is not necessary or even very wise to become too self-conscious about it. People who try too hard to act naturally are not very convincing to others. Forget these things. Think only about your idea, the material and tools, and what you are making. It will be yours, and yours alone, if you work honestly.

SOME EXPERIMENTS WITH IMAGINATION

We shall experiment with imagination without forgetting that all of your earlier practicing and experimenting and all of the experiences of your life up until now have indeed made of you a perceptive individual. Insight, intuition, emotional reactions, reasoning, and play enter into it. A good rhythmic pace and the beginning of control of both hands and materials sometimes set the mind free to play. Before we begin, here are some important suggestions about practicing and experimenting. Be sure that your working space is uncluttered, that you can see and reach all of it. Have your materials and tools in good shape. Work at ease—

relaxed but not limp. Move rhythmically, forcefully, with confidence. If you are afraid, don't let anyone suspect it, least of all yourself. Make yourself believe that you can do whatever you have clearly in mind. Work by yourself. Later you will want others to see what you have done and you will also want to see what they have done. Follow your own path of thinking to the end before you stop. It will not be of much interest to you or to others if you do not feel it is finished, at least as far as you can imagine it.

In the experiments which follow, you will find three kinds of suggestions: subject matter, or themes, media and tools, and ways of expressing things visually (such as lines, areas, tones or colors, and textures). It would be quite possible to interchange all three with those suggested for another experiment. Do not hesitate to do so. Their purpose is only to start your own thinking, not to limit you or stop you at any one problem. For instance, the first experiment might be done with clay instead of by drawing; the second might be done from a recent incident which was very exciting instead of from a remote childhood memory; the third might begin with silhouettes or shapes of things in the story instead of the rhythm of the poem. You will see many other possibilities. When you do, try them.

REORGANIZING NATURE FORMS

Make a large line drawing of a nature form. Turn your drawing upside down or sidewise and look for an entirely different form which the lines suggest. Forget the one you drew. Even the spaces between your lines may suggest something. Develop the new form you see in three or four colors. You may extend, add, or erase lines if you feel the new form is not clear without making some changes. Try to use the same kind of rhythm for anything you add so that you do not lose the wholeness of the original form. You will learn that shapes and forms in nature often resemble others; for instance, compare the head of a turtle with the bud of the lowly skunk cabbage.

TACTILE AND VISUAL MEMORY

Look back to some incident which you remember clearly from your childhood. Try to see it as you did then. Begin with yourself, what you were wearing, how your hair was combed, what you were doing. Then go to the things you touched frequently; remember their feel, their size, shapes, and colors. Use a medium which will give you a quick, easily applied color effect such as crayon or chalk; for it is important to let the images flow quickly as soon as they come to you. One remembered detail will lead to another. You are summoning back to consciousness sensations which once were closely related to each other as part of a total experience. Put things down directly, without erasing. Use simple shapes with inner detail. Do not make things up; just coax back the dormant images. It is said that underneath the consciousness of the present lie all the images and related sequences we have ever experienced. We forget them (do without them, or store them in our minds) but do not lose them. Make a book about your childhood for some young relative.

TELLING A STORY BY RHYTHM

Select a narrative poem or song, one that tells a sequence of events. Briefly experiment with one line or more that will fit the rhythm. Is it a meandering kind of tale that wanders and turns back on itself? Does it march in rigid, drumlike beats? Does it rise and fall like the coming in and going out of the tide? Begin your design with these lines. They will suggest some of the characters, the things, and events of the story. Develop forms to fit and fill the spaces between and along the lines. Tool them into separate linoleum pieces. Experiment with many different colors before printing on cloth. You could make an interesting wall hanging.

CAPTURING A MOOD

Try a poem or music that really has no images, events, or characters yet conveys a feeling or mood by the way the author rhymes and repeats move-

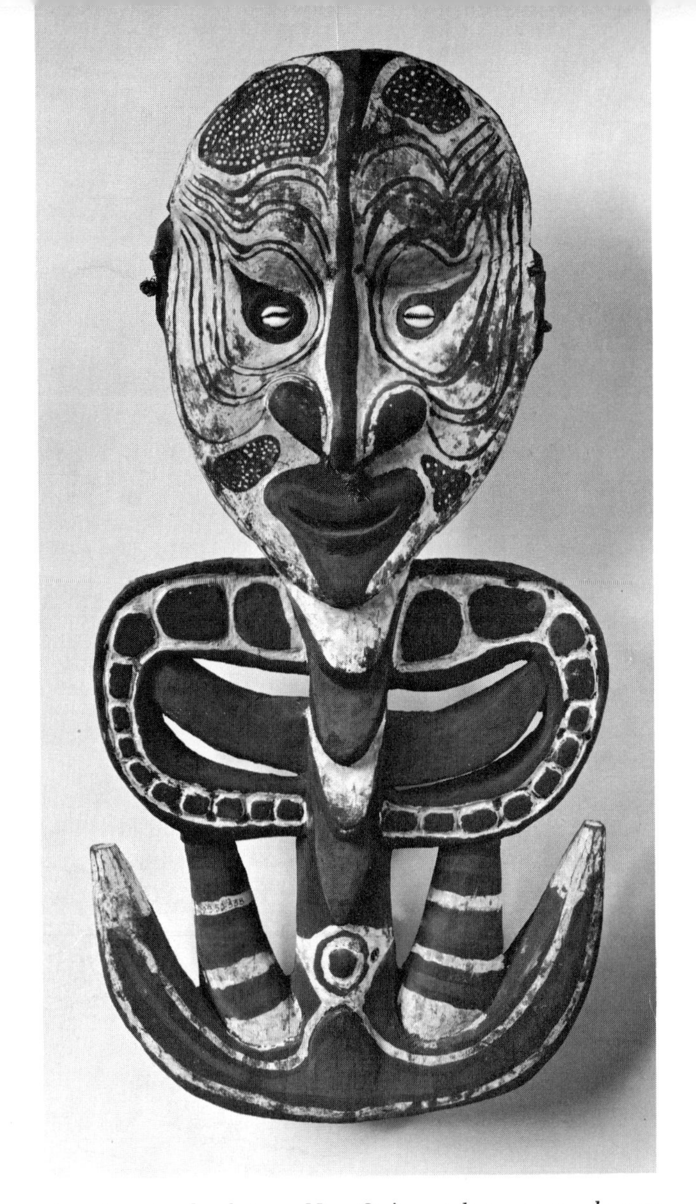

A suspension hook from New Guinea takes on some human characteristics. (Courtesy of the University of Pennsylvania, Philadelphia, Pa.)

ments. Find your lines, and this time fill the areas with colors, textures, darks, and lights which the mood suggests. You will begin to see differences between visual and verbal communication. Select a medium which is suggestive rather than precise, like colored dye or chalk on very wet paper or cloth. You might be well satisfied with this for background effects, such as a stage curtain, or a screen. It will suggest mood without making one conscious of something pictured. It gives everyone a chance to summon his own images.

ANIMATING

Find a piece of wood which has a noticeable grain with a knothole. Imagine the hole is the eye of a living creature and begin to carve his head, wings, body, tail, and feet out of the rest of the wood. Cut away only enough to bring out the form you see; try not to lose the original shape. Keep its wholeness. Keep its woody character. Something very interesting happens when we imagine an inanimate object is alive. Because an eye seems to have expression, we begin to feel that inside the wood is a thinking, feeling creature, like ourselves. This is why sculptors often live with a block of stone or wood a long time before they work on it. This feeling is rather like the primitive man's belief that each object in nature has a spirit which struggles for escape. Perhaps this may be why we are so sure that man, too, has an inner creature or soul which will sometime be set free from material things.

STORY TELLING

Make some people out of anything you have handy (a few clothespins, pipe cleaners, or even sticks will do); make some short, medium, tall, straight, one curved, one an irregular one. Make a character out of each of these by adding a head, hands, feet. Dress them up. Choose one for your hero or heroine, one for the villain of the piece and the rest for extras. Give them names. Make them dance, fight, work, and play together. Tell the story to a child, or let him tell it. Make it a serial, or a comic strip, with plenty of exciting incidents. Get your hero into trouble and get him out of it. You will find that soon your imagination will begin to build human situations around them which go with their characters. This is something which lonely people often do to populate their inside world. It is interesting to find how many make-believe people have become almost as familiar to us as members of our own family. "What is worrying Charlie Brown today?" we ask. "Pogo has the integration problem in hand," we say. Everyone knows them. They do some things which remind us of people we know and of ourselves. They even make us laugh at ourselves, no mean contribution to civilized society.

INTERPRETING ABSTRACT IDEAS

The passing of time has a great deal of imaginative appeal. One way to think of it is in the way things change. The forms whose life-span we can see and understand within a few hours or days such as insects or fast-growing bulbs suggest a great deal to us. In some way they become a symbol of all change and all time. Study one of them carefully. Each stage seems to be complete in itself, possibly grotesque but nevertheless full of beauty. One can see in the next stage some of the forms in the first; they are not lost, but changed. From sheet metal, paper, or foil cut each of the stages separately. Bend or twist the pieces into forms in so far as the material will respond. Try combining them geometrically or very simply in a nonobjective sculpture which combines in a whole the entire life-span and all its changes. Perhaps you will understand in a new way why, although time seems to change the appearance of everything, nothing is ever lost. Sculpture often brings this idea to our imagination in a very tangible way. We usually find that all the material we have is usable. What we take out of one form will make another.

INTERPRETING HUMAN RELATIONS

Some subjects have stirred the imagination of man since time began. These are the human relations which are vital to man's existence: the mother with her baby, the family, a youth setting forth on a journey, the homecoming, discovering love and passion, grieving for a loved one. So old and yet so ever-changing and new are these that sooner or later in the course of every artist's development he is impelled to attempt them, perhaps many times. They may be in different styles, and media, and perhaps many years will have passed between the several interpretations. But they will be much alike. We can see that the same person is giving us a glimpse of human life through his own individual life.

Because many very great artists have done this does not make it impossible for us. Probably even the greatest artist feels humble and quite inadequate when he is doing subjects like these. You will not need any kind of suggestions or instructions for this experiment. Do it alone. It is only necessary to have really experienced these feelings. When you feel that this is the one thing you must do, don't wait. Begin. Perhaps you will almost be able to see it, before you begin, as being a painting, a wood sculpture, a pen drawing. If this happens, do not hesitate to use that medium even if it is for the first time. You will find your way with it very fast; for you will have much to say.

Mask from New Ireland. (Courtesy of the University Museum of the University of Pennsylvania, Philadelphia, Pa.)

OBJECTIFYING

It is as human to hate as to love. To suffer, to fear, to be destructive or ashamed, to scorn and mock are all too much a part of human lives to be denied. They affect us inwardly as do their opposite and stronger counterparts like love, endurance, pride, and pity. Because these better feelings are stronger and we believe them to be good (they make us feel more wholly ourselves), we sometimes do not allow ourselves to admit the others. They seem to get the upper hand, make us feel unlike or less than ourselves. In art when you put into a tangible form the well-loved images and sensations you feel as good, you find you understand them better. This can happen also if you give some visible form to things you hate, fear, or dislike. It is an imaginative process called objectifying. Once we have made these things real, we are no longer at the mercy of the destructive, disintegrating effect they have on us. The very fact that we have the power to shape the material in their likeness helps. We may find that they are not real, but unfortunate combinations of experiences in our minds, freak associations. Whatever we discover, the act of forming, organizing, and then taking a good long look at the thing we hate gives us an insight into ourselves. It may be downright ugly or quite beautiful. Some of the things we make in art are for throwing away, and some are for keeping.

SUMMARY

This chapter has been rather like a short excursion into the strange world which exists within everyone. It can only serve us as a travelogue does, which is not very much like living in a foreign land. We all know that our enjoyment of beauty, our human understandings, and our sense of the meanings of all these things exist inside, not outside, ourselves. No one can live in this inner world of the mind but us. The arts of man are the means of communication in this country inside ourselves where everyone else is a foreigner. Yet we do not each speak a different tongue. We can accept the art expressions of others; for they confirm what we, too, think and feel. The love for the feel of materials, tools, and the enduring mark of the hands are there; even in the work of children and of the masters we find the quality of play and struggle which we know to be true of our own work. We see that the greatest artists often choose to portray the things we, too, love and even those which we all fear and hate to think about. Thus in artwork we feel less strange, less alone in our own inner world. We can understand to some degree the strange, challenging visions of contemporary thinkers who are now using the power of imagination supremely well, not only in the arts but in science and in social concepts. They make us believe in our own minds and in what we ourselves can do.

TOPICS FOR READING AND DISCUSSION

1. In Leonardo da Vinci's notebooks and sketchbooks you will find innumerable drawings and comments upon nature forms. It is said that deformities in nature also interested him. Why did he study these exceptions with such care? What were some of his inventions which have now become commonplace to us?
2. What do present-day scientists say about the importance of the artist's viewpoint and ways of thinking?
3. What do psychologists say about reaching conclusions by intuition; do mathematically minded persons ever use the imaginative faculty of the mind and later prove their conclusions with figures?
4. It is said that one cannot imagine something he has never seen or known. Can you remember dreams in which you put familiar things in a new sequence or relationship? Can you do this purposely, for fun?
5. Read what such poets and artists as John Keats, William Blake, Samuel Coleridge, and Charles Lamb have said about their compositions which came to their minds fully formed, perhaps while they slept.
6. Why is it that you can do things better if you make a game out of a difficult or monotonous task?
7. How is it that a so-called child prodigy can create compositions which even accomplished musicians respect and admire? How can a child interpret faithfully the work of the great composers?
8. In the products of modern manufacture many synthetic materials are proving as useful as natural ones. How many can you identify by their own appearance? How many are still made to resemble natural materials for the sake of tradition?
9. Choose some theme or thought which stirs your imagination. Collect pictures, stories, music, plays, sculpture, and other expressions which seem to center around this idea. How does each reveal different and personal expressions?
10. Choose some artist whose work really stirs your imagination. Collect reproductions of his work and arrange them as nearly as you can in the order in which they were made. What changes and development do you notice in this work? Can you connect these changes with different episodes in his life? Do you notice any recurring themes? Can you see any connection between his work and the prevailing social or political aspects of his time? Does he have a counterpart among writers, musicians, or others of his time?

IV

Our Eyes: Perceiving Lines, Shapes, Forms, and Depth

If a man can learn to see more than he now sees, and see further, and see more beauty, and see more clearly the shape of his own nature and destiny, then he should not hesitate to starting learning.

RICHARD H. GUGGENHEIMER
Sight and Insight

THE IMPORTANCE OF VISION

One hour spent with our eyes covered will teach us more about their importance than reading any number of books on vision. We would probably realize first that it is almost impossible while awake to keep them closed. Even the act of waking itself shows first by movements of the eyeball. Our instinctive question on returning to consciousness is "Where am I?" We usually find ourselves with our eyes, unless we are blind. In that case we resort to the even more instinctive sense of touch. No one not born blind can realize what it means to lack vision. One who loses his sight will find that hearing and touch become much keener; for they must assume the important business of keeping his balance, taking note of his surroundings, and guiding his movements.

While we are sleeping, all our senses are on guard to protect us. They waken consciousness (brain reactions) by reflexes (involuntary body responses). Particularly is this true of the sense of touch and of sight. Even when we cover our eyes willingly for a short time, we notice a feeling of unsureness. This builds up into an emotional state of panic or confusion unless we can reassure ourselves of safety. Although we know we are safe, we may become inert and depressed in the darkness within a short time. So closely knit together are our sight, mind, and emotions that we say "I see" when we mean our eyes can distinguish or that our minds understand and our hearts sympathize. We see again in memory. Prophets are called seers of the future. We try to see some purpose in our lives. Not only does man use his eyes to discover the nature of the physical world and to work with it for his own well-being, he also depends upon vision to understand the communications of others and their attitudes toward him and what he does. Therefore, a thorough knowledge of the eye and how it works is very important to the artist.

STRUCTURE AND FUNCTION OF THE EYES

To understand the structure of the eye, we should use a book especially devoted to its physical makeup and functions. It is an intricately built organ, highly sensitive to light, and really an extension of the brain. Uninformed experimenting with our eyes would subject us to painful experiences which can destroy the very sensitivity we need so much. We can, however, learn a great deal about eye structure by experiences with which everyone is familiar. We know that we see a nearly complete circular area around each eye, obstructed only by the nose, the forehead, and a little of the lower face. Looking straight ahead without moving the eye, we seem to see the center of the area more clearly than the outer rim. Although we are seldom conscious of it, our eyelids contract and expand, raising and lowering automatically according to the degree of light. We also experience a similar involuntary movement within the pupil of the eye itself. Here we recognize structure built upon the principle of inward and outward movement from a center.

EYE MOVEMENT

We can direct the movement of the eye consciously so that this center of vision will rest upon anything we wish to observe more clearly. The center is equipped with a lens, a transparent membrane which has the power of contracting and expanding in thickness. Because of this we can bring into focus (clarity) very small things and those at a distance. By focusing at different places we can follow with the eye along the edges of things and understand their length, depth, and height; this gives us our sense of shape or silhouette that is basic to drawing. We can also follow a moving object, because we can bring it into focus at different distances. Even when it moves too fast for us to focus, the outer, less-sensitive area of the eye gives us vague changing images of its shape.

FIELDS OF VISION AND FOCUSING

With each eye we have a slightly different field of vision; we see two fields which overlap. The focusing action of each eye can cause the one field to coincide with the other on a limited area. The outer rim of the eye still reports the effects of light on surrounding things to the brain. This was how we discovered the similarity between the whole tree and the leaf structure. We compared the sizes of parts to the whole in the same way, which is the basis of our sense of proportion. We can understand the whole object somewhat even when we are focusing on a part of it. In looking at a painting or a piece of pottery, a beautifully lettered page, or an architectural work, it is this ability which gives us the sense of wholeness in the design.

UNDERSTANDING FORM

Because we do see a slightly different field with each eye, we see more than the face of a three-dimensional object. This is how we see around things, or perceive form. We usually call upon our sense of touch and bodily movement to verify what we see. We explore things with our hands, or we walk around them to get a collection of images from different viewpoints which our mind will combine. Our frustration when we tried to draw the leaf may have been partly due to double vision; for we could put down only one image and we may have held the leaf too close for the two images to coincide in focus. Some of the trouble was probably due, also, to lack of skill in following the leaf shape with the eye. If the mind did not direct our hands to coordinate with the eye, we had even more difficulty, as much in seeing as in drawing. If we had tried to reproduce the form of the shell in clay, we would have been able to turn both the object and the clay around in the hand. In this way we would have seen many different contours of both to follow with the eye. The reproduction in clay would probably have been more nearly complete.

The eyelids control the area of vision and therefore the amount of light we see. This is helpful when we wish to study a particular object as well as when we need to sweep a large area. The eyelashes place a softening screen around the outer rim of the area of vision. Opening and closing of the eyelids is usually a reflex action (one that occurs without conscious thought and will), but we can also use the action of the eyelids to help us to focus consciously and to prevent distracting sensations from outside the small area of clear focus. This is why we sometimes half close our eyes to study the general effect of an object we wish to draw. It is especially helpful to a painter in simplifying light and shadow. The pupil of the eye controls the intensity of light which enters it; strong light causes contraction, and weak light allows expansion of the pupil. We see most clearly when the pupil is neither entirely open nor closed very tightly.

Our eyes contribute a great range of sensations to the brain for several reasons. They can focus more accurately than any other organs of sense. They can move very freely, although within a limited range unless we ourselves move. They respond to light which permeates everything and usually persists longer than other kinds of contact. Not only do they respond to amounts of light (darkness and lightness), they also distinguish separate hues, which are the effects of different wavelengths of light. They measure the intensity of light as well (the strength, energy, or degree of saturation) in each hue at different levels of darkness and lightness. So far as we know, the eye's report on color cannot be verified by any of our other senses.

CARE OF THE EYES

Without the protective structure of the eye itself and without proper care the nerves of the eye would be destroyed by constant exposure to light. Once destroyed they cannot replace themselves, as muscular tissue does; therefore, it is of utmost importance to us to protect them.

These are some of the recommendations by oculists and optometrists in regard to care of the eyes and efficient use of them.

1. Keep them clean, cool, and moist. Avoid exposure to dust and heat.
2. Use them in uncramped positions only. Avoid prolonged focusing at close range. Sit or stand relaxed when concentrating on small things.
3. If your vision is not naturally good, invest in the best glasses recommended by a competent oculist or optometrist.
4. Wear your glasses when and in the way you are advised by your oculist. Keep them clean and in the right position on your head.
5. Avoid glare. Do not draw, read, or work on very light or shiny surfaces without adjusting the light to prevent reflection.
6. Sleep regularly.
7. Rest your eyes often. (You don't have to stop thinking, do you?)
8. Inflamed eyes are often indications of illness. Consult your doctor.

SENSING AND PERCEIVING

All of our sensations stem from some kind of physical contact. The skin reacts to pressure and heat, the ear to sound waves, the tongue and nose to chemical makeup of matter, the eye to light waves. Distinguishing between degrees and kinds of contact is *perception,* the business of the brain. It connects into a whole all the information gathered by the sense organs.

Perception is going on when the mind has more than one item to deal with. It is clearer when there are few rather than many items. It is more exact when the items are similar in some respects but quite different in others.

It is helpful to be able to isolate some particular kind of sense experience from other kinds which are reported at the same time (we often close our eyes to listen intently). When more than one kind of sense experience is to be examined in the same object, perception is more sure if the senses do not contradict each other's report (as when we expect shiny things to be smooth or wet). In other words, to perceive clearly with the mind, we must have some similar past or concurrent experience with which to compare the immediate sensation. We must also have a real difference between the two. We identify each sensation with the object which produced it (association). We compare it with other like sensations (evaluation).

Another and simpler way to state all of this is that we have a scale of perception for each of our senses which we ourselves have built; it consists of all the sense experiences we have had. The more experiences we have, the more complete is our total sensitivity. All artists strive to increase their own store of sensory perceptions, because they depend upon reaching the minds of others by sensory perceptions.

A pretty good indication of the completeness of your own scale of perceptions is found in how you can identify the perceptions by words. Make five lists of words concerned with sight, taste, smell, hearing, and touch. Notice how one list borrows words from the others. Notice, too, how often we give names of things in nature to identify certain sensations. Your lists may be quite short under the headings of smell and taste. So far we have few words for these sensations which are not simply derived from the names of the objects which emit them, like salty or musky. Your list will probably be the longest for the sense of sight. Thus, one sense is by no means a real substitute for the other; instead, each contributes to the total perception necessary to the artist.

VISUAL ARTS

Here we are concerned chiefly with visual perception, with learning to make good use of our eyes in doing things which have a good visible result. In all of the visual arts the eyes are constantly in demand to select, manipulate, arrange, measure, fit, and adjust materials and tools. They also give the final judgment on the finished work. A particular function of the eyes, however, is important in *representation* (drawing and forming three-dimensionally whatever we actually see and any design we may imagine). In this activity, our ability to focus our eyes and to see the relation of parts of things to the whole contributes to the making of an image, or likeness, and in any scale we wish. Our ability to select the most important elements of what we see (perceptive vision) derives from the close relationship of the eye and the mind itself. And long practice in this perceptive selection of the essential shapes, forms, and movements of things has resulted in the visual langauge: meaningful and recognizable symbols for the forms of the visible world.

It is difficult to say just when in his development man discovered that he could make a line on a flat surface which would recall the shape of something he had seen. The next discovery was that he could also represent its solidness and its texture by marks that were also made by his hands and various tools such as charcoal, lead, graphite, paint, and quills and ink. We know of no primitive peoples now living who do not draw recognizable shapes. Our children begin to do so very naturally between their third and fifth years. It seems to be a good means of communication without words and also a means of self-discovery. By their drawings, children often reveal their understanding of things, and teachers often use those drawings to understand the children's needs and their progress. If the ability to draw is used, it will develop, just as talking and writing do. We know that our written language developed from pictographs (the outlines of familiar objects). Letter forms are the remnants of the shapes of things which have now been simplified into symbols so that reading and writing can be faster.

REPRESENTATION AND DESIGN ARE INSEPARABLE

At this point we should consider rather seriously an important concept already suggested in the Introduction and in Chapters I and II. Our sense of design as it is found in all nature and our urge to represent what we see and feel about it can never really be separated, no matter how realistically we work. Nor should they be. The very act of hands, pencil, brush, or chisel at work means that one's mind is translating nature, not duplicating it. The result is our own symbol, embodied in some kind of material. We hope that symbol will be understood by others. We know that it will be if we seek in nature the essentials which everyone feels to be there. *Design might be defined as the search for and use of the essential.* Representing helps us to find the essential, to record it, and to use it. Designing and representing should never be thought of as separate.

To convey some meanings, we must use nature's form recognizably but not necessarily literally. Thus it is that ways to represent nature forms have come to be so important to us. They are a part, but not all, of the language of art. Accurate representation may or may not convey the meaning we wish. Just as our spoken language is full of the names of things, so the language of art is largely made up of recognizable shapes, forms, and colors. When men wished to give words to some more abstract ideas such as love, hate, and rebellion, the spoken language developed and changed. When we wish to express in art something we understand, rather than see, about a nature form, literal representation will not do. We must refine and enrich our art vocabulary too. So long as we have something important to say, we shall find that the ways of saying it will come to us.

We do not have to invent for ourselves the basic language of art. Like the spoken language, it is already in use, and has been for a long time. Learning to use shapes, forms and depth, colors, and textures is like learning to speak. It is easier for some to learn than for others, but it is essential to everyone. An artist must learn to draw and to design at the same time.

It is futile to argue about which came first, the power to draw or to model or carve. Like the argument which shook the medieval world about the number of angels who could stand upon the head of a pin, it seems to us a little ridiculous. There does seem to be a common origin for drawing and for forming three-dimensionally. A young child's impulse is to reach for and touch each new thing he sees; he makes gestures to show us something of its size and shape; he will also show us that he saw movement by running to the place or pointing with his finger. These natural gestures may well have been the origin of both two- and three-dimensional representation. Parents and teachers observe that children usually see a connection between objects and pictures or models when they are between the ages of three and five. Children's works of art have inconsistencies in scale (large heads on small bodies, or large people with small houses) because the children become more interested in some part of a thing, such as faces or hands, than in representing the whole. They subconsciously exaggerate one and ignore the other. We, too, as children and also as adults meet problems of scale and proportion both in recording our ideas and in making finished work. Learning to draw and to design alike require the same kind of attention, judgment, and feeling, and our eyes are the instruments of our perception.

The suggested experiments which follow will combine forms and movements we see in nature. Some will be experiences in observation, representative in intent. Others will use nature only as a sort of springboard, beginning with real forms and movements but using them as symbols, not pictures. All of the activities have one purpose, to discover how to use our eyes in artwork.

GOOD VISUAL WORKING CONDITIONS

Here are some suggestions for good visual working conditions.

1. Keep your working space uncluttered. (Your eyes will help your mind to concentrate.)
2. Be sure that you can see and reach the whole surface on which you are working without moving your head. (You can focus on any particular part and still see the rest on the outer rim of your vision.)
3. Tilt the surface somewhat, so that you do not get a perspective view. (Even a desk top may be deep enough to distort the shapes of things.)
4. Your light should be so placed that it does not create deep shadows. Two lights (from left and right) are better than one. Shade them so that the bulbs are not visible; be sure that the surface (especially a shiny or a very light one) is not reflecting them. Avoid glare.
5. Stand or sit straight and at ease. Avoid slumping, leaning, habitual tilting of the head. Your eyes work better together than separately.
6. Focus on your work rather than on your hand and tool, and form the habit of looking all over your work before you focus on a particular place. Do this again after you have worked on a detail. Your eyes help you to visualize the whole effect. Spend more time looking (at your subject and at your work) than you do in drawing. The image must be in your mind before your hand can make it. Look, shut your eyes and try to see it, then open your eyes and work.

THE EYE, HAND, AND MIND WORK TOGETHER

Practicing with the hands, materials, and tools cannot be beneficial unless we form the habit of using our eyes effectively. In the first handling of any new materials our eyes guide the movement. In repeating movement rhythmically, we explore the area first with our eyes to determine its shape, size, and depth. Our eyes guide the hand about the same distance and in the same direction each time. In moving parallel to something (the edge of the table or the piece of material) the eye measures along the path of movement. Because we can see over a large area when focusing on a small one, the eye can maintain the hand's direction, even when it sees the outer shape of the material vaguely. This is the reason why peering at close range at each small movement which one is making often results in meandering lines of marks which never come out even.

CONTROLLING DIRECTION

You will learn faster if you do not use guide lines. Try instead to follow the shape of paper, the grain of wood, or the weave of fabric on which you are working. Unprinted newspaper is a good inexpensive surface for preliminary work. Use large circular or triangular pieces, as well as the usual rectangular ones. Then work on cloth, wood, and clay surfaces and on solids such as cylinders, cones, and spheres. Practice first with hand movements, with and without a tool, almost but not quite touching your surface. This helps your eyes to guide hand and tool at the pace you want to work. Work standing, swinging your body; or swing your material, keeping your body still.

Brush patterns reveal the character of the medium, the tool, and the artist.

Student experiments with repeated movement.

CONTROLLING REPEATED MOVEMENTS

1. Repeat rhythmic movements derived from the sea, using brushes and ink. Keep them parallel to each other, very compactly spaced, and fill the area completely as you work. You will tend to compensate in each row for the natural variations of the one above, getting a satisfying total effect which is not monotonous.

2. With colored chalks repeat a simple movement such as a bird makes in flight. Gradually increase or diminish the size of each stroke. Fit them together. Fill the area.

3. Imagine the movements of an animal in action. This time alternate forward and reverse directions. Lay out a "grid" of stripes or squares. Fill the grid with pen or brush strokes. Interlock the movements.

4. Try a simple movement around a sphere, cone, or cylinder, turning it as you work. Completely fill and fit the form. Poster paint with sponge or cloth with give body and good coverage.

5. Develop your own experiments, keeping in mind the important movements we recognized in nature: inward and outward from a center, upward and downward from the earth, spiraling ascents and descents. Use a variety of tools. Fill a great number of different shapes.

SEEING GEOMETRICALLY

The more smoothly circular a shape is, the more easily the eye travels around it. Other shapes very easily traversed are the square, triangle, and spiral. Irregularities in contour seem to slow the eye's movement. It prefers, however, to stay on the track. This is the reason why we are said to seek geometric shapes in even the most complex array, for instance, in constellations of stars. Using our eyes in this way helps us to see things whole and also to achieve wholeness in what we make.

Find a place where there are many objects of one kind growing together, such as a stand of spruce. Ignoring the few branches which are irregular in length, each tree would fit within a cone. These are the geometric shapes and forms we are trying to see. Compare spruce trees with cedars. Here we have a differently proportioned cone, high and not so broad at the base. It more nearly conforms to the perfect cone, because the branches and needles fill out the surface. This preliminary search is to make clear just what your eyes do when they recognize geometrical relationships. You will find many forms in nature which combine two or more geometric forms, but few which are so irregular that the geometric is hard to find. Collect them; take pictures of them; draw them with this in mind. Look for your own concepts of geometrical forms in each thing. They are not necessarily those seen by others. Even when you cannot stop to model with clay, draw, or cut paper, keep looking for them wherever you are. They will come to your aid when you try to visualize for designing. To be really useful, the memory of form has to have the essentials, not the unimportant details, of the original. Then proceed with the following experiments:

1. Make some cones, spheres, and cylinders of clay. Experiment with finger movements on their surface to see how much you can vary the outer silhouette without destroying the geometric form. Try combinations of cones, spheres, and cylinders. How many fruits and vegetables can you suggest with geometric forms without adding any detail? Try some animals, some people. Press the clay together firmly but without destroying the basic geometric shapes. Where the shapes join, leave the natural distortion from the pressure of your hands. You will often make transitional forms which remind you of those in nature.

2. Collect leaves from one plant which differ in size and variations on the edge. Make sequential arrangements (large to small, irregular to regular, etc.). Find the geometric shape basic to the whole plant, including the roots. Make an interesting arrangement of the leaves within this large basic shape. Add the basic shapes of seeds, flowers, buds of the same plant. Where do they fit into the geometric scheme?

3. Select a number of different nature forms which are often seen together. Build a three-dimensional landscape of colored papers using only the geometric forms you discover in nature. You will find that the earth, too, can be seen in spheres, pyramids, and intersecting flat planes. How could you suggest the sky?

SEEING INNER STRUCTURE

A cross section is a flat plane, as though cut with a knife, across a solid form. A perfect ball will slice into perfect circular planes, no matter where it is cut. A cone will slice into circles if cut horizontally and into triangles if cut through the center vertically. Each of these cuts would resemble the outer silhouette from top or side view without perspective. Trying to visualize a cross section is more difficult when the total form is a combination of two or more geometric ones as they often occur in nature. The following experiments will help you to see in imaginary cross sections. This will help you to draw and to shape three-dimensionally with sound structural feeling, rather than becoming dependent on outlining the outer shapes of things.

1. Slice a pear in half vertically (a). The upper section is like an elongated circle; the lower part is larger and more nearly circular. Where the stem (a cylinder) must be strong, the circle seems to follow its axis. Where the seeds were centered in the lower part, it has spread out fully to cover them. This shows how the function of the stem and that of the seeds are evident in the total silhouette. Take note of the proportion of one part to the other and also the new shape which is made where they join. Slice several irregularly formed fruits to help your eyes to visualize structures inside outer silhouettes. Examine carefully any so-called imperfections in the outer shape. Nature often provides a good solution for irregularities in growth. The pepper segments illustrate this (b).

2. Slice some of the combinations of geometric forms you made in clay to see what their cross sections reveal. You will probably notice that they have a tendency to fall apart unless the pressure has welded them into one piece. Potters often make preliminary trials of their work in this way to be sure that they are using their hands and materials well. They are trying to make a sound structure in which the parts seem to grow out of each other naturally.

3. Along a wire, place at frequent intervals some paper cross sections of a simple nature form, such as a long-necked squash. Now bend the wire in the familiar curve of growth. Watch how the outer silhouette of the whole changes. Do you recognize some of the various squash forms you observed in the market? The cross sections give us a clue to the outer, total silhouette; the wire gives us the clue to the inner direction of growth. If you can learn to see in imagination the most important cross sections and the central axis of growth, you can draw any form you understand, from any point of view or in any action. If the cross sections you made were simple geometric ones, you will be able to draw the basic three-dimensional form, a geometric abstraction of the form (c). If you included the irregularities, you will have a more "naturalistic" result (d).

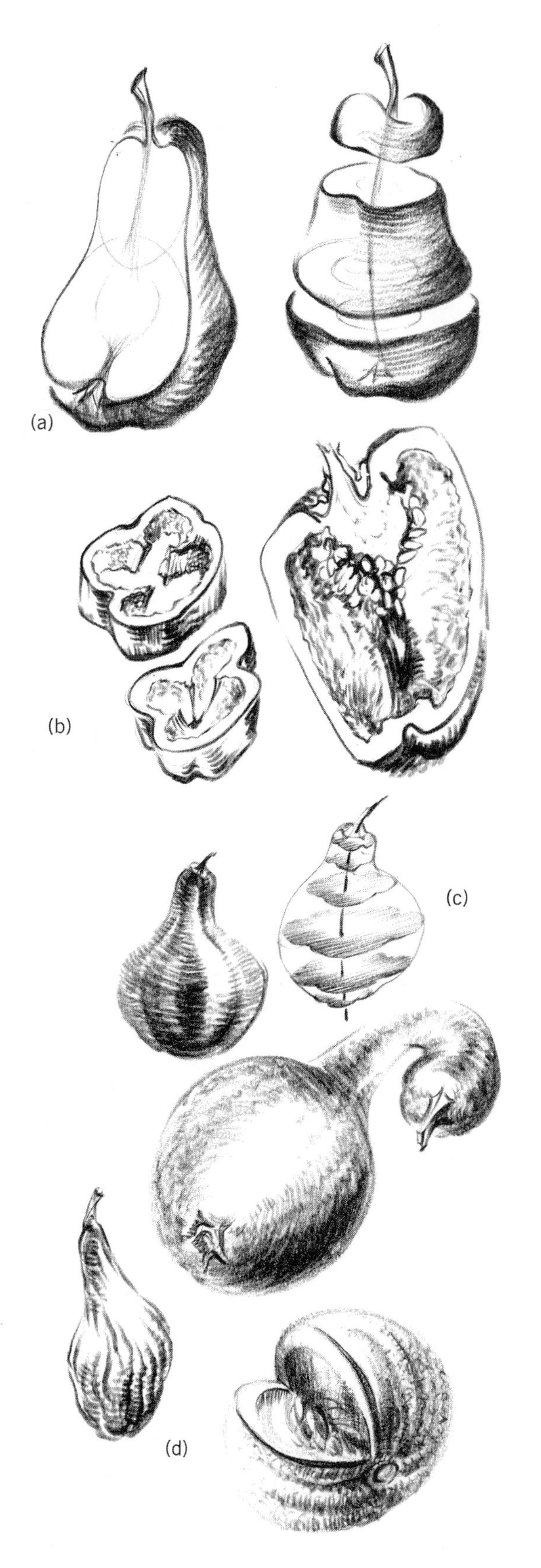

4. Objects in nature which are symmetrically formed from every point of view are rather easy to analyze geometrically, even when they are somewhat distorted. Animals and human beings in action as well as many irregular nature forms can also be seen geometrically. Try combining cross sections through the head, neck, waist, hips along the line of the backbone when drawing a living creature.

CHARACTERISTIC SILHOUETTES

Think about the shape of an animal as seen from the side, the back, front, top, and bottom. Which view in silhouette with no inner detail gives us the best idea of what kind of animal it is? Probably you will see some advantages in the side view, where the shapes of head, body, tail, and legs are easily recognizable. If the animal is in action, we can also see the changing directions of legs, body, and tail without losing their shapes very much, nor the way they attach to the body. There are, then, certain viewpoints which give us more of the essential character of a form, a better idea of the whole. The experiments which follow are planned to help you to see *characteristic silhouettes.* Using your eyes in this way is essential to both drawing and forming in three-dimensional material. The things we make should be readily understood; choosing the best viewpoint and the most characterful silhouette helps us to keep them simple and meaningful.

1. Pose your classmates behind a screen which is lighted from the back. Try to identify them by their silhouettes, in profile and in front and back views. Try the front view of body with head in profile. Next try the side view of body and head facing front. Whom did you recognize by build and height alone (larger geometric relations)? Of what help was the head in profile? What happened to the basic geometric shapes in the last position suggested?

2. Make a study of the human and animal figure as drawn by different primitive peoples.

How did they distinguish between male and female, adult and child, king and commoner, priest and warrior? How did they identify members of the cat, deer, dove, or hawk families? In case you do not believe that all the parts of a living creature belong together, try combining parts of various animal and human forms. Some of the fantastic creatures of mythology and legend were conceived in this way by early man. This experiment is interesting in two- and in three-dimensional material.

3. Draw or paint a design combining the front, side, back, top, and bottom silhouettes of some nature form. Use a differently colored line or area for each, so that the pattern does not become confused. You may want to change scale, overlap some with others, isolate some entirely, or use one silhouette for a background to hold them together. You may discover some reason in the improbable inventions of Picasso and Miro in painting; sculptors have also experimented with arbitrary combinations of characteristic silhouettes.

4. Select a simple form such as a tree which you see clearly in its most characteristic silhouette. Stand far enough from it so that you can extend your arm and trace around it in space with your index finger. Memorize this movement by doing it two or three times. Have a large enough surface of paper, sand, or flat board on which you can repeat this movement still at arm's length with finger extended. You will discover how it feels to make it on a flat plane. Alternate between doing it in the air and on the surface until the movement feels the same. Try faster and slower speeds to discover your own best pace. Take anything that will make a mark (pencil, charcoal, paint brush) and repeat the process. You are drawing; your mind, eyes, and hands automatically time and space the movements. You are also designing; for you are interpreting your subject instinctively as you and no other person can see it. You are also making it conform to a flat plane.

Chama vase, Guatemala, A. D. 600 to 900. (Courtesy of the University Museum of the University of Pennsylvania, Philadelphia, Pa.)

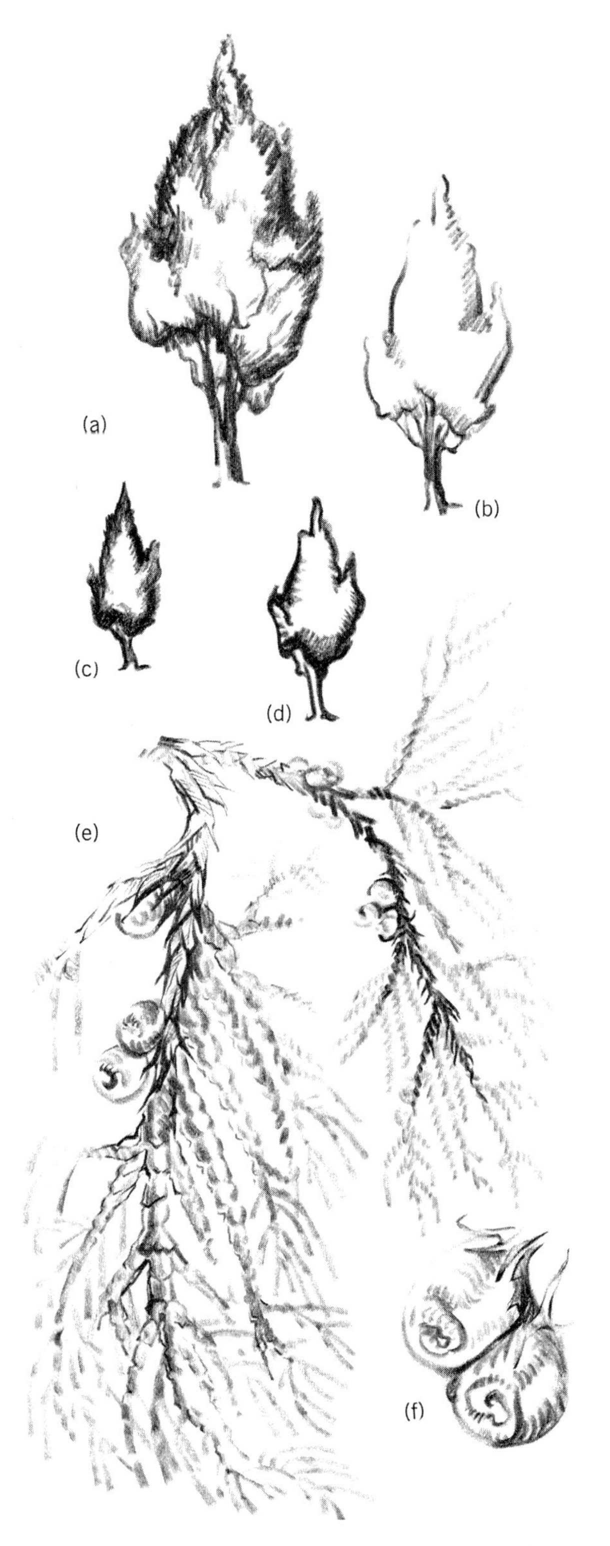

Drawing in miniature and also enlarging a detail gives one control of the image.

SEEING SCALE

5. Now experiment with scale. This time draw at arm's length in the air around a rather large object (a) still in the air, repeat that movement getting smaller and smaller (b, c, d). You are "focusing" your movement; it still feels the same. The parts of it are still going the same direction; you take the curves and angles in stride, faster on the long stretches, slower on the irregularities, but the whole movement is there, just as it was before. Now gradually reduce size until it fits; take your marking tool and use it on the surface where you need it. Drawing large things much smaller helps us to see the whole rather than the parts of things.

6. Reverse this whole experiment (e and f). Beginning with a small object, enlarge your movements gradually in the air. Finally, draw them on a surface much larger than the original movement. It will still feel the same. Every movement of your fingers affects and is affected by the movements of your arm and of your eyes. Your mind is directing all at the same time and selecting what you feel is most important. Drawing larger than the actual object often makes your work more expressive, especially if it is full of intricate and beautiful detail.

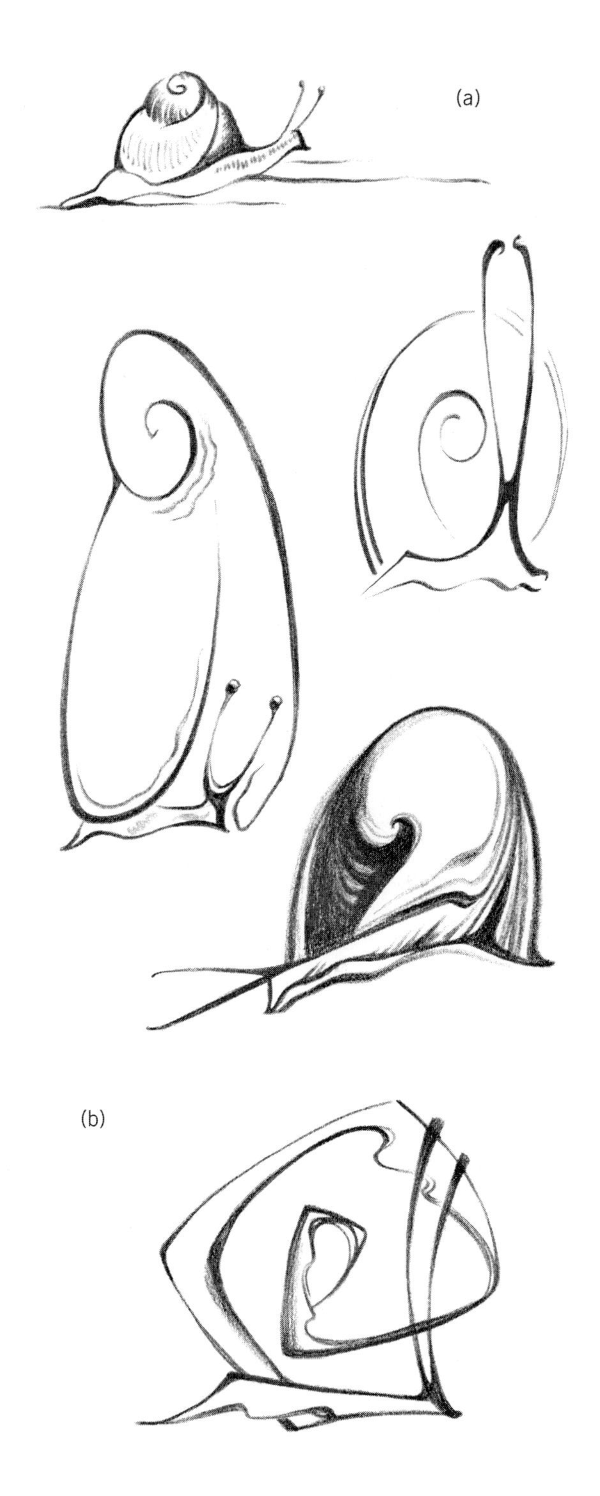

Fanciful interpretations of a snail within different given areas.

FILLING A GIVEN SPACE

7. Now experiment in another way. This time make the surface on which you will draw much longer and narrower than the object seems to be (a). You will pull it out to fit the area in one direction and hold it in to fit in the other direction. It will be an elongated image but still in proportion within itself (b). You may have noticed that certain of your classmates tend to elongate naturally. Elongation is a characteristic of the paintings of Modigliani and El Greco and of the sculpture of the Egyptian and the Gothic periods. It is a very common characteristic of certain people's handwriting. Fashion illustrators use it to make clothes look smart; for women like to look tall and slender.

Quick, intense studies from life result in unrealistic but expressive drawing.

EXAGGERATING WHAT YOU SEE

8. Try this time to change the original silhouette so that some parts will be exaggerated, some minimized. Perhaps a simple human face will do, in profile, which is easy (a). Then try an animal or human figure in a characteristic silhouette or line. Go about this as before, first the actual form in the air; take your time on the important parts, simplify on the less important. Perhaps you will discover something about how cartoonists "see." The movement will feel the same, but there will probably be a grotesque, fantastic quality about the image you get. It may remind you of children's work because in spite of being out of proportion it still is remarkably like the actual thing. It is not unnatural or deformed, just exaggerated (b, c, d).

If this has been your first experience with drawing something you actually see, you will begin to realize how long it may have taken for primitive man to develop this skill with the eyes and hand which many of us take for granted.

Base line illustration on Chama vase from Guatemala. (Extended drawing by M. L. Baker, courtesy of the University Museum of the University of Pennsylvania, Philadelphia, Pa.)

Steer drawn by kindergarten child at Kutztown State College Laboratory School.

SEEING AND EXPRESSING DEPTH

Learning to transfer a simple image to a working surface leads inevitably to a desire to show it in some detail and to tell a story. Some truly ingenious ways evolved historically just from the purposes for which drawings were made. For instance, if they were intended for a record of events, they might be lined up like a parade on the baseline of any convenient wall. If the story was to be told with symbols on a bowl, they might begin at the vessel's center and expand. The most important person was placed in the middle, with objects, animals, and other human forms on a circular baseline around him. A very good solution; but since the most important character could look in only one direction, the artist sometimes has given him several heads.

In the round, on a rock or tree trunk, for instance, a sculptor could put the front and back silhouette on opposite ends, fill in the two side profiles and cut away the extra material. But to represent the entire animal just as completely on a long flat surface, (for example, in low relief) he might have to begin in the middle with the front view, placing the two side views appropriately to the left and the right. The logical conclusion to this method is that the animal has two tails, probably a disturbing thought even to a primitive; a five-year old child might find it perfectly understandable.

Dancing male figures on a shell breast ornament from the Spiro Indian mound. (Courtesy of the Stovall Museum of Science and History of the University of Oklahoma, Norman, Okla.)

Within the total silhouette of an animal from the side view the inside structure is sometimes shown by outlining the separation between legs, tail, neck, and head. Such invisible parts as the heart, the teeth, and the tongue appear in appropriate places. Some primitive drawings even include what the animal ate or the arrow with which he was killed. By placing the legs in appropriate positions the primitive artists showed that the animal had four, not two legs, and also that it moved. It was very easy to fill in the nearest legs, covering up the farthest where they seem to overlap in contour. They represented another animal in back of the first one, simply by seeing to it that the second silhouette did not quite coincide with the first. The feet of all the animals, if they are four or five abreast, remained on one level, as though they were walking a tightrope. Objects such as trees and buildings also appeared on the same line. This is a very satisfactory solution when the area in which the artist works is a long narrow strip, like a wall or a border on a blanket. A succession of humans, animals, and objects can tell a pretty complete story and can be made to fit whatever space is available.

Probably the next discovery in representation had to come when the tightrope became too full. If one could put the nearest things on one line and those in back on another above it, one could explain depth more clearly. This satisfied the Egyptians very well. It served to make use of high walls, columns, and the upper slabs of stone in the roof. The objects on the higher levels were usually smaller than those on the lower levels. This must have suggested depth in perspective very convincingly when looking up from the ground. The disadvantage of this method of showing depth is that each level looks like a separate picture. Almost all early architectural forms bear some representative decoration. Usually any effort to show depth appears either in the overlapping or the tier format.

The reason for including these historic experiments with showing depth is that we ought to recognize in them perfectly logical thinking. They are ways of coordinating eyes, hands, and mind on the problem of representing the world we see. That they no longer satisfy us is quite apparent from the fact that they need to be explained for us. They did, however, express sufficient realism for man for centuries uncounted.

PERSPECTIVE

In the Western arts since the Renaissance we have an invention for showing form and depth which we call "true" or converging perspective. Other experiments very closely allied to it developed at a much earlier date in the Oriental world. Considering that they have been using their perspective about 2000 to 4000 years compared with our 500, it is perhaps natural that we are still not very skillful. There is no reason to insist, however, that ours is true and theirs untrue to life. Certainly their solution seems to be beautifully harmonized with their drawing or painting surface, whereas ours sometimes is not. It is quite unlikely that we actually see differently than either the primitives or the Orientals. Most of us understand what we call true perspective in a picture, that is, we know when it is wrong, but we are not very sure how to make it right. Perspective drawing is rather like a language which we understand but cannot speak. Some of us use this language without very much skill, just enough to make ourselves understood if others are not too critical. There are those who speak it correctly (they draw things just as they see them) and a few who speak it with great beauty. The power to communicate the sensation of form and depth whether in two or in three dimensions is an exciting one.

CONSTRUCTING PERSPECTIVE MODELS

Practicing converging perspective can only give us a little more insight into what we need to see and how the coordinating of eye and hand with our minds can help us. The constructions suggested here have proved useful in learning to see in perspective.

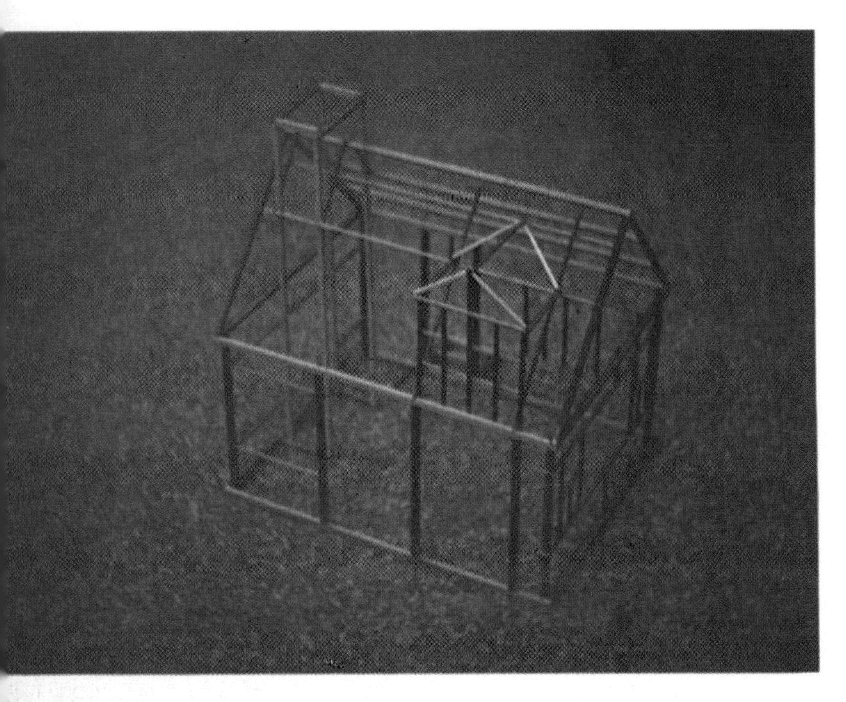

Model formed of balsa strips.

1. By joining balsa wood strips with cement, construct the skeleton of a simple house, perhaps with an adjoining L or shed. Do not fill in the walls, roof, or floor. Build some doors and windows to make the skeleton more interesting. Try to keep visible the most important cross sections, such as where the shed, a chimney, or flight of steps joins the main walls of the house. Now paint the ends of the house and the parallel sides of the chimney, steps, shed, etc., with one color. Paint the sides of house and all the other strips parallel to them with another color. You now have all the lines you need to draw your house correctly in perspective. The parallels are clearly distinguishable because of color. Building this house has given you a clue to what you must do in imagination when you draw a real house. The color helps you to use the correct vanishing points. (See pages 90 and 91.)

2. Build some other skeleton forms of toothpicks or balsa wood strips which combine cubes, pyramids of various heights, octagonal forms, star forms, and others which will suggest themselves as you work. Because these are like the combinations of geometric forms you feel in nature, they will help you to master the perspective views. Keep the important cross sections visible; do not fill in.

3. Make of reed other skeleton forms which include round, oval, and spiral parts; combine them with vertical and horizontal straight sections. Cross sections are very important. Do not cover them. They will help you to see what happens to curves in perspective.

Any or all of these experiments might be done with glass, cellophane, or any other transparent material.

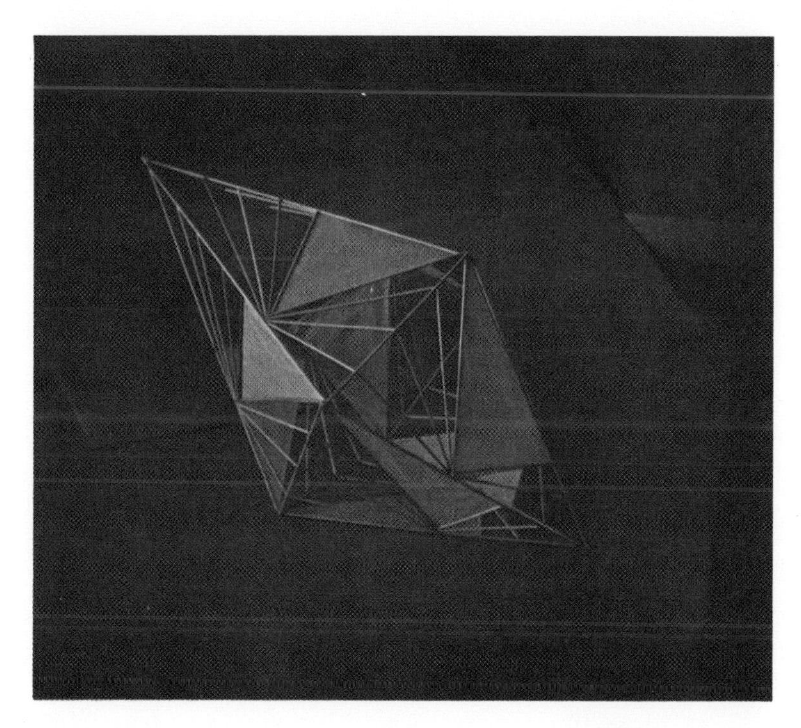

Constructions of balsa strips and paper. (By Susan Harbold, Linden Hall School for Girls, Lititz, Pa.)

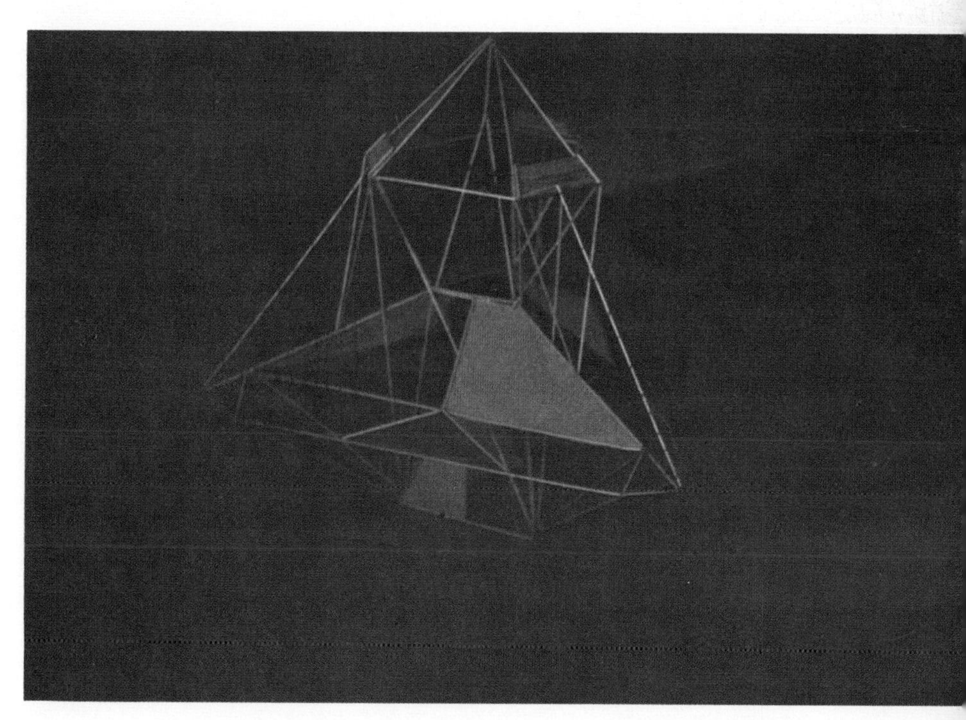

(By Judy Alspaugh, Linden Hall School for Girls, Lititz, Pa.)

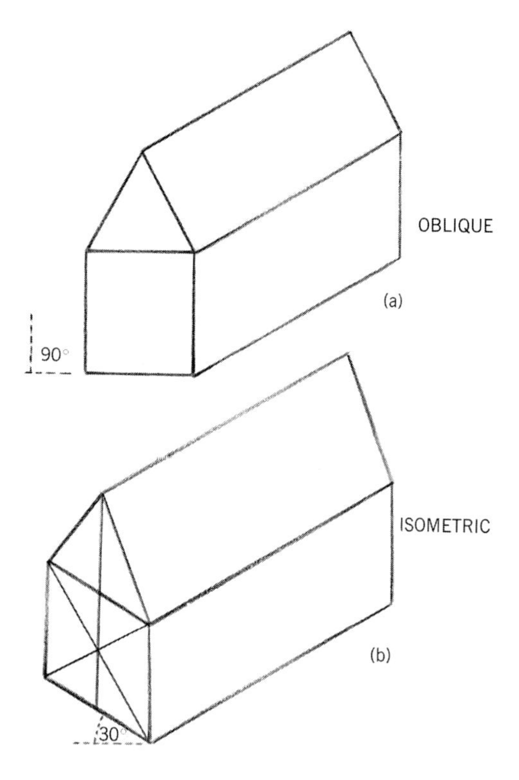

Bahram with Chinese Princess in the Yellow Palace on Sunday; from manuscript "Khamsah" by Nizami (1574 A. D.). (Courtesy of the University Museum of the University of Pennsylvania, Philadelphia, Pa.)

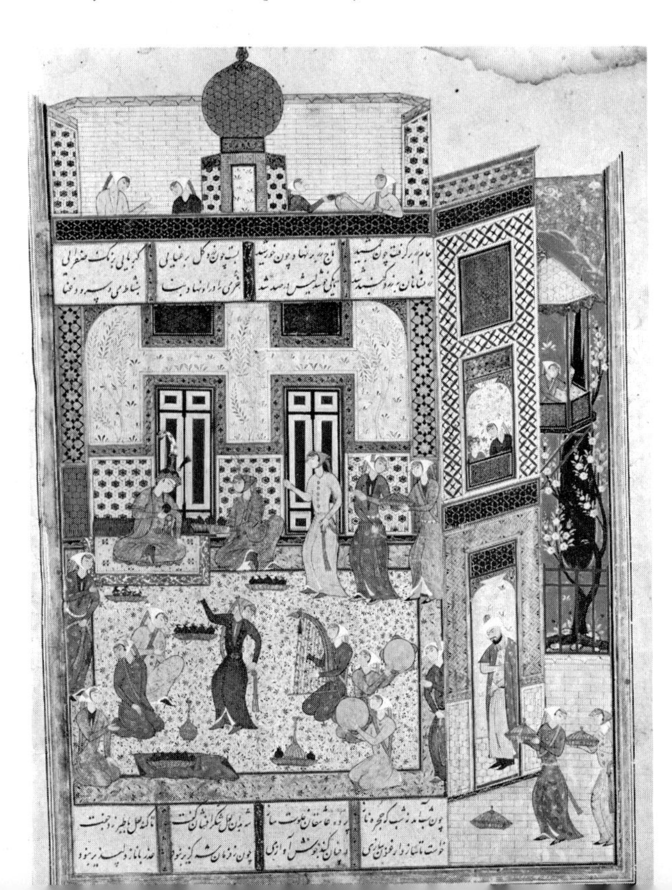

OBLIQUE PERSPECTIVE AND ISOMETRIC PERSPECTIVE

We shall explain briefly two ways in which some illusion of form in space may be obtained by drawing the skeleton of the house you made exactly as it is.

1. Begin with an elevation of one end of your object in actual size. From each corner of this draw lines at any angle, using the actual lengths of the sides which meet this end. Connect the ends of these lines, thereby making the other end (a).

2. Begin with the corner nearest to you. Make the elevation of the end an angle of 30 degrees. (Find the center of this end by diagonals to erect a gable.) Project the side of the house on an angle of 30 degrees; measure off actual lengths of each line. Connect the ends of the lines to obtain the far end of the house (b).

You will observe as you work that the near parts seem to give you a good idea of form as you know it. The farther you project into space the more unconvincing the drawing becomes. It does not feel right. This is partly because you have become accustomed to the convergent method of perspective more commonly used in the Western world. Oblique and isometric perspective are the bases on which the Oriental arts of representation were developed. We use the same method when we wish to visualize a form on a flat surface and still be able to measure actual lengths of lines at any distance from the eye. Architects and engineers make use of isometric perspective because the actual measurements are used and can be read on the drawing.

CONVERGING PERSPECTIVE

In converging perspective we are trying to represent the way our eyes move across and around, over and through the solid objects we see *from where we stand.* We need to know how these eye movements can be coordinated with those of our hands in space. The so-called laws of converging perspective were discovered in this way. To understand it thoroughly, you will need to consult a good textbook on perspective drawing. The following experiments are intended only to help you to use your eyes correctly when you are actually trying to draw what you see in perspective. The convergence of receding lines is due to the focusing power of the eye.

1. Select a simple building of which you can see two sides plainly by facing a corner (a). With arm extended trace in the air around one side of it. Transfer this movement to your drawing area just as you did with the outer silhouette of the tree (see page 79). You will find that you do not have a rectangle. The near corner of the building is definitely a longer movement than the far corner. The ground line slants upward, the eaves downward. Retrace in the air the first side and then cross over to the other side of the building. When you are sure you feel the two together, add the second side. This helps to keep the sides in line and in the right proportion to each other. It is important to keep your eyes level and to stand in the same place each time you draw in the air. With this kind of practice in coordinating hands and eyes you could learn to make a perspective drawing without benefit of a textbook, but it is a slow task. Mechanical perspective from a book, however, can never be a substitute for the actual feel of it on the spot.

2. Choose two subjects which are cylindrical, like a silo above your eyes and a wagon below your eyes (b). Repeat the experiment. Begin with the silo, tracing it in the air and transferring the movement to your paper.

a) Feeling the convergence of shapes. b) Feeling the elliptical appearance of round objects.

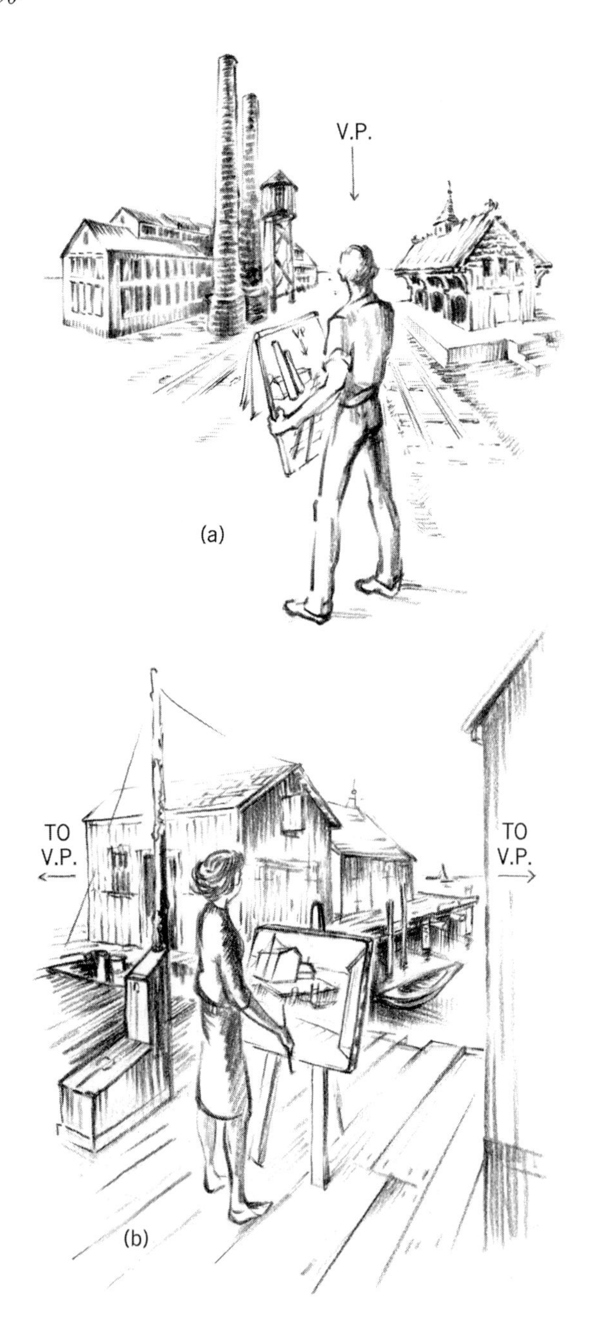

Locating one's eye level helps to unify a sketch.

You will have to feel the full roundness by imagining it is transparent. It will not feel like the complete circle for you will have an ellipse at the top and at the bottom. These two ellipses will be different. Probably the bottom will be more nearly on the level of your eyes (making a shallow ellipse) than is the top (making a deep ellipse). Try the large round wheels of the wagon. When you trace them in the air, you will again get an ellipse but not a vertical-horizontal one. It will seem to tilt toward your center of vision. A drawing textbook will explain the reason, but you can feel it in the way your hands and eyes move.

3. To make good use of a textbook on perspective, you need to know how to locate your eye level and so-called vanishing points wherever you are drawing. Stand or sit straight, and extend your arms horizontally level with your eyes. Move them in a full arc. Focus straight ahead for a one-point perspective view (a). For the vanishing points in two-point perspective (b) use the place on each side of the arc where your finger tip comes into view on the outer edge of your vision. You still focus straight ahead while you place these points. They determine the angle at which lines above your eyes seem to slant downward and lines below your eyes seem to slant upward. All lines parallel in a building are drawn toward the same point. Use the same points when the forms you see are arranged parallel to each other, as in a neatly laid-out town. Buildings built at a different angle determine their own vanishing points: begin with the nearest corner and by arm movements in the air carry the ground line on each side upward until it seems to meet your eye level. The eaves on each side, being parallel to the ground lines, will slant downward to the same two points on eye level. All of the receding lines come to rest on the same eye level, but you might have several vanishing points along that line.

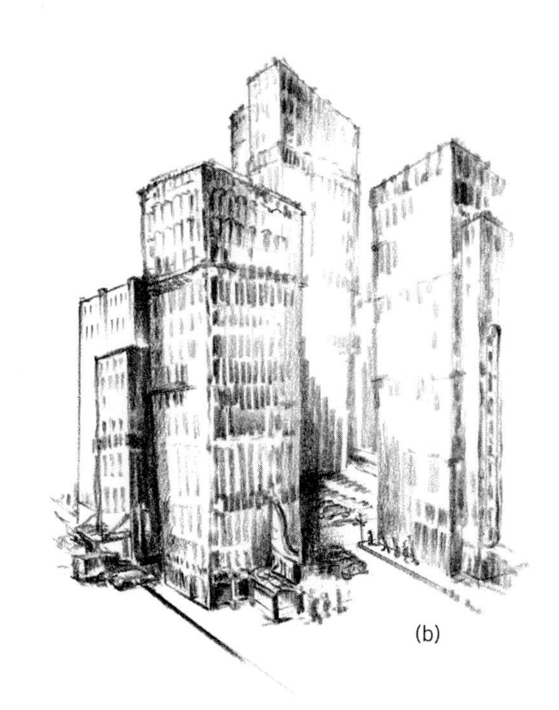

4. Tall rectangular forms also show the effect of distance upward, and if you look down through an elevator shaft, you will see the same effect of depth downward. This can only be achieved on a flat surface by making the vertical corners also appear to be drawn toward a vanishing point. Your perspective textbook will explain this at great length. It is easy to verify if you point a camera upward at a skyscraper. It is very apparent when you choose a position which is very close to even a small building (a). Some people exaggerate this effect of receding upward to make forms look large and heavy (b). Some even reverse this effect to make forms seem to overhang (b).

a) Adobe house seen both above and below eye level. b) Exaggerated convergence emphasizes the bulk of tall city buildings.

As we have stated before, the various ways of showing form on a flat surface are not true in the sense that real forms are. They simply are useful or not useful depending upon the purpose of the drawing. The most important advantage of using converging perspective is that seeing everything from one point of view gives you a better sense of the whole scene. It helps to unify your drawing. The disadvantage in using converging perspective literally is that the picture frame seems like a window through which you are looking. You feel outside rather than inside your subject. Sometimes you forget that the surface on which you are drawing is a design in itself and the converging lines may touch the frame at inconvenient angles or corners. The lines must be reconciled to the frame, so planned that they do not distract from the whole picture. Just as the natural focusing action of the eye makes it possible for us to see any object, or even any small part of it, more distinctly than the surrounding areas, so in looking at a picture will the eye seek a focus which the artist has chosen. It is here that he must concentrate attention by clarity of shapes, by contrast, and by adjusting all of the other shapes in such a way that nothing will interrupt the instantaneous total perception of the whole.

It is unfortunate that in studying particular characteristics of visual perception and functions of the eye one must separate the seeing of lines, shapes, and directions from the perception of forms and color. Actually, there are no lines in nature; one would see none of these, were it not that light reveals them as the edges of forms. We would not be conscious at all of the myriad shapes surrounding us were it not that the movement of the eye informs us; still less would the movement of the life about us be perceived without the changing shapes and aspects of lighted forms. This chapter and the one which follows, therefore, should be read and the experiments attempted without undue interruption of their sequence.

POINTS FOR DISCUSSION AND EXPERIMENTING

1. Read about Helen Keller and her teacher. How did she learn through her other senses even though she was born both blind and deaf?
2. Why are we unsure of ourselves when our eyes do not focus properly? If a design or picture has no focal point, does the observer feel that it is unsure or confusing?
3. How far to your right and left and above and below can you see without moving your head? Why do very large works of art need to be planned carefully because of this limitation? How do mural painters solve this problem?
4. Before slide projectors and screens were invented, we used stereopticon viewers. Why were the slides made with two pictures rather than one?
5. Why does a painter back away from his work and study it with half-closed eyes?
6. Why does a sculptor walk around his work or place it on a turntable?
7. Why do people instinctively reach for and handle a material which is new to them? Why do they often touch a very realistically rendered picture?
8. Why do children often draw and model or carve objects rather geometrically?
9. Why do primitive artists' works seem to fit into any space they have, whereas we often have trouble with composition, no matter how well we can draw?
10. Study some Japanese prints and some reproductions of Chinese paintings. How did the artists express depth and perspective? Would you say the artworks are well drawn? or well-designed? or both? or neither?

Our Eyes:
Perceiving Tone, Color, Texture, and Movement

V

All Arts are one, howe'er distributed they stand;
Verse, tone, shape, color, form are the fingers on one hand.

WILLIAM WETMORE STORY
The Unexpressed

REPRESENTING FORMS WITH DARK AND LIGHT

We have been chiefly concerned so far with how eyes move and how the hands can be taught to follow them. This results in delineation, or line making. Now we shall attempt, in a very elementary way, to study the artist's use of the sensitivity of the eyes to light and dark, to colors, and to textures.

Light and shade, like the use of converging perspective, were especially interesting to the European Renaissance artists and have characterized the arts of Western civilizations. We shall first consider the obvious fact that we do see dark and light and many intermediate tones inside a total silhouette. Everyone has experienced how important it is for the outer contour of a thing to be of a different tone from the background. Within that outer contour we find that flat objects vary in tone very little if they face us. If they are turned on a decided angle, however, we see a great difference between the near and the far part of that same face, a swift gradation of the tone. To represent this on paper, we must make a gradation of some kind. To make it convincing, we must be sure that the near part is easier to see than the far edge, but the whole silhouette must be different enough from the color of the background to be visible. You will probably have to exaggerate the gradation you see. Our eyes are very keen, but drawing materials have limitations.

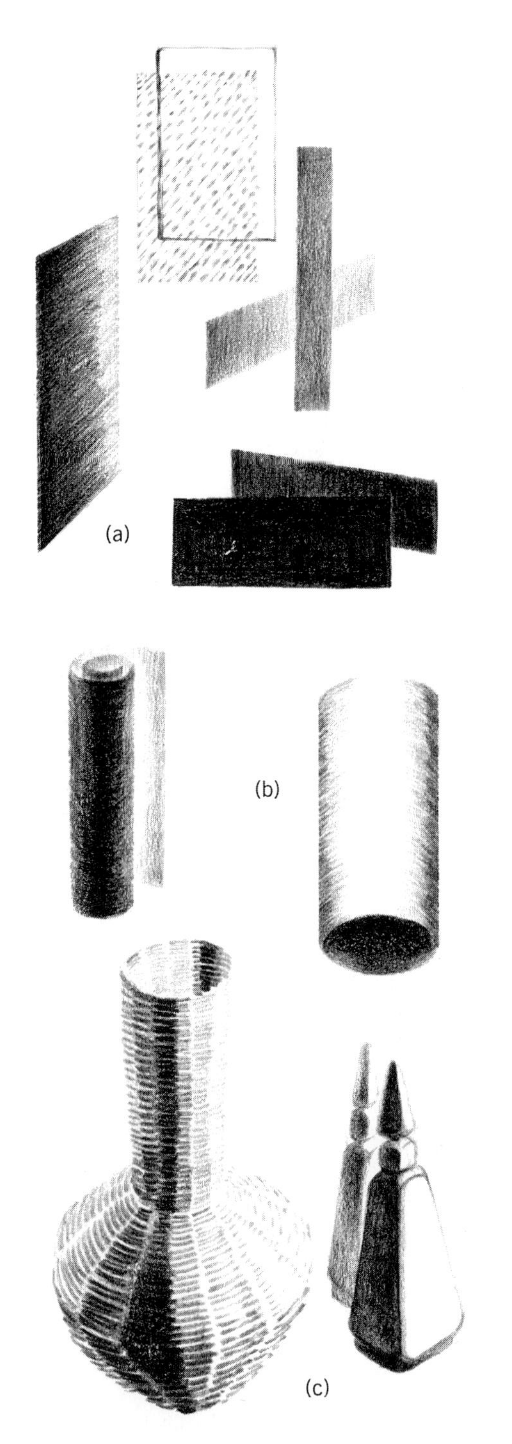

Gradations of tone reveal form and suggest light direction.

DIRECTION OF LIGHT

1. Experiment with this basic principle. Make it work on light, on medium, and on dark backgrounds; observe pieces of cardboard standing on edge to help you to see the gradation of light. Apply this simple device to some of your first experiments in perspective (a).

Suppose that the object is not flat but round like a cylinder. The center of this round surface is the closest to our eyes; other parts recede from that part, and those receding surfaces are visibly graded in tone. To make this convincing on paper, therefore, we need a gradation in two directions, to the right and to the left of the center (b). This would give us an illusion of a solid cylinder but not a logical effect of light from a particular direction. Practice this effect on dark, on medium, and on light paper.

The eye can distinguish very closely related tones; our scale of perception of light and dark might include a hundred or more. Hence we could use a gradation of light tones to the right, a gradation of dark tones to the left (c). This would give us something like the effect of light on a solid cylinder. However, we must still arrange these tones so that we see the near surface more plainly than the far surfaces. We begin, therefore, on that near surface with a good strong dark and a clear light near each other. If they touch each other, the form will project sharply like the near corner of a box. If they grade swiftly but smoothly into each other, they will seem to be round like the near part of a cylinder. It will be necessary to practice this, too, on light, on medium, and on dark backgrounds to thoroughly understand it. Do not be surprised if you cannot see these tones clearly in a real object. You will find them after you have learned to look for them.

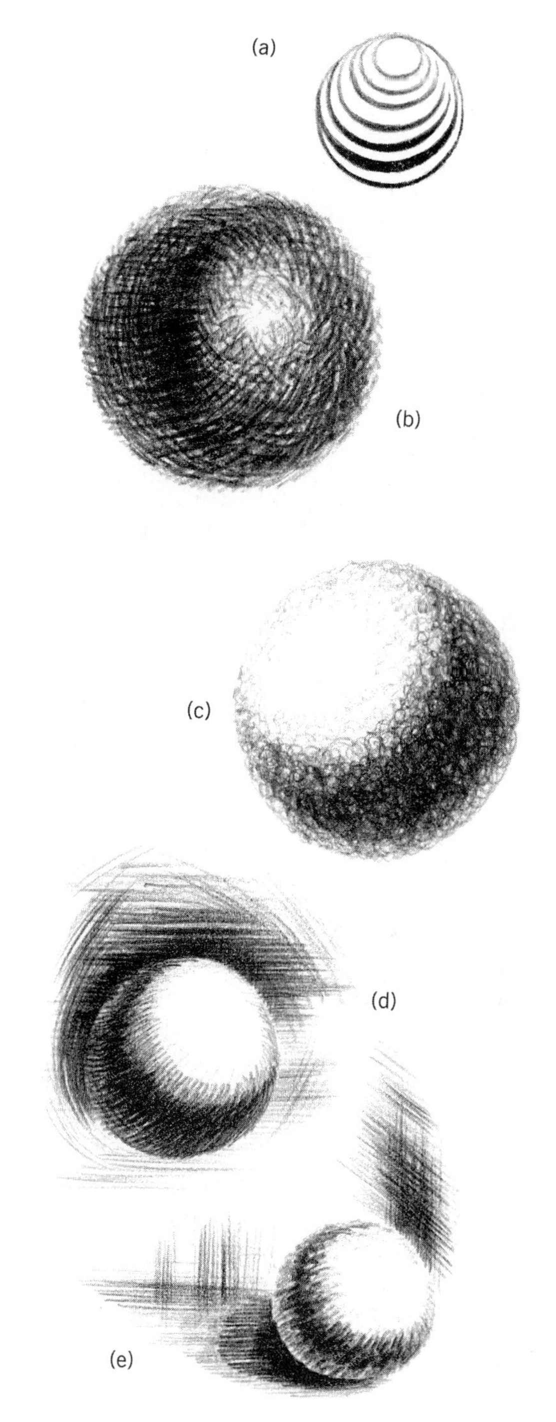

Round forms in space are more tangible with background gradations.

2. Suppose that the object is round like a ball. Find the spot on this object which is closest to you. All the other parts must invite our eyes to move back into the picture. One can make a fairly convincing sphere even with a few simple shaded lines (a). To make a solid one, (b) use a strong dark and a bright light first on the near surface to be sure that our eyes catch this area more plainly than anything else. For all the other parts, to the left and right and above and below, use gradations for our eyes to move upon. To make it look lighted, proceed as before; first, be careful to blend the strong dark and the strong light on the near side if the object is smoothly round. Use light tones in regular succession on the lighted side, reserving all the darker ones for the shadowed side (c). We do not allow any tone which is just like the paper to be used on the outer contour; for this would destroy the unity of the total silhouette.

REVEALING FORMS BY BACKGROUND

It is possible, of course, that the background, too, might be more helpful if it seemed to recede in back of the object; our round object still looks as if pinned to a flat surface. This change in the background should now be very simple. Make use of gradations of tones to invite the eye to move from each edge of the picture to a place in back of the ball. It should now float in space like a planet (d). If you wished to express a sphere standing on a flat surface (e), you would also need the shadow it casts on the table. Study these effects of lighting with actual objects. Experiment with different directions and distances from the source of light.

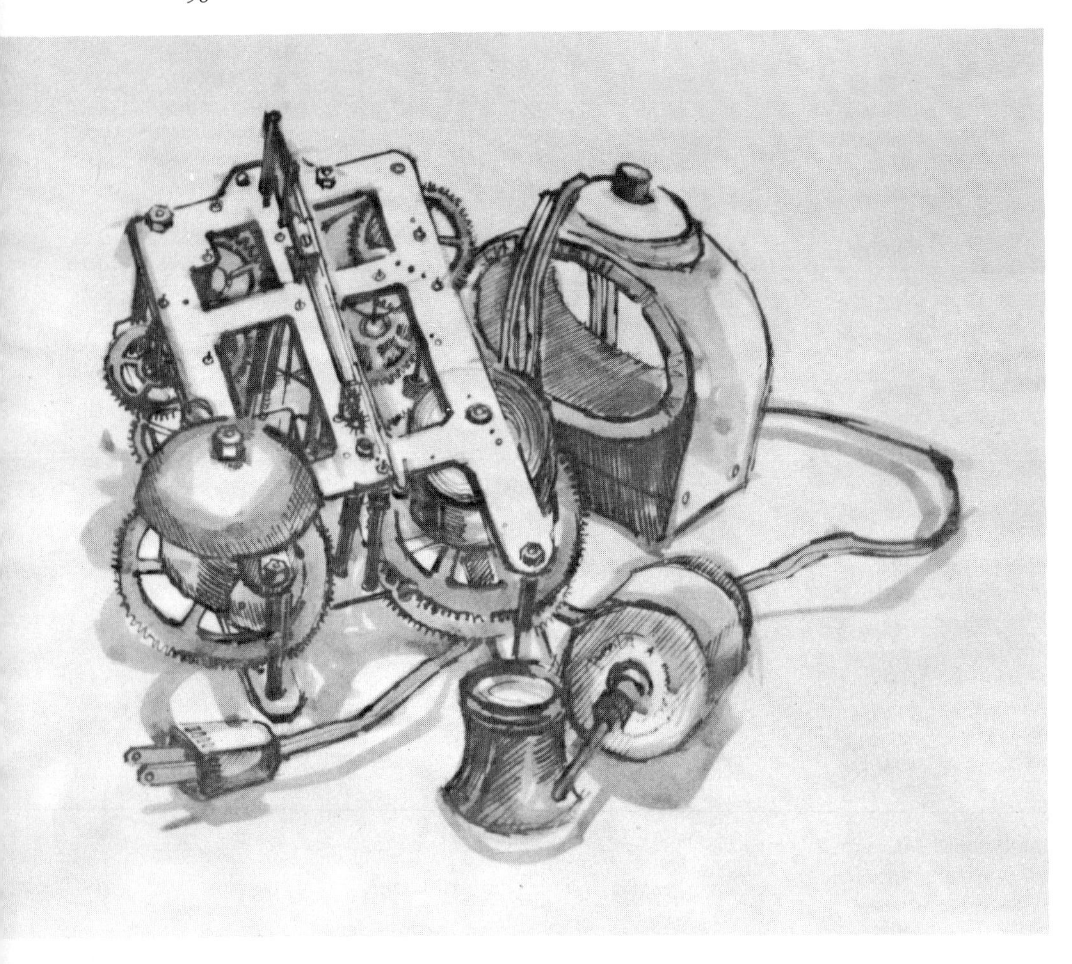

Forms may be revealed by a studied freedom of values and line. (Ink wash drawing by Phyllis Ritter, Kutztown State College.)

Experiment with various media, projecting forms by the use of *values* (darks and lights). Black and white poster paint mixed in various proportions will give you about ten different steps between black and white. Try charcoal, soft pencil, water color, or diluted India ink for a more smooth gradation. Try projecting a form by pen strokes or stippling. Tooling strokes cut with a gouge in linoleum will give you another experience. Try to discover in each medium how a solid form can be expressed as fully as possible. As you practiced with lines and areas in Chapter III, you realized how important it was to maintain rhythmic movement. Keep this in mind. Let your hands and eyes move around, across, and in back of the object, feeling the form with every stroke.

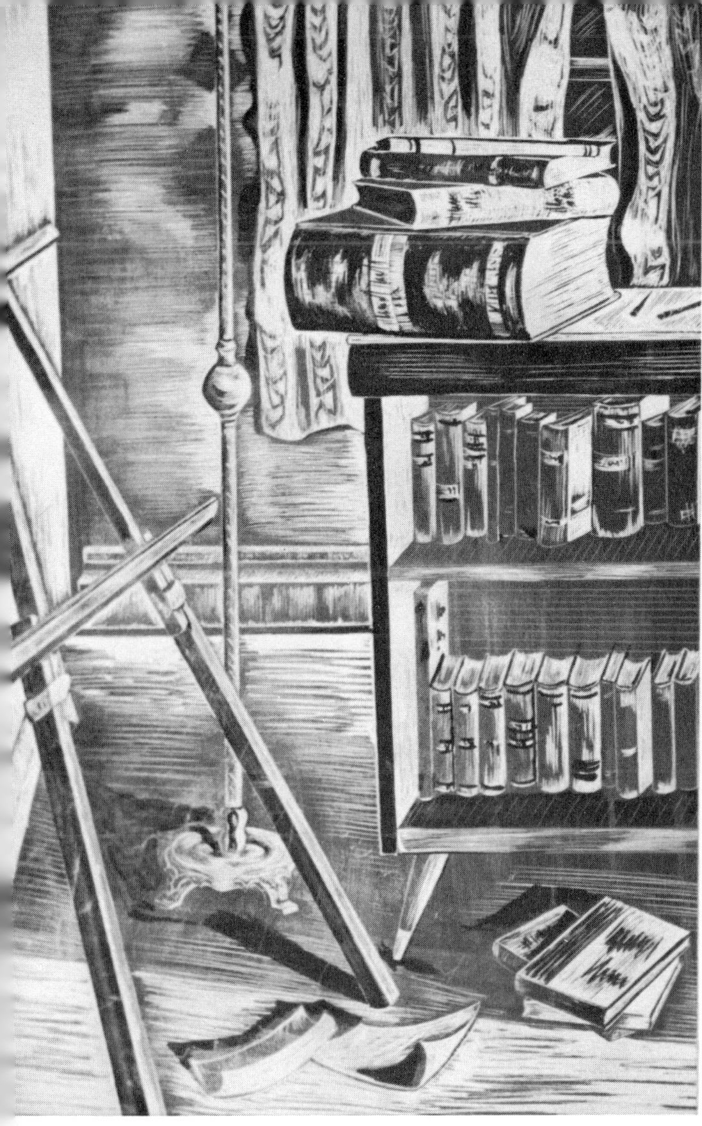

(Scratchboard by Boris Dudchenko, Kutztown State College.)

Forms may be studied in textural detail or simplified into flat values.

(Cut paper by Susan Curlett, Kutztown State College.)

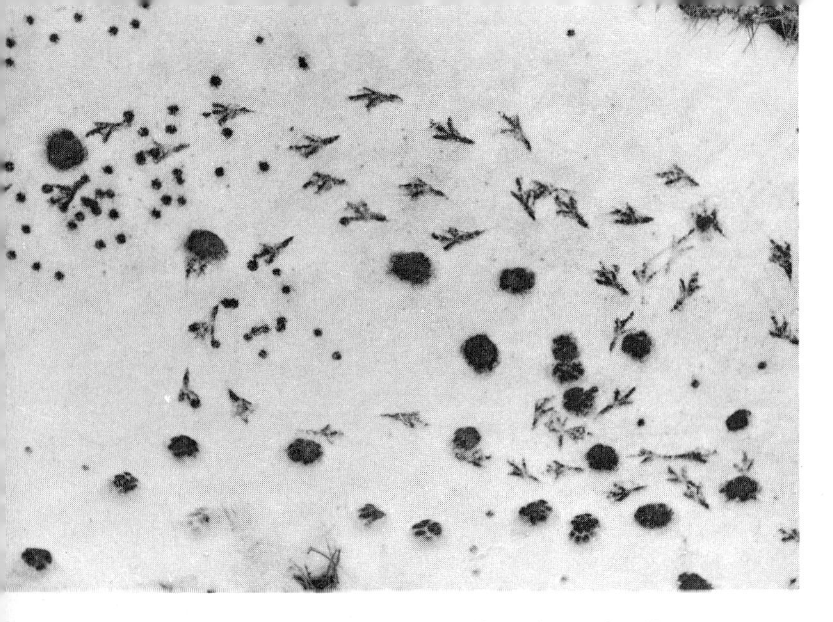

The tentative prints of small feet in newly fallen snow.

The dry crispness of a sun-baked beach.

The moist softness of ferns and lichens among boulders.

The bulging leathery cushions of fungi on paper birch.

The imprint of living creatures on an age-old rock.

SEEING AND USING TEXTURE

Our eyes report to us a fairly clear idea of the materials out of which things are made because the sensations of color and of dark and light are caused by various surfaces which reflect light in different ways. The green leaves of a tree are seen as green planes some of which face the light and others of which turn away. Glass reflects almost pure light at one angle and permits almost all the light to penetrate at another angle. The myriad facets of sand grains throw off tiny flecks of color and pure light, resulting in a soft, vibrant, neutralized tone as a whole. Fur picks up light on the small hair tips and absorbs a great deal close to the skin where the hairs are closely packed together. The reports our eyes give us and those which we get from touching verify each other, and we have come to use the word *texture* not only for what we feel but also for the look of materials.

Just as we express a form by making use of light and dark, so we can make use of textures we see. In nature the textures are evidence of inner structure. The grain of wood, the hardness of the heart wood, and the roughness of the bark are as they are because of the varying cell structures of the tree, each structure being suited to its function. When we wish to express the essential qualities of a tree in a drawing, we must discover some way to use strokes of the tool to suggest these important differences in feel. Without them our interpretation of the form would not be as meaningful. The object is not to invite someone to touch the drawing to make sure that it is not an actual tree. It is simply to recall the interesting experience of touching because it reveals so much of the essential nature of the tree.

Perhaps this will be more clear if we make use of a rather gruesome example. Consider for a moment that we have a really fine example of the taxidermist's work, a mounted fox. We also have a fox which has been whittled from soft pine with a jackknife. The stuffed animal is entirely lifelike in action and, of course, bears his own beautiful fur. The carved fox is full of life, too. His foxy nature is perfectly apparent even though we

The taut strength of tendrils and the vine.

The lush and hairy leaf of a garden border plant.

(By Patricia Snyder, Kutztown State College.)

Linoleum responds to tooling in individual ways.

(By Diane Riu, Kutztown State College.)

recognize immediately that he is made of wood. The hackles rise sharp and clear, his back is sleek, his brush tail is flaunted but soft, like a plume. If we touch the little carving, we experience both the remembered form of a real animal and the satisfying feel of the warm wood. We are not fooled; we are intrigued by the way the carver has translated the real experience into wood for us. But when we touch the mounted fox, we cannot help but feel first that he is not alive but dead. Let us look also at two pictures of a fox, perhaps a Japanese brush drawing and a painting of the English school of the nineteenth century. In the one we have him in a few sure strokes. In the other we have as faithful a copy of the sad, hunted creature as human eye could ask. In the brush drawing we have the remembered experience of pure foxiness and also the rewarding new experience of enjoying the artist's translation; we see foxiness as he sees and feels it. The painting would make us feel almost impelled to shudder were we not forewarned by the frame that it is, after all, only a picture. Much as we admire the skill of the realistic representation, we can only compare it unfavorably with the real thing. It does not give us a new experience; instead, it rather painfully recalls an old one.

In your own experimenting with textures as they can be suggested or simulated you will probably need to try many different tools and media. Some that are especially rewarding are pen, or brush, and ink; tooling linoleum or soft wood; and scratchboard (an inked, clay-surfaced cardboard that is scratched with a sharp point to give clear white strokes). Try some of the less traditional tools, such as feathers, sponges, or fur with paint. Each will give you a different translation of textures you see.

(Chalk drawing by James Goodhart, Kutztown State College.)

(Charcoal drawing by Helen Huffington, Kutztown State College.)

Each medium reveals materials in its own way.

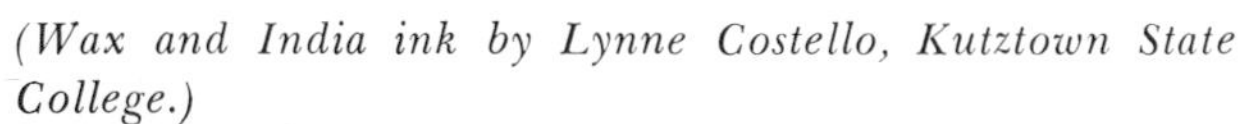

(Wax and India ink by Lynne Costello, Kutztown State College.)

(*Photograph by Jeanne Horn, Kutztown State College.*)

(*Photograph by John Uram, Kutztown State College.*)

Textural beauty is where you find it.

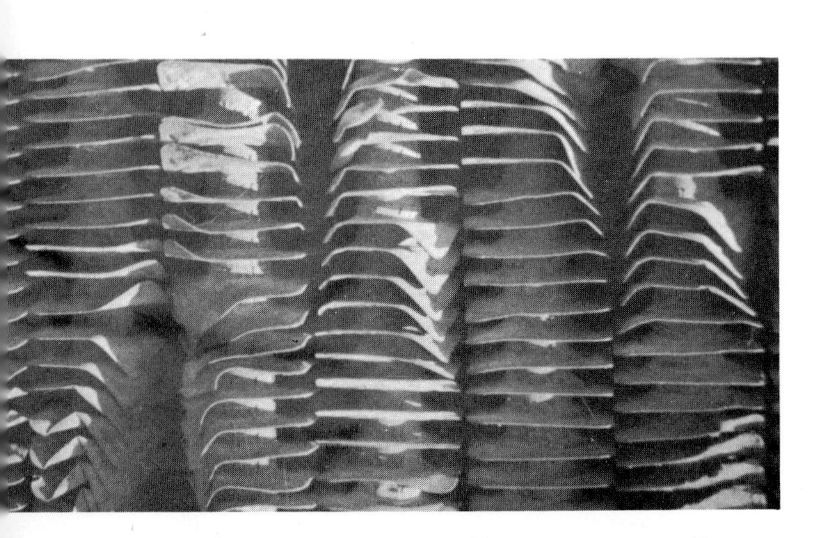

(*Photograph by Edward Barili, Kutztown State College.*)

You will notice a very close relation between simulated textures and producing the intermediate values we need so much in rendering form. It is very helpful when one is experimenting with textures to arrange them carefully alongside a good value scale. In this way we can make the best possible use of them as tones in showing a form. Now that you know the importance of practicing with each tool and medium rhythmically, and understand your needs as far as darks and lights are concerned, you should be able to translate forms and textures together. They should help each other in your work in much the same way as they belong together functionally in nature forms.

DISTINGUISHING COLOR

The human eye is said to be able to distinguish at least forty thousand changes of hue, value, and intensity when they are placed in order closely enough together for accurate comparison. As we have said before, it is very easy to be mistaken about colors. They appear quite differently when seen against various surrounding colors, in varying degrees of light, and when made of varying materials. People vary, too, in their sensitivity to color. Almost everyone has some lack of sensitivity to one or more hues. This is called color blindness. Inability to distinguish between red and green is probably the best known form of color blindness. Some persons have difficulty with blue and orange, and some with purples and yellows. The defect is more noticeable when one has to distinguish between light or dark tones of the particular colors or between weak and strong intensities of them. Intermediates can be confused more readily than primaries and secondaries. Color blindness is said to be more common in men than in women. This could be attributed to lack of interest or need for distinguishing colors in daily life. Although it was once thought of as an unfortunate physical defect of the eye, color blindness, like tone deafness, is now conceded to be at least partially curable. One can exercise or practice discriminating between colors which are not clearly distinguishable. It is certainly true that some persons do not see color at all, but are simply aware of darkness and lightness. They are quite helpless when the need arises to see the difference between two hues of the same value and intensity. On the other hand, the person with poor color preception may be highly efficient at distinguishing forms in spite of their color. This has proved very helpful in spotting camouflaged guns, buildings, and boats in wartime. They were painted in broken areas of bright color to break up the silhouette, but this did not confuse a color-blind observer. To confuse persons with normal vision, the shadowed underneath areas were painted light, and the lighted tops were darkened. This almost obliterated the form. Both methods were borrowed from defensive coloration in nature.

COLOR MEANINGS AND TRADITIONS

In keeping with the scientific interest that has been characteristic of all of man's efforts to understand and control nature since the eighteenth and nineteenth centuries, color has been the subject of theorizing and experimentation by artists and designers. As with all of man's inventions to communicate with others, there are more or less commonly accepted color meanings. That is, there are certain colors which generally affect people as being exciting (like brilliant red or orange) or calming (like green or medium blue). Some colors are said to be dismal (like dull purple or brown); others gay (like pink or bright yellow). Meanings like these are founded on common associations. Every social group has devised traditional meanings for color; for instance, the color for mourning is black in our tradition, white in the Chinese. Other color meanings are purely personal; that is, they are founded on the associations that go with particular color experiences in the individual's mind. Climate is said to have considerable to do with color preferences. For instance, a tropical environment is supposedly more likely to produce a liking for hot, rich, brilliant colors with strong value contrasts. People who live in temperate or cold climates are said to prefer subdued colors and less contrast. Some of these characteristic preferences may have originated in physical needs for clothing and shelter which would blend into the environment, for primitive people generally use the materials around them in their natural state.

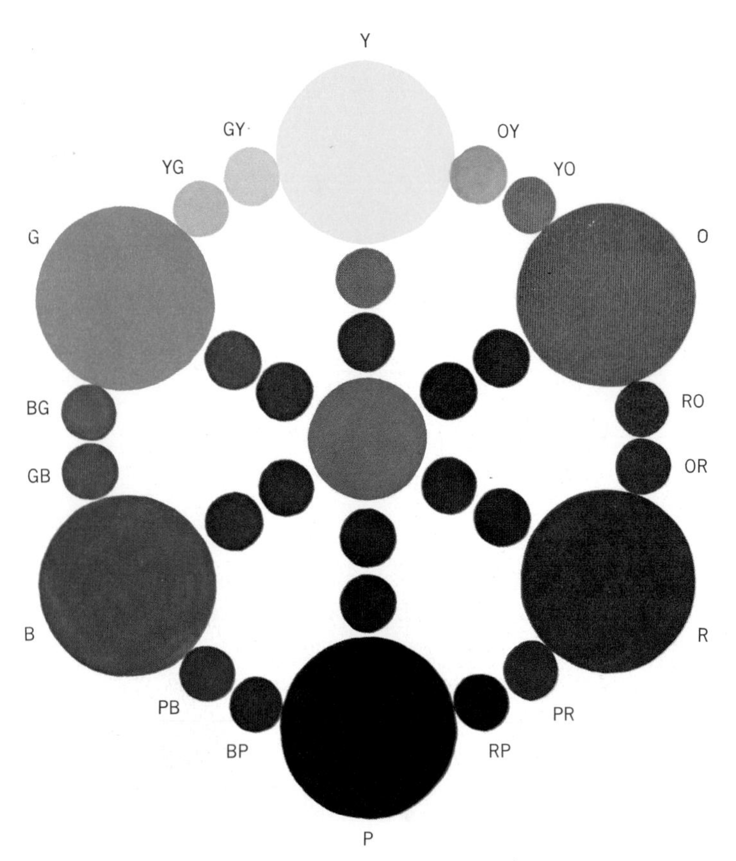

Prang color wheel showing primaries, secondaries, intermediates, and complementary sequences.

THE PRANG SYSTEM OF COLOR

Primary Colors and Value Scales

All the color sensations with which we are familiar can be organized around three basic unmixed hues: red, yellow, and blue. They are called *primary,* for with them artists have made all of the others. This is the organization which is based on coloring matter such as clays, minerals, and vegetable stains. The addition of white and black to red, yellow, or blue and to mixtures of these three will make a tone scale or *value scale* for each hue. This scale would be adequate to represent a form of that hue in light and shade very simply. The eye would move smoothly on the gradation of tone (see the illustrations on page 167).

Secondary and Intermediate Colors

Mixing equal amounts of primary red and yellow makes orange, of blue and yellow makes green, and of blue and red makes purple. These are the *secondary* colors. They seldom appear as pure or intense as the primaries, because the coloring matter is not entirely pure, often containing ingredients which counteract or dull each other. Some coloring matter is stronger and some weaker; therefore, we cannot measure drop for drop, by weight or size. We must measure by the way the colors affect the eye. Unequal mixtures of two primary colors are called *intermediates.* We could make many of these transitional steps between each pair of primaries. The eye will move smoothly from one to the other if the steps are kept in order. We can also make each intermediate color into a complete value scale if we add black and white.

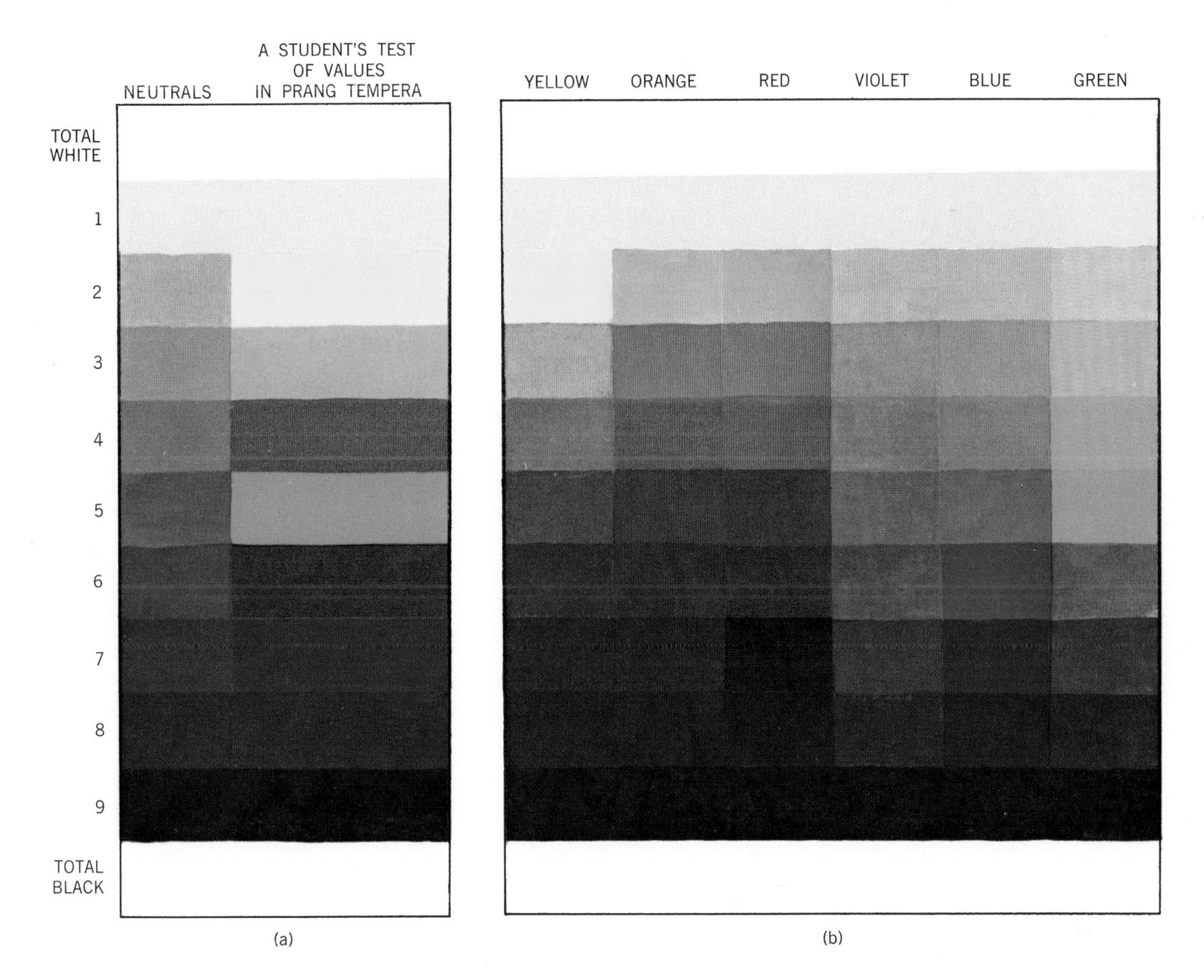

a) A student's test of values in Prang tempera. b) Value scales of primary and secondary colors. (By Wayne Cardinalli, Kutztown State College.)

Neutralizing Color

Mixing equal amounts of redness, yellowness, and blueness makes gray, a *neutral* tone. This happens because the three primaries tend to counteract each other; the warmth and coolness in them cancel out the intensity, and the mixture becomes even more dull than the secondaries. Mixing primaries of light value makes a light gray, and mixing dark primaries makes a dark gray, almost black.

Tertiary and Quaternary Colors

The chemical ingredients of coloring matter also tend to darken and dull the mixtures of three primaries. Mixing unequal amounts of redness, yellowness, and blueness makes a "near neutral" which may reveal more of one of the primaries such as maroon (dull red), ochre (dull yellow), or navy (dull blue). These are called *tertiaries.* Or the mixtures may resemble the secondaries, such as olive green, mauve (gray purple), or brown. These are called *quaternaries.* By adding black and white to the neutral gray, we can get a complete neutral scale. By adding black and white to any tertiary or quaternary color, we could make it into a complete value scale also.

Of the three primaries, yellow is the lightest. Primary red and primary blue are almost equally dark. If we place the secondaries between them and the intermediates in their appropriate order (see Prang color wheel) between primaries and secondaries, we find we have another scale of values made of pure, brilliant color. Beginning with yellow we can move progressively darker as we go through orange to red and to purple. Or we can move through green to blue and to purple. As long as we keep the transitional hues in order, our eyes will move smoothly on the gradation of hues. We could even represent a complete form in light and shade by using the pure colors without mixing them with white and black; for all the values are there except white and black (see page 167).

Complementary Colors

Because red, yellow, and blue mixed together make gray, we shall find that red mixed with green (yellow plus blue) will also make gray. Likewise, yellow mixed with purple (blue plus red) will give us gray; blue mixed with orange (red plus yellow) produces the same result. Because various color materials have different chemical makeup, the grays thus obtained are not quite alike. Practice proves somewhat different from theory, as it often does. When the paints, chalks, crayons, or dyes we use do prove to balance or neutralize each other, we have a *balanced palette.* This means that we have hues which *complement* each other. Red is complementary to green, yellow to purple, and blue to orange. Each intermediate has a complement, too; the redder the orange gets, the more greenish the blue must be. Each pair represents wholeness or completeness; they contain within themselves all the possible hues and combination of hues. "Complementary" means the perfect balance of opposites, like male and female in nature.

Student's experiment with complements in Prang tempera. (By Mary Schum, Kutztown State College.)

Intensity Scales

Imagine a scale of redness. Step by step it becomes less red because it is being mixed with green. It changes finally to neutral gray. If we keep on adding green, the mixture will become more and more brilliantly green until we cannot see any red in it. We could not paint a complete form with this scale; for we would have little or no value contrast, since red and green are both medium tones or values. Yellow and purple would make a better balanced combination; for these two complements are different enough in value to make a gradation of tone. Blue and orange would also be complete. Black and white would be helpful for value contrasts in both the yellow-purple combination and in the blue-orange combination, but not as necessary as in the red-green combination.

Working Palettes

The Prang system of color has been the basis of almost all the so-called sets of paints, crayons, chalks and pastels, and dyes used by artists. Some sets include intermediate hues, neutrals, and near neutrals. Some do not. One should always test a set of colors to discover whether it really does include the hues needed to get a complete range. This is especially necessary when one is buying colors separately rather than in sets. You can make almost all the intermediates and the light and dark values of each hue if you have the bright red, yellow, blue, black, and white. There are a few very intense ready-mixed colors such as magneta, chartreuse, and vermillion which you cannot make from red, yellow, and blue very successfully. They are derived not from natural "earth" colors such as clays, minerals, and vegetable stains, but from man-made combinations of them. The earth colors were used by all primitive peoples, since they were readily available. A notable exception was the much sought-after purple derived from purpura, a sea creature living in the Mediterranean. Earth colors seem to belong together, and those synthetically derived are difficult to blend with them. The masters of the Renaissance used natural or earth colors. Apprentices mixed them from the closely guarded recipes invented by their masters. Until the period of scientific experimentation in the nineteenth century, the earth colors were almost the only ones known. The discovery of aniline colors in 1856 and the manufacture of powerful coal-tar colors has increased tremendously the variety of hues available. There are so many that one really needs to keep some kind of organized system of color in mind and to experiment on that basis. The Prang system is probably the simplest of these systems. It has been presented first because it is based on familiar materials and practice rather than on the science and theory of light.

THE MUNSELL SYSTEM OF COLOR NOTATION

Numerous color systems have been devised to make more complete use of all the hues now available from natural and synthetic sources. Mass-production methods have made it necessary to identify exactly a particular hue, value, and intensity of a color and match it perfectly, even when the original sample is not available. This led to the invention of color notation, which is somewhat like musical notation. Each hue, value, and intensity has been given not only a name but a number. This is a symbol by which others can identify and reproduce it as a musician identifies and can reproduce the sound of a note by its position on the musical cleft. The Munsell system of color notation, perfected by Albert H. Munsell, of Boston, in 1912, is an example of an organization of color sensations which includes a system of notation. It has contributed considerably to our understanding of the three dimensions of color (hue, value, and chroma or intensity). It is in use by major departments of the United States government and many other governments, the Encyclopedia Britannica, the International Printing Ink Corporation, the Lakeside Press, *Fortune,* and Walt Disney Productions. Industrial ceramists and dye makers use the notation widely to ensure matching color in products nationally advertised. Designers for every branch of science, industry, advertising, and television make use of both the notation and the complicated method of color selection. The latter is made possible because The Munsell Color Company, Inc., Baltimore 18, Maryland, supplies charts, manuals for teachers and students, colored papers, and color-measuring devices. A brief description of the Munsell color system follows. One should, of course, refer to the Munsell Company for complete details and experimental equipment.

The Hue Circuit; Value Scale; and Chroma Scale

All the visible colors we know are organized in the Munsell system with respect to five principal or basic hues placed at equally distant visual intervals on a circle. The principals are named red, yellow, green, blue, and purple. Between each principal and the principal next to it are placed the five first intermediates, which are the hues yellow red, green yellow, blue green, purple blue, and red purple. Further subdivision creates nine hues between each principal and intermediate hue, a total of one hundred separate and distinct hues.

Each hue is represented in nine distinct value steps between black and white. A complete chroma scale for each hue, at each of the nine value levels, is made by adding to the hue a gray of the same value. These scales would vary in length; for not all hues are capable of wide range in chroma. Red, yellow-red, yellow, and red-purple give us the widest range at present. The invention of new synthetic colors may add to or change any statement of this kind.

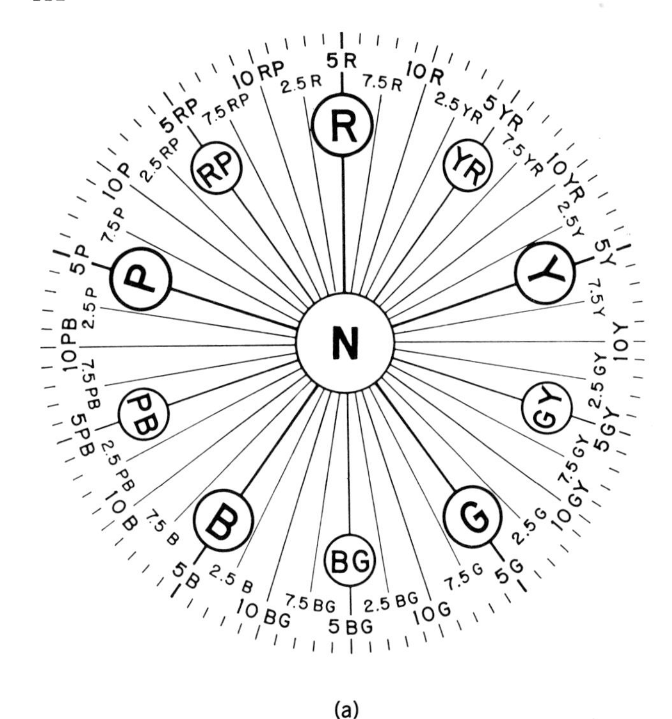

(a)

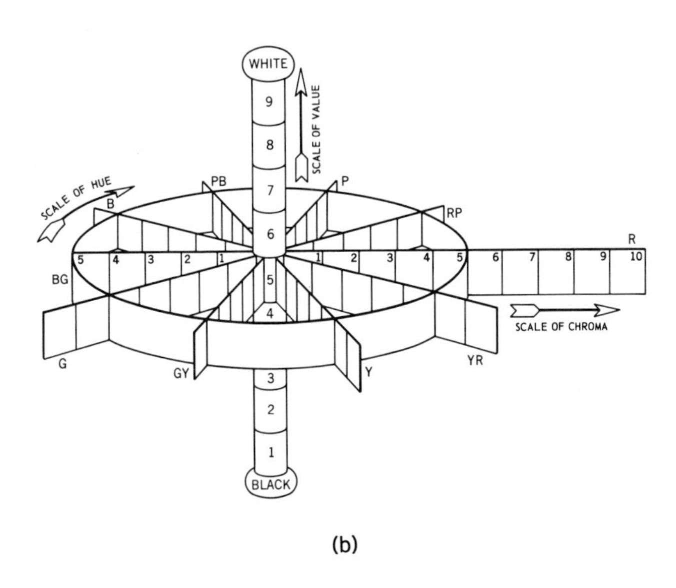

(b)

a) Hue symbols and their relation to one another. b) Hue, value, and chroma in their relation to one another. (Reproduced by permission of the Munsell Color Company, Inc., Baltimore 18, Md.)

The Identifying Notation

To identify a particular hue at a particular value and a particular chroma, these are the symbols used.

1. Hue is indicated by the initial of the color name on the hue circuit and by its number also (a). Numbering is in groups of ten proceeding clockwise. Principals and first intermediates are numbered five, which places them centrally in the area containing the intermediates (1, 2, 3, 4 and 6, 7, 8, 9, 10) which they dominate. Example: 5R is the principal red, 8R is an intermediate red–yellow red, 2R is an intermediate red–red purple. When a hue is initialed but not numbered, it is 5, a principal or a first intermediate hue. Observe that the numbers of hues directly opposite (complementary) are the same.

2. Value (darkness or lightness) is indicated by a number from 1 to 9. A particular color sample is compared with a neutral value scale which begins with 0 (total black) and reaches 10 (total white). The value number is written as the numerator of a fraction (b). Example: 8R2/ would be almost black (dark maroon) and 8R8/ would be almost white (light pink). Neither of them would be a very strong red, because red must be about middle value to attain its greatest saturation (the degree of departure from a neutral gray of the same value).

3. Chroma (intensity or degree of saturation) is indicated by numbers from 1 to 19. A particular color sample is compared with a chroma scale which begins with 0 (neutral) and reaches as high a number as the hue can be made at the value level chosen. The chroma number is written as the denominator of the fraction. For example, 6R4/12 would be very brilliant but 6R4/2 would be very nearly gray. Notice that their value is the same.

4. The complete notation for a specific color sensation is written as follows:

	Examples
No. Hue Value/Chroma	Aquamarine = 6BG6/8
	Terra-cotta = 2YR5/10

Color notation is for identifying purposes only. It is only the first step, but a very valuable one, in the artist's experience of color. It is hoped that by now we are agreed that any visual experience which can be developed in sensitivity as well as organized in the mind will be of use in art expression. Identifying the colors and using the symbolic notation does not, of course, do the selecting of color for us. That is the combined work of the physical, mental, and emotional capacities we have. Most of us have scarcely begun even to identify colors with any degree of accuracy. Even professional designers and great painters select combinations more by instinct than by reason. We may also use certain color schemes which we find effective until they become habitual, just as we may use certain words or phrases continually until they begin to lose their meaning or impact. It is very important to keep on developing color sensitivity by studying scientific systems of color and by frequent experimenting with new combinations.

DEVELOPING COLOR DISCRIMINATION

To learn to use a system of color, even as complete a system as the Munsell, for choosing color schemes would be for most of us a little like using a dictionary to carry on a conversation. It would be possible, but rather cumbersome. We prefer to use both colors and words which most people understand even if they are not exactly defined. We trust intonation and common associations to convey shades of meanings. It is probably more important for us to use a color system as we use a dictionary, to help us to expand our color vocabulary (to see more steps in hue, value, and intensity and more combinations of these). Even the most complete color systems we have yet devised are rather like a dictionary which might contain only common nouns, verbs, and adjectives. They do not help us to express very much; for no agreement has been reached as yet on the combined meanings.

Both the Prang system, which is based on coloring matter, and the Munsell system, which is based on psychological color spacing, are closely related to the science of light. All color sensations are a direct result of the sensitivity of the eye to light. Architects, stage designers, and display artists recognize the need for an organized system of color in light, since they achieve their effects not only with actual materials and textures but also with the amount and quality of illumination. Light can be analyzed as consisting of three basic colors: *red, blue,* and *green,* which are called the primaries. When these are superimposed upon a neutral surface, they produce a neutral color, just as the primaries are assumed to do in pigment. However, in light the result is lighter than any one of the primaries, whereas in pigments the result is middle gray. Therefore, the process of mixing colors in light is called *additive* (it *adds* to the total illumination). In mixing paints, dyes, and other color matter the process is *subtractive* (beginning with the lightest hue, such as yellow, mixing with other hues *subtracts* from the apparent illumination or value). Superimposing red and green light results in a *yellow* or straw color; combining red with blue results in *magenta;* and combining blue with green results in *blue green.* The three italicized colors are called the secondaries. They are complementary to the three primaries. As in the Prang and the Munsell systems, complements (opposite primaries and secondaries) produce a neutral when superimposed on a flat neutral surface. A complementary color of light will tend to reduce the intensity of a colored surface, and light of the same hue or a similar hue will make it more intense. These effects are often used to modulate as needed the various actors, properties, and scenery items on a stage. When complementary lights are directed from opposite positions upon a three-dimensional form, they tend to increase the sensation of the forms because the warmth or coolness of the two hues intensify each other. However, if they are equally strong lights, they tend to flatten the form by destroying the shadows. For practical use in stage lighting No. 2 Light Pink and No. 25 Daylight Blue, No. 17 Light Blue Lavender and No. 57 Light Amber, and No. 29 Steel Blue and No. 62 Salmon are considered useful complements. These are to be found in Brigham Gelatines, Randolph, Vermont, and they have the approval of lighting experts of the General Electric Company.

The source of colored light in common use is an incandescent lamp which is not white, but a very light yellow. This is intercepted between the source and the object by colored glass, lamp dip, gelatin, or a synthetic such as Transolene, Transpara, or Cellophane. These substances have the power of absorbing some of the light rays and allowing others to pass, as in a filter.

The diagrams which follow show in a simplified way how the source light is modified by passing through single filters or combinations of filters.

A yellow filter absorbs blue light, transmitting green and red light.

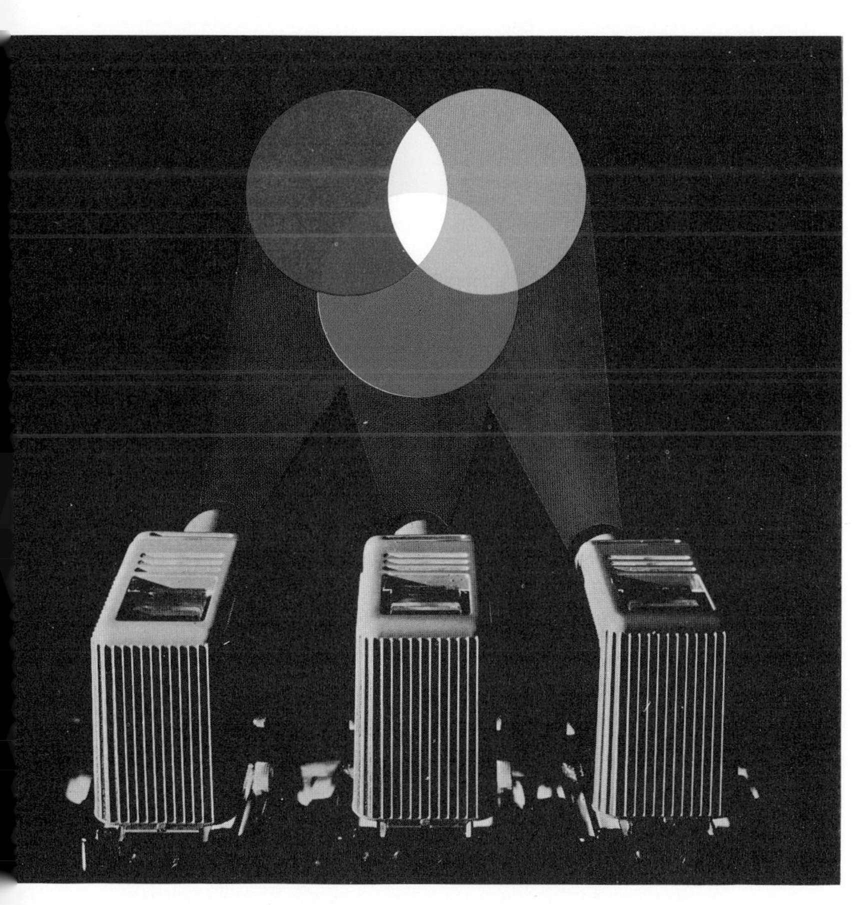

Additive mixture of the colored light from projectors covered by red, green, and blue filters. Combined in pairs, the beams give cyan, magenta, and yellow. Where all three beams overlap, all three of the visual receptor systems are stimulated, and the screen appears white. (Reproduced, with permission, from the copyrighted Kodak publication "Color as Seen and Photographed.")

A magenta filter absorbs green light, transmitting blue and red light.

A cyan filter absorbs red light, transmitting blue and green light.

Secondaries Obtained Through One Medium

1	Source	Filter	Result on Stage
	Blue Red Green	Y	R G = Y

2	Source	Filter	Result on Stage
	Blue Red Green	BG	B G = BG

3	Source	Filter	Result on Stage
	Blue Red Green	Magenta	B R = Magenta

Primaries Obtained Through One Medium

4	Source	Filter	Result on Stage
	Blue Red Green	B	= B

5	Source	Filter	Result on Stage
	Blue Red Green	R	= R

6	Source	Filter	Result on Stage
	Blue Red Green	G	= G

Primaries Obtained Through Two Secondary Media

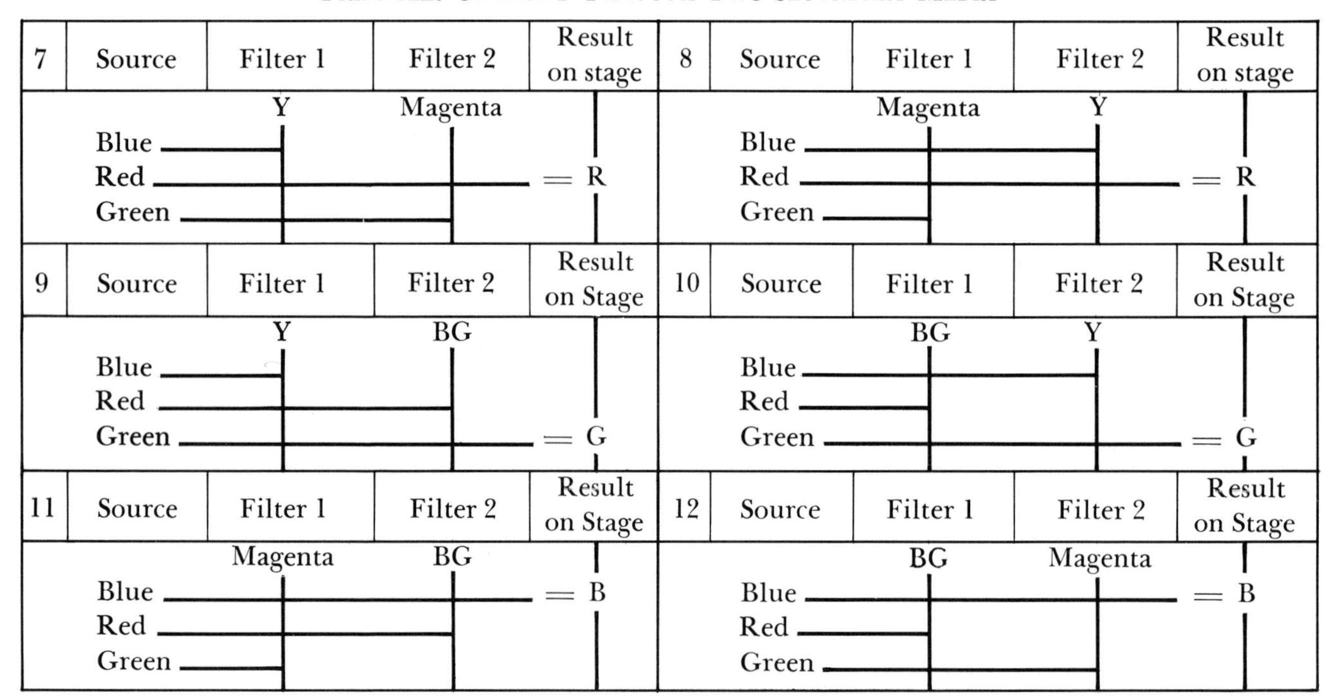

Primaries Obtained from Secondary Sources

13	Source	Filter 1	Filter 2	Result on Stage
		Y	Magenta	
	Magenta R		R	Red (low illumination)
	Magenta B			
	Blue green B			
	Blue green G			
	Yellow G			
	Yellow R		R	

14	Source	Filter 1	Filter 2	Result on Stage
		R	B	
	Magenta R			
	Magenta B		B	Blue (low illumination)
	Blue green B		B	
	Blue green G			
	Yellow G			
	Yellow R			

15	Source	Filter		Result on Stage
		G		
	Magenta R			
	Magenta B			
	Blue green B			
	Blue green G		G	Green (low illumination)
	Yellow G		G	
	Yellow R			

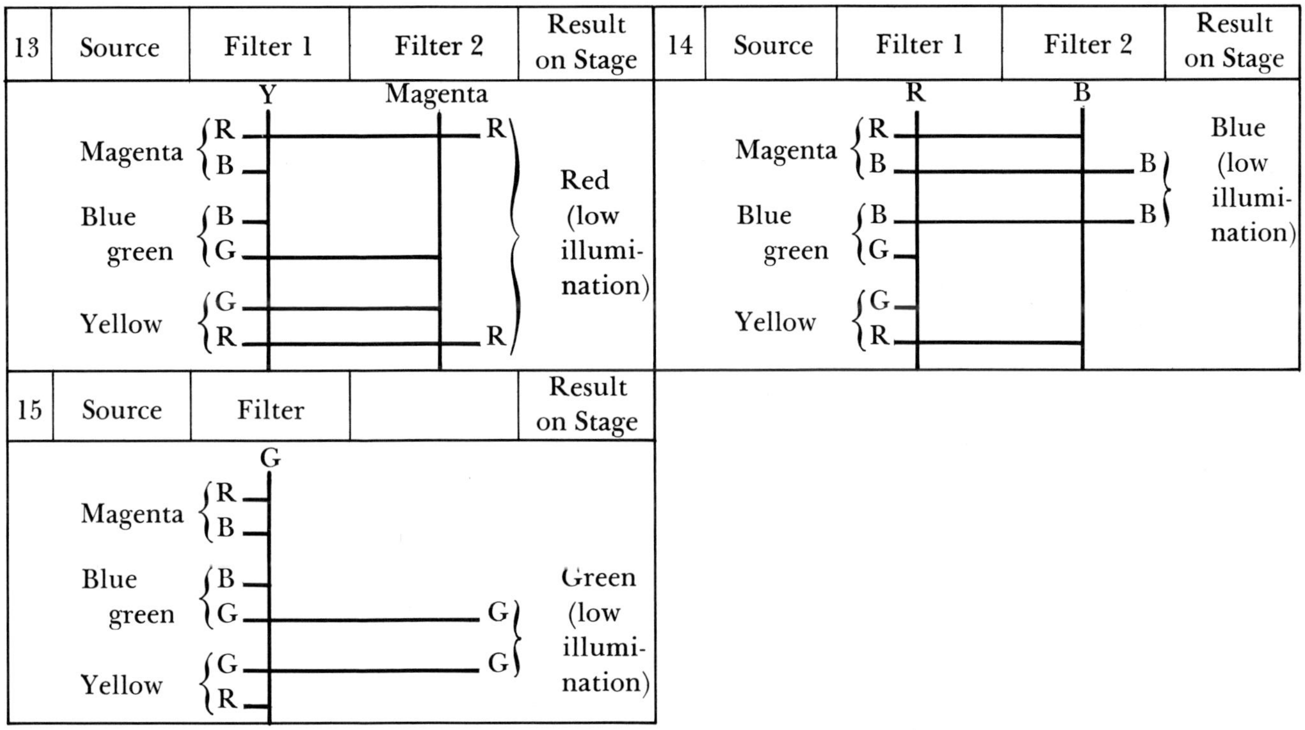

Secondaries Obtained from Secondary Sources

16	Source	Filter		Result on Stage
		BG		
	Magenta R			
	Magenta B		B	= BG (high illumination)
	Blue green B		B	
	Blue green G		G	
	Yellow G		G	
	Yellow R			

17	Source	Filter		Result on Stage
		Y		
	Magenta R		R	= Y (high illumination)
	Magenta B			
	Blue green B			
	Blue green G		G	
	Yellow G		G	
	Yellow R		R	

18	Source	Filter		Result on Stage
		Magenta		
	Magenta R		R	= Magenta (high illumination)
	Magenta B		B	
	Blue green B		B	
	Blue green G			
	Yellow G			
	Yellow R		R	

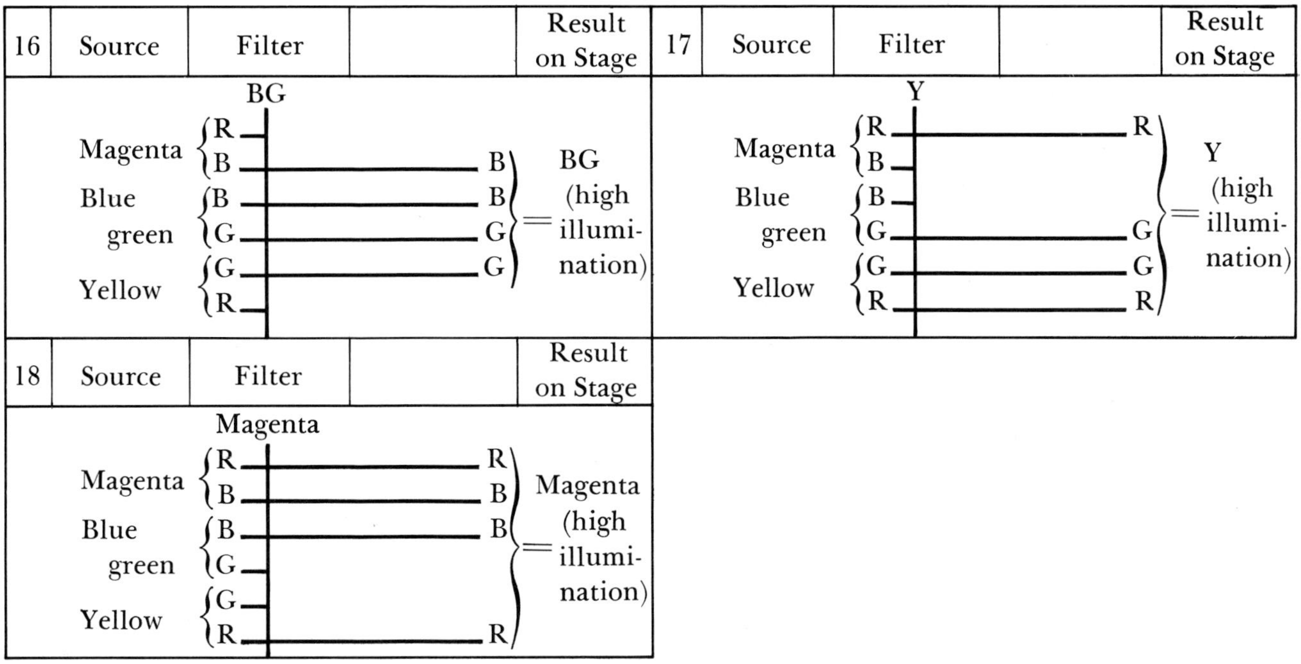

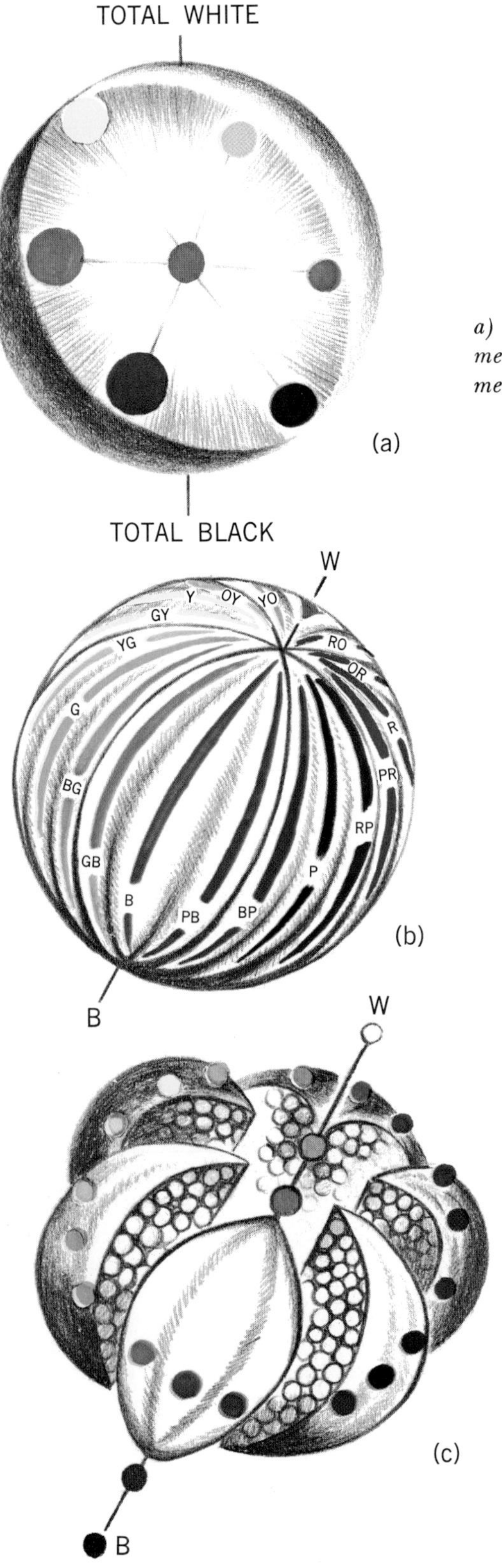

a) Standard color wheel inside the color sphere. b) Segmented color sphere with primaries, secondaries, and intermediates. c) Segmented color sphere with neutrals on the axis.

SEEING COLOR THREE-DIMENSIONALLY

Color, like form, is three-dimensional, but it is measured in hue, in value, and in intensity (rather than in length, width, and depth). Imagine a sphere packed full of all the possible colors. Along the vertical axis are all the neutrals. All the light-valued colors are in the top half, all the dark ones in the bottom half. A color wheel as usually painted with standard colors would tilt inside the sphere, because each one is a different value (a).

If the color sphere were cut into six vertical segments (b), all the reds, yellows, blues, oranges, greens, and purples would fill a segment apiece. Eighteen segments or more would make a segment for each intermediate color as well (c). About 2200 different values and intensities of each color would fill each segment. (A monochromatic harmony would be chosen from one segment; an analogous harmony from neighboring segments; a complementary harmony from opposite ones. Each harmony would include some darks from the bottom of the sphere and some lights from the top, some near neutrals found near the core of the sphere, and some intense colors found near its surface. True neutrals from the central core could also be used. (See the illustration on page 163.)

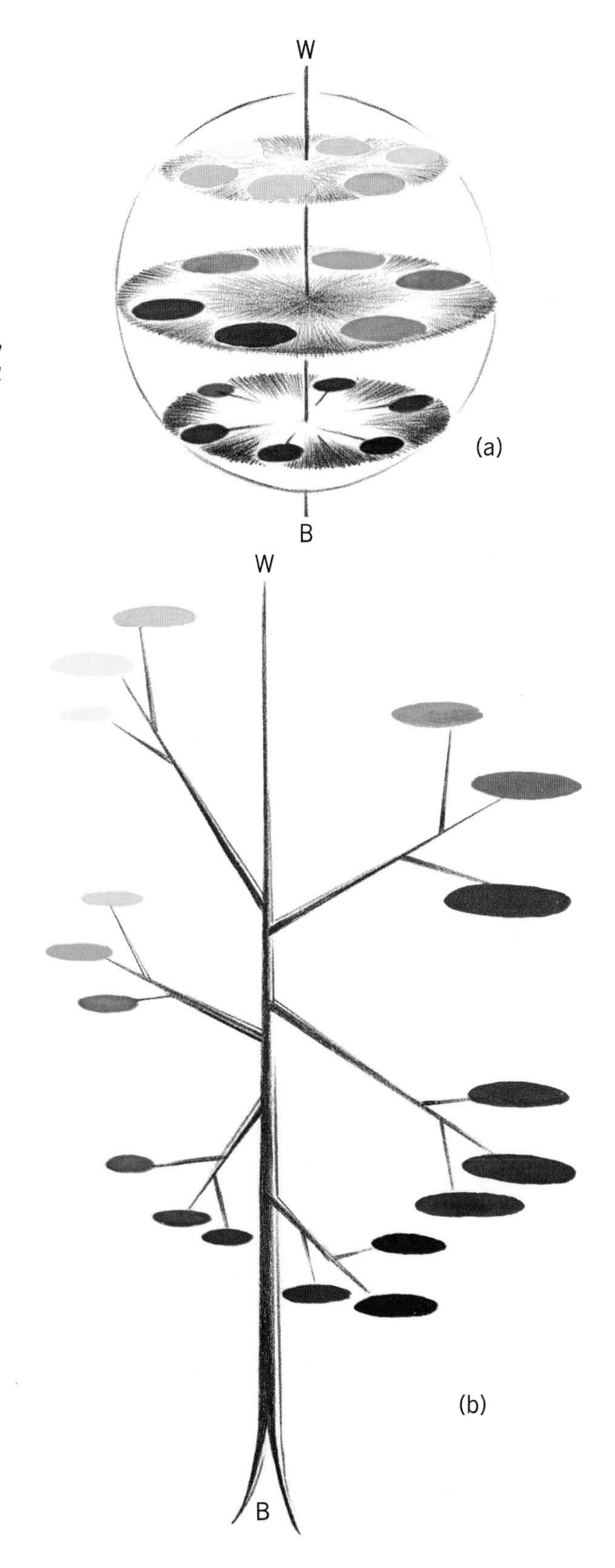

a) Color sphere with color wheels of high, medium, and low tonality. b) Color tree showing how far various standard hues extend from neutral axis.

Horizontal slices would reveal a complete color wheel on each level, but each wheel would be composed of colors of equal value (a). (High-tonality color schemes would be chosen from the top slices; low tonality ones from the lower slices.)

A color tree shows the dimension of intensity (b) better than a perfect sphere does. Certain hues (like yellow and red) are capable of great intensity; others have much less (like blue green and purple). The trunk of the tree is neutral black to white. The main branches show how far from neutral each pure color can grow, at its own value level. Imagine the color tree with 40,000 branches. It would not make a perfect sphere. Like the earth, it would have many irregularities on the surface, but the interior would be compactly filled.

MIXING COLOR

Systematic practice and experimentation in the use of color could be so extensive that one might spend a lifetime in pure analysis without ever producing a beautiful color scheme for any particular purpose. This would be rather like learning all the sound effects of many musical instruments but never playing or singing a tune. Probably the best way to begin would be to test immediately all of the colors, combinations, and mixtures of any set of colors you have against black, white, and middle-gray backgrounds and against each other. This would give you a working knowledge of what you have at hand. Most commercial sets of pigments (oil, water color, crayon, chalk, casein, and dyes) are based on three primaries, like the Prang system. You first should try to make a complete color wheel and a value scale for each color by mixing with black and white. Then determine which colors are complements (when mixed, they should make gray). If you do not have true complements, try to find out which two colors you must use to obtain a true complement for each pure color you have. You need to know this in order to control the intensity of each one.

Testing Equal Mixtures

Y	O	R	P	B	G
	Y+O	Y+R	Y+P	Y+B	Y+G
		O+R	O+P	O+B	O+G
			R+P	R+B	R+G
				P+B	P+G
					B+G

Testing Complements
(Numbers mean proportions of each)

Y	$Y^5 P^1$	$Y^4 P^2$	Gray $Y^3 Y^3$	$Y^2 P^4$	$Y^1 P^5$	P
YO			Gray			PB
O			Gray			B
RO			Gray			GB
R			Gray			G
PR			Gray			YG

Scale of Neutrals	Value of each Pure Primary and Secondary Hue	
W		
	Y	
	OY	GY
	O	G
	OR	BG
	R	B
	PR	BP
	P	
B		

Value Scale of Each Primary, Secondary, and Intermediate Hue
Place the pure colors as shown. Mix with white above; with black below.

White →											
Y											
	OY										GY
		O								G	
			OR						BG		
				R				B			
					PR		PB				
						P					
Black →											

On white, gray, and black paper paint a separate dab of each mixture to discover how backgrounds affect it. Try colored backgrounds also.

Test of colored chalks applied directly on warm, medium ground.

USING COLOR TO EXPRESS FORM

Begin using color to express a solid form (see illustration on page 167). Translate the simple forms you have already made in black and white into several values of one color. Follow the important points you remember from that experience:

1. Flat surfaces which face you will usually be of one value throughout.
2. Any surface which recedes from you must be graded in tone to make your eye move.
3. Any surface which both advances and recedes (like a corner or a rounded form) will have to be graded both to the right and to the left and possibly above and below.
4. You may want to make use of several light values on one side and several dark ones on the other to express a definite light direction.
5. Be sure to use more contrast on the part of the object nearest you than in any other place, including the background.
6. Avoid using a color of the same value as your paper anywhere on the outer contour of the object. Try using dark, medium, and light backgrounds.
7. Colors used pure (without mixing) will give you considerable range in value in and of themselves. Decide which pure color spot looks the closest to you on each background. Which seems to recede the farthest? Try substituting the pure colors for the neutral values on a simple form and then on a picture you have already done in black and white. You may discover why Cezanne painted green on cheekbones and red on trees.
8. Our eyes sometimes come up with very contradictory reports about color. Even though we think we know exactly what color we have, we find that it is quite possible to change our minds about it if we see it in several different surroundings. This is especially noticeable with neutral or nearly neutral tones. Make several identical shapes out of one piece of gray paper and lay them on some pure-colored backgrounds of several values. Take note of the way the gray shapes seem to change color, value, and even size. You may also notice a difference in their apparent distance from you.

ADVANCING AND RECEDING COLORS

9. One of the most useful color illusions is that warm colors seem to advance toward our eyes and that cool colors seem to recede. Suppose we are painting a gray stone wall. Natural stone does vary in color, some being warmer with subdued orange and red, some cooler with greens, blues, and purples. Nevertheless, the total color effect of the wall is gray, because our eyes report a rather even distribution of all these colors. Try making the wall look closer to us at the near end and recede at the far end. You may use a medium-gray ready-mixed paint and add small amounts of warm and cool colors to it.
10. Here is a problem for the "experts." A farmer has painted all of his farm buildings with the same red paint. Some are close to you, some far away, some face you directly, and on others you see the receding planes. It is obvious that you cannot borrow his paint and fill in all the areas he painted with it! You need lights and darks, and also warm and cool reds to show the forms and distances. Experiment with mixtures until you have enough different reds to keep the buildings where they belong in space. Use neutral grays for all the other areas. You will have enough to do without using other colors in the picture.

a) Seeing this group from above aids the circular movement.
b) Gradual changes in the direction of movement help to bring the horses closer.

SEEING AND EXPRESSING MOVEMENT

We have already pointed out that the movement of objects can be understood because our eyes follow the objects and report numerous images to the brain. If the movement is very fast and direct, we do not have time to focus upon the silhouette. We see a more or less continuous blur from one side to the other of our area of vision. If the movement is irregular, changing direction and speed, we get varyingly clear and blurred images.

We have the same tendency to see movement geometrically as we had with shapes and forms. Spasmodic movements interest us, but we try to understand the whole movement by more or less ignoring the irregularities. We instinctively relate the movements to our own vertical standing position. We try to hold them together centrally as from a source, or around it. We look for the gradual rise and fall of spiraling objects. Examples of these movements are readily observed in a wind-blown tree, in a fountain, a wave, or the flight of a bird.

There are also certain points of view in which the real nature of a movement can best be seen. For instance, circular movement can be understood very clearly if we ourselves are at the center. If we are not, then we need a viewpoint either above or below the moving object (a); for at eye level it would seem to be moving in a straight line. Receding or advancing movement must be seen from off-center to be understood (b); for if the object moves directly toward or away from the eyes, we see only a gradually enlarging or diminishing silhouette. Here, too, a viewpoint above or below the object is helpful.

Like representing form, expressing movement is an exciting way to convey the essential nature of living things. Unlike the dancer and the actor, who use actual movement, the painter or sculptor traditionally must resort to suggesting movement by exaggerating the way he suggests form and distance, by rhythmic lines, by a succession of images, and by gradations of tone and color. Using very perceptible textures on the near images and flat tones on the far ones will also contribute to the illusion. In other words, anything which invites our eyes to move faster on a gradation of any kind will imply that we mean to express a moving object. As in all kinds of representation, we are not concerned with confusing or deceiving the mind. We must be satisfied with what the material and our hands will do to suggest and interpret, rather than to imitate real movement. Sculptors, however, experiment with actual movement of objects in space, making use of weight, balance, and mechanization to convey the exciting experience of movement. Of course, although these experiments are relatively recent, such use of movement is not new. Moving parts have been used by primitive peoples in ceremonial objects, architectural constructions, masks, and the like. Even in our own history, moving advertising "eye-catchers" were forerunners of mobiles (moving sculpture). They were the beginning of the motion picture and of television, two outstanding modern arts that are based on the fact that slightly different images following each other in sequence are reported to the brain as a moving object. When the images are drawn simply (using characteristic animal and human silhouettes, often almost geometric in shape) we get a satisfactory feeling of motion even though relatively few images are shown. When many images are photographed and exposed to our eyes very rapidly, the illusion of moving, living form is almost complete.

Experiments with drawing movement are even more closely related to gestures than are those concerned with drawing shapes. We often resort to representing not the image of the object but the line we instinctively make with our hands or bodies in imitation of the moving thing. Sometimes we combine the two, attaching direction lines to the silhouette of the object in action. This is a fairly satisfactory solution often used by cartoonists and advertising artists. To them subtlety

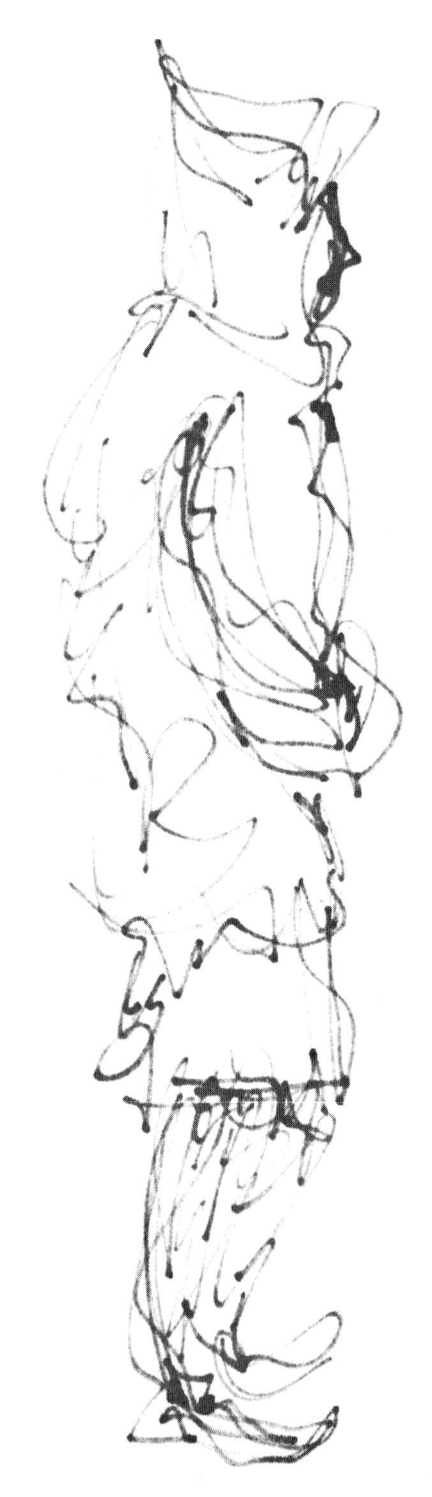

(By Errol Smeltz, Kutztown State College.)

Gesture drawings without attention to detail often capture a movement from life.

is not so important as suggesting movement very simply and quickly.

Go through some large movement which you have practiced, such as skating or the serve in tennis; do it several times in the air. Try to translate this movement into one line in such a way that the rhythm feels right from beginning to end. Accent the places where the action is forceful. Make use of any way you know (tones, color, perspective) to make the line seem to move in the right direction. Experiment with smooth, heavy, light, and both regular and irregular movements. Try some movements you use naturally in emotional states such as striking, caressing, running away, and pleading. Try several silhouettes diminishing in size to help the illusion of distance.

The image of a moving thing which the eye reports cannot very well be studied at leisure, but we can to some extent stop the motion with our eyes somewhat as a very fast camera makes an exposure on sensitive film. We try to focus on this fleeting image consciously. The action in these images is often suspended (off balance as though hanging in space). When we draw objects off balance, some movement is implied. By making use of rather extreme gradations of tone and color both in the object and in the background, the illusion of movement is much enhanced. However, any flat surface, especially if it is rectangular, tends to contradict even the most forcefully drawn movements. We are sometimes "of two minds" about this solution. Our eyes and minds are uncomfortably aware of the conflict, which eventually becomes tiresome because it is never resolved. We catch ourselves wishing that the movement would get finished. Suspended action is just as annoying, if not more so, when used in standing sculpture. Artists often use suspended movement to excite the observer or to guide the eye swiftly to some area or object they particularly wish him to see, as in an advertisement or poster.

1. Try some drawings from a parade or line of march (the uniformity of the silhouette will help you).
2. More difficult but very exciting, try to pick out the repetitive movements of a child on a

swing, stopping the image at various places along the arc. Do not try to complete each image; be satisfied with the details which are most noticeable. Exaggerate them and ignore what you do not catch.

3. Animals in action seldom repeat their movements exactly, but their characteristic gait and swing make interesting subjects. (Do not expect too much of yourself in this case. It requires long practice.)

Probably the most effective use of suspended action is in mobile sculpture. Even though the shapes do not represent any recognizable form (they are usually nonobjective), we enjoy watching the play of planes moving through, around, and opposite each other, giving us an infinite variety of viewpoints on each form in relation to the others. We have a satisfying sense of whole movement to which each part contributes its own. Being suspended and balanced, we have no uneasy qualms, as we have with "stopped" action in drawings or photographs.

1. Begin with a simple experiment in balance. Suspend several sizes and shapes of one material (glass, wood) from the arms of a balanced rod hanging from above. The problem is to judge the weight of the pieces and their distance from the suspending wire. When one is set in motion, the others should swing without striking each other. They will all eventually return to their original positions.

2. Experiment with concentric shapes cut from one piece of cardboard or metal. Cut away enough material between them to be sure they will clear each other when in motion. A twisted string from which they are all suspended, one inside the other, controls the movement, which reverses itself. Hold the bottom of the string and wind the top of it, like the mainspring of a clock.

3. Try a construction which works on a descending plane or spiral path. An object of the right weight and stability with a smooth, rounded base will move downward. Balancing arms are added to make the movement more interesting, and these are used to set the object in motion.

(By Louis Rosenberger, Kutztown State College.)

(By Christopher Ripnak, Kutztown State College.)

SUMMARY

We can now understand that to an artist, seeing involves more than simply opening his eyes. They are, indeed, truly marvelous instruments of perception, almost indispensable to our physical, mental, and spiritual wholeness. Recognizing and learning to distinguish between all the visual and tactile experiences we have is only the beginning of effective thought. The eyes contribute innumerable units of perception concerned with shapes, forms, colors, textures, and movements of the world we live in. But what we see is not as meaningful as what we are looking for, and why. Relations, similarities and differences, connections between cause and effects, changes and sequences give thinking its organized form. Because our eyes are so directable, they not only focus in their physical mechanism but concentrate the attention of the mind. What each of us needs and wants to see is personal and unique, and our eyes are selective instruments faithful to our purposes and desires. They help us to store up the images of well-loved forms and to seek out fresh and meaningful experiences of beauty. They ignore the trivial in favor of things important to us. They speak a language of their own in personal contact with others.

Learning to see has become one of the most important parts of human living. We have immeasurably extended our power to see and record what we see by the remarkable inventions of the microscope, the telescope, and the camera. All of the ways we have to communicate with each other depend upon sight except actually touching another person, the spoken word, and music. We have even invented visible symbols for the latter two. Thus the visual arts have become a more and more complete, comprehensive language through which we can reach all human kind and persons still unborn. Primarily through our eyes we reach for the fullest realization of the primal urges of man: to understand the realities of the universe, to deal with it to fulfill his needs, to communicate with others, to belong to and contribute to the society of man, to understand man's own nature, and to seek out his own destiny.

SUGGESTIONS FOR READING, DISCUSSION, AND EXPERIMENTATION

1. All drawing and painting is said to give an illusion of form and depth. Can art media make this illusion convincing? Compare media: which of them have the greatest power of expressing form and depth?

2. Real textures in natural materials are evidences of actual differences in the physical structure of things. How do architects and interior designers take advantage of this? Do they ever attempt to conceal or contradict it?

3. Textures in living creatures can be an effective means of concealment in their environment. How many examples of this can you find? Are textures in nature used also to draw attention to certain forms? Do textures change according to times of year or stage of development?

4. What experiences which are memorable, particularly in respect to color, have you had? Do you see color when dreaming? When hearing music?

5. Does color play an important part in one's emotional well-being?

6. How have industries and businesses made use of color to improve working conditions and increase the efficiency of employees?

7. Why are some artists' works identified according to certain color periods?

8. What kind of color usually predominates among primitive peoples?

9. Do social and political conditions ever seem to be manifest in the kind of color which designers use? How would you characterize the colors popular in our predominantly industrialized society?

10. We are said to be an unusually mobile people. How many products of modern living which are designed specifically to satisfy our love for motion can you name? What new art forms have resulted?

VI

Our Hands, Tools, and Materials

(Courtesy of the American Museum of Natural History, New York, N. Y.)

We are neglecting the gift of comprehending things by what our senses tell us about them. Concept is split from percept, and thought moves among abstractions. . . . The inborn capacity to understand through the eyes has been put to sleep and must be reawakened. This can best be done by handling the pencil, the brush, the chisel.

RUDOLF ARNHEIM
Art and Visual Perception: A psychology of the creative eye

Stamping and printing are basic hand movements. (Print from painted cardboard by Linda Bloom, Kutztown State College.)

THE NEED TO TOUCH

The urge to understand and control the things of nature for his own purposes had to be satisfied by primitive man largely by means of his hands. We ourselves have an impulse to examine any new thing with our hands even if we see it quite plainly. This is because we try to verify the evidence of our other senses by that of touch. We usually learn in childhood the characteristic *textures* of things about us. Textures are the weight, smoothness or roughness, softness or hardness, warmth or coolness, in other words, the physical makeup of things. Thus we see that our hands are the means through which we first understand the world. This is very important in fulfilling the first creative urge in man to make a safe, satisfying, and beautiful environment for himself. Touch also plays an important role in the second urge, which is to communicate with other living creatures and to help us to identify ourselves with other human beings. An animal which trusts us will allow us to touch him, but other animals stay out of arm's reach or take flight at any movement on our part. Animals recognize differences in touch, too. Before a man can teach an animal to obey a spoken word he must build up a set of responses to touch always accompanied by certain sounds and certain tones of voice. Usually he rewards obedience not only with food but also by an approving touch.

COMMUNICATING BY TOUCH

Human babies, like other young animals, manipulate the mother's breasts and soon learn to respond to her movements and touch. They explore their own bodies with their fingers. Deaf children can be taught to speak, even if they are also blind, by feeling the vibrations in the throat and movements of other's lips. Complete hand languages are in use by the deaf-mute, and they are very readily learned in any part of the world.

THE LANGUAGE OF GESTURE

Gestures of the hands play a part in human communication long after the spoken and written word are in common use. We offer our hand in greeting, point a finger in scorn or derision, and fold our hands in resignation. A soft clasp of the hands accompanies comforting words; a vigorous slap on the back goes with encouragement. We raise our hands to acknowledge our leaders, turn thumbs down on those we blame; we keep score on our fingers, put a man out of a game by one gesture, and reward him with another. Our fingerprints are better signatures than we can write. We seek divine help with hands together, or part them in fear and awe.

Alternating right and left hands creates a balanced pattern. (Paint and sawdust by Sandra Ambrosius, Kutztown State College.)

Kneading movements result in a shell-like form of clay.

STRUCTURE OF HUMAN HANDS

Because hands are every artist's most responsive and effectual tools, it is necessary to understand them thoroughly. They are like, yet different in structure from the forepaws of animals and the wings of birds. We notice that the bones of the shoulders, arms, and hands are so fitted into each other that they move at one time and yet in a different arc. So intricately interwoven are the muscles that even a tiny movement of one finger requires a combination of contractions and expansions of all the rest. A touch on the hand is recorded accurately as hot or cold, rough or smooth, heavy or light by a system of nerves so interdependent that they set off a reaction almost at the same time they report the cause to the brain. These are precision instruments we have inherited. Structures like these have been modified to serve other living creatures for swimming, flying, burrowing in the earth, striking and clawing their enemies, running, jumping, and bracing themselves to climb.

Our own hands show the results of what men do, too. To begin with, we have a "good" thumb, long enough to give us a firm grasp even on little things and spreading out for a good hold on larger ones. It swings in an arc larger than the fingers do, and independently of them, whereas they tend to move with each other. The thumb makes it possible for us to lift and manipulate a tool. Without a good thumb, the arts of man probably would never have begun.

HAND MOVEMENTS AND THE FORMS THEY MAKE

It is interesting to discover what shape we make when we squeeze tightly a ball of clay just large enough to hold in the palm of the hand. It is very much like some sea shells. This is because the hand exerts a spirally directed pressure. The outside shape of a fist also suggests a shell, the knuckles projecting in the largest spiral band and the joints in diminishing ones. The curled palm is like the lip of the shell, and the nails are like the corrugations through which the water is strained. The spiral construction, therefore, may account for the difficulty we have in building a perfectly symmetrical form with one hand. It is obvious that the common complaint "I can't even draw a straight line" is quite justifiable, nor can we expect to change matters; for the hand is not built for it. Fingers move in a small arc, the hand in a larger one, the arm in two still larger ones in different planes.

When we use the hands together, however, we have a powerful, flexible pair of pincers. They operate, if we let them, in perfect symmetry (the same movement, in reverse balance). Every move of the one is compensated for in the other by a reverse movement. Pressure and pulling movements balance through our arms on the fulcrums of our backbones and breast bones. With both hands together we could successfully draw a perpendicular line were it not that continual practice with the right or the left has made one more responsive than the other. Our legs and feet work in the same way through the hips, but they have been modified, or adapted, for other purposes such as locomotion and balancing of our bodies to keep them erect.

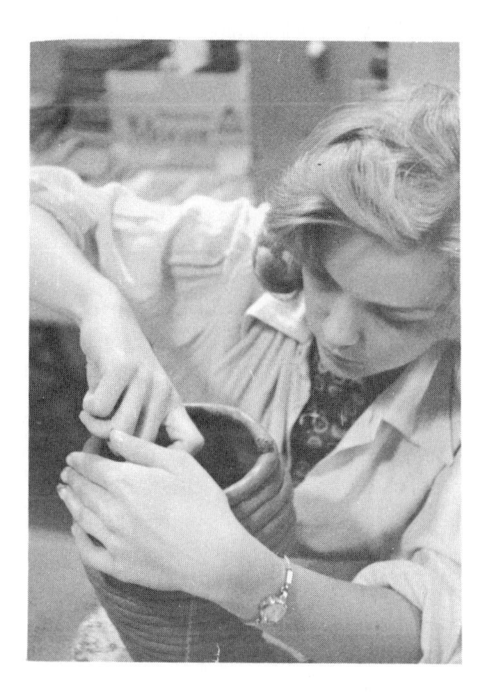

Students building and blending with coils of clay. (Courtesy of Linden Hall School for Girls, Lititz, Pa.)

SENSITIVITY, STRENGTH, AND FLEXIBILITY

Weaving, piercing, squeezing, pointing, drawing, pounding, twisting, and smoothing the objects we use have all had their effect on the hands of human beings. We often hear it said that certain kinds of workers can be identified by the shapes of their hands. Some people believe that the particular kinds of work for which children will be gifted can be predicted, that they are born with good hands for learning the piano or for the use of certain tools. However true this may be, it is certain that anyone who expects to handle the materials and implements of the arts will do well to develop in his hands sensitivity, strength, and flexibility. The perfect control of their movements is essential. They respond to almost every directive from the mind and to emotional states of being as well. We would have very little success in dealing with physical matter without them. We

would have even less with the difficult business of thinking out problems and communicating our feelings if our hands would not do our bidding.

HANDS, WORK, AND HEALTH

One of the things which we usually discover about ourselves early in life is the fact that we can work off many of the impulses within us, which would otherwise be expressed in actions not very acceptable to others, by keeping our hands busy. Of course this is not a very good reason for learning any kind of artwork. That will require that we keep more than our hands busy. Much thought and feeling is necessary, and also intelligent solving of practical problems. In fact the whole idea is a misconception. The therapeutic (healing) value of art activities is there by reason of this very combination: in artwork, the physical, mental, and emotional capacities are involved at one time and for one purpose. Meaningless activity of the hands usually only intensifies the distress of persons who are irritated, ill, or confused. Purposeful activity in which they can succeed is helpful.

Nor is it fair or even true to say that a person who cannot do arithmetic, read, or write intelligently is therefore gifted with his hands. On the contrary, his hands are usually as loath to do his bidding as his mind, and for the same reason. He has had no practice and no success with either. What is true is that many school learnings are based on word and number symbols whose meanings must themselves be learned. He has probably learned them by rote, that is, without associating them with any real action on his part. This in itself is a weary business for a human child. For instance, the numbers above zero and one, so hard to copy with his hands, do not look like three, four, five, six, seven, eight, or nine of anything. He sees no connection. He is not even given time to count them with his fingers often enough to remember them by touch. As for words, they are easy enough to remember when he can connect them with pictures. But again, the words he writes do not look or feel real. So he becomes more and more involved in using a language he does not understand. It is no wonder that he cannot use it to communicate with others. Sooner or later he may become convinced that teachers are intent upon making him unhappy (he hates school) or worse yet, that he himself is stupid.

ONE-SIDEDNESS AND ALL-SIDEDNESS

All of this has come about because in learning he has not been using his hands and body at the same time as his mind and spirit. He would reach much the same conclusion had he tried to use either of them separately. We all know persons who resign themselves to do repetitious, manual tasks with no pride in them. Their skills never improve. We are also very familiar with persons who retreat within themselves or who throw tantrums when they cannot communicate with others. Perhaps we recognize a few who are too "gifted" to need practice or too "spiritual" to earn their own living. We also know others who are "all brain." They know all the answers except the important ones like how to do something themselves and how to make themselves helpful and loved by others. These are, of course, extreme examples of equally unhappy, incomplete human beings, each stupid in some ways.

Because artwork does involve us very completely and uses all of our skills of hand, mind, and spirit at the same time, it does often help us. We not only become more skillful but also become better thinkers, better able to figure, talk, and write, and more understanding of others and ourselves. In school we are sometimes rewarded because failures tend to disappear, low marks rise, good marks get better. Even if they never reach the top, we know that they do nevertheless present a pretty fair picture of the work we have put into them. This happens when all our school experiences allow us to use our bodies, minds, and spirit together. It can also happen when we balance carefully in adult life all the things we do, including work, play, and inspiration.

In whatever work we may choose after we leave school we shall be fortunate indeed if it calls upon the combined physical, mental, and spiritual capacities we have. Our total health or well-being depends upon using them. It is interesting to know how many persons who do repetitious physical work, how many desk workers, how many highly trained doctors, lawyers, ministers, and writers do find that art experiences help them to do these things better. They have a more complete report card, too. It consists of marks which others place upon them, such as better wages, better working conditions, bigger responsibilities, better relations with others, and a growing recognition which comes to them of their value to others. More satisfying than all of these things is the mark they place upon themselves as more nearly complete human beings. Each person has to be his own teacher in this.

HANDS AND THE SIX URGES OF MAN

Since our hands are our first tools of learning, it seems natural and important to begin our study of art with them. We have already found out how important our hands are, first, in making us sensitive to the forms, materials, and movements of nature. Second, we need to know how they will help us to manipulate materials for our purposes. We shall learn a great deal from the early arts of man which were done without the use of tools. Third, we shall need to find out how much our hands can do with tools and how to practice to improve their skill. The fourth important thing is to learn how to use our hands to communicate with others in the graphic (two-dimensional) and the plastic (three-dimensional) vocabulary of art. We may find some answers to a fifth question, how do hands help in identifying our work as our own? All of these things will be useful in the important sixth realization we are seeking, which might be expressed in the simple question, "Just who and what am I?"

PRACTICING

After you have read the next page or so, close this book and work. What follows you will learn better without it; for a book is, after all, words. Words are only symbols which can have no meaning unless they stand for experiences we can see and feel. If you need directions and examples, you might later open the book to see what others have done and thought. The chances are that you will eventually work out your own conclusions. Unless you are working entirely by yourself, you will see how others work better by watching them and listening to their reactions than by looking at pictures and reading.

MATERIALS

You will need some materials such as clay, wood, metal, straws and reeds, paper, and fibers. You should begin with the ones which will respond easily to your hands without using tools. They may be either in their natural state (these give the greatest satisfaction and are necessary to understand the others) or they may be man-made (you will have to understand them eventually). Work with one material at a time. Do not clutter up your working space.

An experiment with thin sheet copper. (Student work, Lancaster High School, Lancaster, Pa.)

WORKING SPACE

You must have more than elbowroom; arm's reach should be about right. Give yourself space to stand as well as to sit; toe room is important, too; for the free movements of your hands are connected with those of your whole body. Be sure that you can reach with your hand every part of the surface on which you are working without stretching or bumping into things. Your eyes must guide every move of your hand by focusing on the hand itself and by directing the hand to any part of the working area you choose. Therefore, you must be able to get close to it as well as to step back away from it. Be sure that you have enough light to see what you are doing.

TESTING MATERIALS AND HAND MOVEMENTS

Take one of your materials in your hands, sense its weight, texture, color, and wetness or dryness. Begin working it with your hands. Test its willingness or resistance to pressure, twisting, sudden blows, scratching, or smoothing. While you discover its responsiveness to the hand, you are getting ready to learn what your hand will do to it which may be useful to you. Discover what happens when you press, squeeze, poke with your thumb and each finger separately or together, pound with your fist or your palm. Put the weight of your shoulders into your hands, even lift yourself off your feet to get the full weight of your body. Flick it delicately with your nails, tap it gently. Do these things fast, at medium speed, and slowly. And watch, take note, and try to understand what is happening to the material and to your control of it.

STUDYING YOUR RESULTS

If possible, save all of your experiments. Then try to separate those which interested you (were good to feel or look at or suggested some use) from those which you would not care to repeat. Discard those which wasted or destroyed the material. You may want to look now at what others have done with the same material and compare reactions. They may have seen possibilities you missed, and vice versa. Ask yourself some questions such as, "How did I use my hands to get the ones I like best? How much of the material can I control at one time?"

Return again to work. This time choose some particular movement of your hand which you liked and practice it rhythmically. Repeat it over a surface just large enough to keep the movement going without losing the flow and consistent pressure. Do not expect your hand to work like a machine, producing identical movements; you are trying to learn what it does naturally as a part of you. Learn to breathe naturally, adjusting to the amount and kind of force the movement needs. The position of your body has a great deal to do with the size of the area you can control. Your feet are not rooted to the floor. Learn to shift weight gradually from one foot to the other. Know where you will begin and where you will stop your repeated movements. Use both hands, separately and at the same time, in the same and in reverse directions. You will not enjoy the places where you break the rhythm because of overreaching, cramping, or losing balance. Relax or rest when you feel this break. Do not force yourself to continue, for you

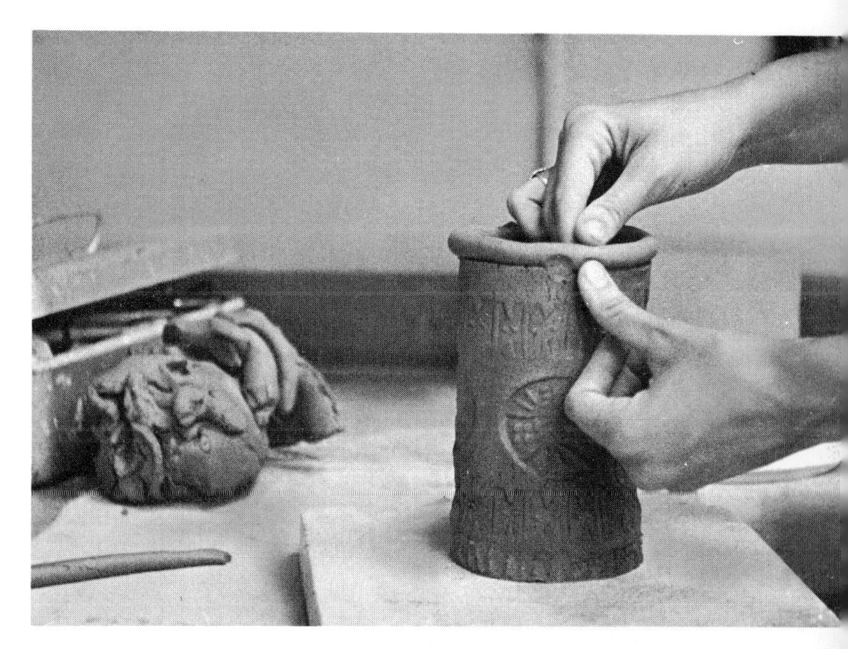

In responsive material both forms and surfaces are undeniably one's own. (From "Hand-Built Pottery," by Josephine Krum.)

Experiment comes before forming.

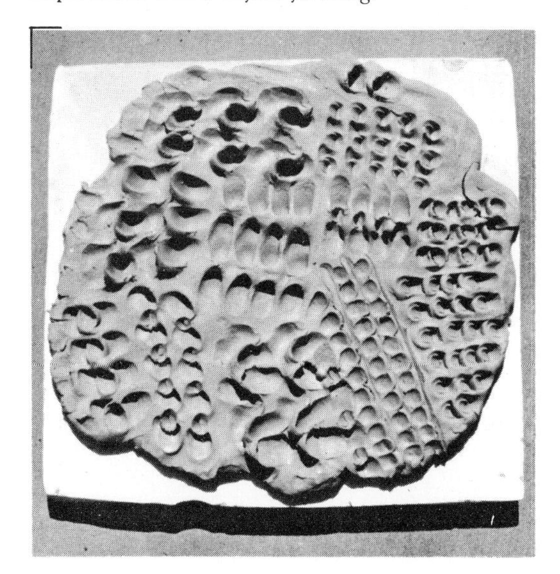

will only form poor habits instead of effective ones. Rhythmic movement has a feeling of beginning strongly, rising to a climax and ending with a gradual decline of force. Learn to accept and use this natural tide of energy. It makes your work seem alive in every stroke.

LEVELS OF SKILL

You will seem to reach levels of skill where you do not feel the break in rhythm and control, but nevertheless do not improve. Here you should *not* stop practicing; for this is the natural place for you to "consolidate your gains" (become accustomed to your new skill). From this plateau you will surely bring yourself up to a new level. If you stop practicing, you will have to begin again at the lower level. There is a better thing to do. From the natural variations, you will begin to see many possibilities for future use which would never have occurred to you had your hand been a duplicating machine. Choose one of these possibilities and make something with it. Do not expect it to be a masterpiece, but do complete it to the best of your present ability.

Again you may want to look at other people working and also at what they have done. You may find some helpful ways to practice. You will certainly see differences among people in pace, rhythm, ability to concentrate, and power to improve. There will be some results which show evidence of the heavy-of-hand, the spasmodic, the slow-deliberate, the uncertain, and the swiftly-sure person. In the things they choose to make you will recognize differences from yours, also.

Sooner or later you will begin to see that there is a certain identifiable quality in what your own hands will do, whatever the material you try out. Not only that but there will be no one else who will be able to do exactly what you do, nor can you reproduce what he has done. No one should touch your work nor should you try to fix or finish the work of others. You have no need to strive to be original or to be afraid that others may copy what you have. The marks you have made upon materials are undeniably your own. You will also begin to recognize differences in your own responsiveness to different materials. You may like those which yield easily or prefer those which offer more resistance. You may like both of these characteristics but for different purposes. Experimenting with your hands has stirred your imagination.

SELF-IMPROVEMENT

No one is entirely unfamiliar with the movements of his hands and the characteristics of some materials. Every contact we make is part of ourselves. Compared with primitive living and working in any society in which everyone makes the things he needs, our tactile experiences are quite restricted. This is the reason why even an experienced artist plans for himself a systematic, thoughtful period of experimenting with every new medium. He also practices before he is ready to make a real beginning on some object he hopes will be useful and beautiful. Sometimes the very process suggests to him ideas he did not even know he had. The period of practice prepares him to meet practical problems which may arise. It also increases his confidence and gives him more time to develop the concept he has. These are some of the important things that experienced artists recommend about experimenting and practice.

GOOD AND BAD PRACTICE

1. Work by yourself at first; then watch and share with others.
2. Keep your hands sensitive, flexible, strong, clean, warm.
3. Explore one material and one movement at a time.
4. Clear away all obstructions to free movement and sight.
5. Use all the natural movements of both hands and of your whole body.
6. Test all the physical properties of the material.
7. Practice rhythmically and often.

8. Work as long at a time as you sense improvement. Relax. Practice again. Don't give in to momentary loss of self-confidence.

9. Think only about what you are doing; set yourself a goal at each level of skill.

10. Renew your understanding of every material before you use it.

11. Respect the nature of your material.

12. Accept and respect the way your hands work.

These are some of the injurious results of the wrong kind of practice.

1. Cramped neck, shoulders (from working tensely, too long, or in poor light).

2. Sore hands, destruction of material (caused usually by unrhythmic or forced movement).

3. Automatic, monotonous movements (usually due to prolonged repetition without thinking).

4. Loss of interest (often because the skills acquired are not put to use during the period of practice).

5. Loss of confidence in oneself (usually the result of trying to make one's hands or the materials do things which are not in their nature).

Simplicity is the tangible result of direct and vigorous cutting. (Carved linoleum by Marian Hinnerschitz, Kutztown State College.)

Contrasting textures call for change of tool. (Portrait of classmate by Donald Strailey, Kutztown State College.)

TOOLS AND THE POWER OF HANDS

Tools were invented to make our hands more effective. They help to prevent injury to the skin, bones, and muscles (tools like files); to cut resistant materials (tools like knives); to make marks (tools like brushes, pens, and pencils); to reach into places our hands are too large or too short to go (tools like needles and hooks); to increase power by adding weight (tools like hammers) or by directing movement (tools like wedges and saws). Some are for measuring movement (tools like compasses and all kinds of scales). Some are for fastening things (tools like nails and clamps) to keep our hands free.

Because our hands are so intimately connected with our minds and emotional states, the tools which are used directly by hand power almost become a part of us. We can sense through them, and guide them. The work we do with them will be almost as personal as that of our hands alone.

NATURAL TOOLS

Experiment first with some natural tools. Find one stone which will scratch or chip another. Polish some clay with a pebble. Use a stick or a stone to make marks in sand or clay. Pierce a piece of leather with a fish bone. Tie a bundle of grass together with a vine or a straw. Make a hole in a shell with a burning stick. Pound some wet bark or reeds flat enough to lie on, but make your own mallet. You may get some idea of how much time, thinking, and imagination went into the invention of the tools we now take for granted. You will probably understand better, too, why tools bear the earliest marks of individual ownership. When we find one or make one which just fits our own hand, we are not very likely to lose it, lend it, or break it.

SENSING THE NATURE OF THE TOOL

Read pages 138 and 139 again and try to remember your own experience in practicing with your hands alone. Then begin, as systematically as you experimented with your hands, to test one tool at a time. First sense its weight, balance, and the fit in your hand in different positions. Feel its shape on the business end, that is, where it will transmit the power of your hand to the material. Be sure that you can see the end of the tool plainly. See that your working area is within reach of touch and sight. Then go to work, as before: what does it do to the material and what does the material do to it? Try it with all kinds of pressure, movements, and pace. You may spoil some material and ruin a tool in the process, but this is better than being afraid of it, uneasy with it, or trying to make it and the material do something they cannot do. Do not expect a hand tool to give you identical repetitions. If you use your tools rhythmically, you will get natural variations as you did with hands alone. The tool stroke will feel and look alive. You will find that many of your experiments will be useful in suggesting ideas to you. You will be able to transmit your thoughts and feelings with them too. Do not cramp your hands or any part of your body. This will destroy your natural rhythm, tire you, and make it almost impossible to improve with practice.

FINDING YOUR OWN WAY

Again, practice often and rhythmically and relax when you no longer feel completeness in each stroke. Seek improvement (more control, more definiteness, better-looking results). Keep those you like to do; discard those which destroyed the nature of the material or spoiled the tool. Return to practice. At each level or plateau of skill make some complete form with it. Do not stop there. Go on practicing. Compare with others' efforts with the same tool and material. Watch others work. Look for the way in which your work with tools differs from that done with hands alone. Also, try to recognize how your handling of tools differs from the ways of others. You are trying to make the tool a part of you; therefore, it will surely be apparent sooner or later. A skilled craftsman can easily show you how he works with a tool, but not how you will use it. You will begin to understand why it is impossible for one person to touch the work of another without leaving betraying evidence. This is just as true with tools as it was with the work of the hands alone.

CARE OF TOOLS

These are some of the important things which good craftsmen advise about taking care of tools:

1. Keep them clean (a rusty, gritty tool is no pleasure to the hand).
2. Keep them in shape (sharp, smooth, pointed, etc. according to their use; fit them to your hand).
3. Keep them ready to your hand (where you use them and within reach).
4. Invest in the best tools which you can afford. Better yet, make your own.
5. Do not lend them (selfish, but necessary; they will feel different after use by someone else).
6. Above all, use them. (It takes long practice to understand tools and your own way of using them. An unused tool is like a stranger. A used one warms to your touch like a friend.)

Form found in wood; an experiment with tools. (Pierced and carved low relief by Bonnie Ling, Linden Hall School for Girls, Lititz, Pa.)

The tool disciplines and strengthens the hand. (Carved linoleum by Georgine Antolick, Kutztown State College.)

SUMMARY

In all of these preliminary experiments we have been concerned only with discovering the nature of our hands, tools, and materials. We also learned how to practice. Except for the occasional trial pieces at each level of skill, we have said nothing so far about what part our hands and tools play in the making of any complete thing which will be useful and beautiful. To understand this, we shall have to return again to some of the experiences we had with nature. One of the most important of these was the sense of wholeness. Each thing had a wholeness about it because of its structure. We sensed this wholeness especially in certain objects which we could hold entirely within the hands like shells or pebbles. We shall find that we can use our hands in the same way with things we make. If they feel complete and comfortable within the hands, they will be very satisfying. Our hands played an important part in realizing the strength of central structures, axial structures, and vertebrate ones. We have already discovered that each hand works separately on the strong spiral principle and that together the hands work symmetrically. Thus it is that our hands are the perfect tools to produce in objects that same quality of strength we love in nature. What we make should feel strong to the hands, even though it is of fragile material and delicate in workmanship.

Flight is built into inner structure. (Papier-mâché by Elaine Fleming, Kutztown State College.)

Form and surface treatment alike are confirmed by the touch. (Branch vase by Paige Brown, Kutztown State College.)

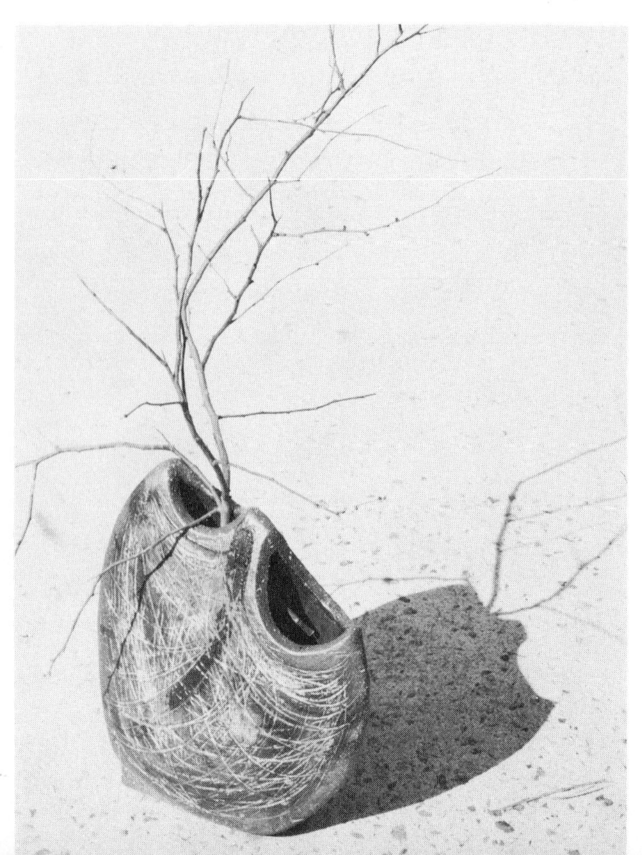

Our work should also feel alive. We know that none of the objects we will produce will move and grow in the same sense that forms in nature do. Yet they must suggest this inner power if they are to satisfy us. The sense of touch is more keen when our hands move and explore forms and surfaces and manipulate them than when we simply keep them still. What we make, then, should invite the hands to move. One part of the form should lead into another, and no part should feel disconnected or broken. In nature for very definite purposes we saw many gradual changes in size and form but very few sudden changes. Our hands can help us to achieve this kind of variety in unity; for whatever we did rhythmically had that same quality of gradual rise, increasing to a climax, and diminishing. The natural movement of the hand seldom repeats itself exactly. Where there are contrasts in the forms we make they must feel as though there is an important reason for them. They should feel like the contrast between the leaves of a plant and its seedpods. To complete this concept of aliveness, we may also trust our hands for another comparison. Whatever we have made we must feel that the material we touch is what we think it is. We were quick to discard experiments which destroyed our material; how much more important will this be when we work with serious purpose! If things look like wood but feel like stone, our hands will soon inform us. If they look heavy but are light, we shall doubt our eyes and believe our hands, a very confusing sensation.

Our hands might be said to be the truth-detectors. They are the reporters of the real character of all materials, the testers of structural strength, of balance and weight in all that we do. Hands verify the evidence of our other senses, especially our vision. If what we make with our hands feels right, it will look right. Our hands reveal a great deal to us about ourselves; for every mark with hand or tool will show the decisiveness or uncertainty of our minds. Our hands reveal the true nature of our feelings toward the materials, tools, and toward our work itself. Our hands speak for us.

DISCUSSION TOPICS

1. Gestures of the hand and body are said to be the origin of all forms of communication. What art form in the theater has been developed almost entirely by the use of gestures?
2. What hand gestures are commonly used instead of the spoken or printed word in sports, in social situations, in worship, in military activities?
3. Compare photographs and make drawings of the hands of man and the forepaws and wings of living creatures. How has nature adapted their shapes to various uses?
4. What art symbols which make use of the hand in some meaningful gesture do you know?
5. By comparison with one who is studying some musical instrument, how much practicing do you think is advisable for a student of the visual arts?
6. Is practicing entirely a matter of technical proficiency? Does it ever suggest or have any effect upon what an artist wishes to express?
7. The shape, size, and material used in some tools have remained almost unchanged since the early days of civilization. Which ones, and why?
8. How and why do hand tools and power tools compare in the extent to which a craftsman can develop an individual style of working with them?
9. Children, artists, and those who have the do-it-yourself urge seem to take a great deal of pride in their accomplishments, even when the results are meager. Is this connected in any way with a lack of money, time, or opportunity? With any other lack?
10. Make a study of the hands in some of the great periods of painting and sculpture, such as the Chinese, the Hindu, the European Renaissance, the classical Greek, the Mayan. How can the styles be identified? Compare them with examples of the primitive arts which predated these great periods.

Design Is Synthesis

VII

Make it thy business to know thyself, which is the most difficult lesson in the world.

MIGUEL DE CERVANTES
Don Quixote, translated by
Peter Anthony Motteux

LEARNING IS FROM WITHIN

Our hands and eyes, our reasoning, and our imagination never do their best work separately, always together. Because this is true, we often find that what we make without stopping from beginning to end has a satisfying wholeness about it. If it does not, we can usually tell why. We may say to ourselves: "My hands were too clumsy." "I never even thought about how to make it stand up." or "I lost interest in it when I thought about something else." This is the reason why it is important to work, often, on impulse and alone. Not only do we often make instinctively the right movement, the best shape, the good arrangement, but we seem to have a kind of check and balance within our minds, a critical center. It is true that we are never completely satisfied with what we make. Probably the reason is that even during the time when we were working, we ourselves were changing. What seemed satisfactory when we began has already become a little too limited for the thing we can now imagine. Anyone who has watched a young child make a drawing or a thing of three-dimensional material will remember how very satisfying it is to him while he is working. When he is finished, how quickly he turns away, or even forgets that it is his! He is growing very fast.

SEEKING MATURITY

We grow more slowly as we mature, but still the most dependable critic is within us. If we ever felt entirely satisfied with what we have made, it would mean that we had stopped growing. Probably the most mature artists are those who are the most keenly disappointed with what they have just made. They are most anxious to get started on a new venture; for they have become very conscious of the verdict of that inner critic. They are very ready to submit their hands and eyes to more experience and practice. They are patient and painstaking thinkers. They study themselves and others for human meaning. But they know the value of keeping themselves whole. They do not practice or experiment without purpose; they do not think without testing their conclusions. Nor do they retreat into themselves and just wish they could do something. They work.

SELF-CRITICISM

As much as possible, do trust the verdict of your own inner critic. It will not fail to tell you when you are losing touch with materials, when you are too tense, too slow, or too fast. It will pass instinctive judgment on the balance and harmony of the things you make. It will bring to mind all that you know and put in place the new sensations and facts you are learning. It will direct every move you make toward one purpose. It will inform you where you are strong and where your weaknesses make you ineffective. This inner judgment makes it possible for you to single out certain parts of the whole process to perfect them. To some extent it will let you learn from other's art experiences as well as your own. This happens because other artists use the same language of line, form, color, tone, and texture that you use, and they have agreed upon some of its meanings.

ELEMENTS AND PRINCIPLES IN ART

We have used the *elements* of this language long enough to have agreed upon certain basic *principles,* the ways in which they seem to work best. We are constantly finding new combinations of the six elements: lines, shapes, forms, tones, colors, and textures. It is not impossible that we may someday discover more than six elements which could be used in the visual arts. The principles, or ways they work, are like the laws of science and of human societies: they stay basically the same but must be interpreted and adapted for each new time, problem, and person. In art, rules or principles are not laws *against* something the artist wishes to do; they are laws *for* doing it better. They are the same for all those who sing and dance, who build homes or places of worship, who write poetry and prose, and who make and use things for daily living; they guide those who teach and also those who learn. They are derived from natural laws. We do not invent new natural laws, but we do sometimes learn of natural laws which were always there without our being aware of them. Each person must become aware of them by himself; he cannot memorize them. He must experience them.

While we know by analysis that what we call principles are enduring forms with that subtle correspondence of parts which is the chief mark of beauty, we find the exercise of these principles helps us but little; and yet we dare not neglect them. We have to trust to our own choice after all, and end with the simple belief that what pleases us is beautiful. Indeed, no other rule is of any use to us, and if we do but honestly please ourselves and make forms which genuinely give us pleasure, we shall find ourselves credited with a power of designing beautiful things.

This encouraging bit of advice was written in 1909 by Richard G. Hatton in *The Craftsman's Plant Book,* which was itself a collection of designer's source material with illustrations drawn as early as the year 1530. It was reprinted in paperbound edition in 1960. Apparently students of art have always been somewhat mystified by the so-called rules of art. Read and study the diagrams which follow, but do not try to memorize or copy them. Make your own experiments and find your own examples. Collect them, analyze them, enjoy them, but always return to your own work with an open mind.

a) Lines differ in character. These are bold. b) Lines vary in movement. These are controlled. c) Lines vary in their impact. These are weak.

The Element of Line

Our hands instinctively make innumerable, different kinds of lines: straight, curved, or combinations of the two (a). It is almost impossible to copy exactly a line someone else has made. Our eyes move along lines fast or slowly, smoothly or with difficulty; it depends upon how easy it is to stay on the track and upon whether we know in what direction to move.

We need a goal. Contrast along the line gives it direction and purpose (b). We do not enjoy lines which lead us weakly, get us confused, or give us no rest (c). A line can also be too easy to travel. Usually when lines feel limp, weak, or monotonous to make, they also look uninteresting. We welcome a change of pace, direction, spacing, softness or crispness, darkness or lightness.

(a)

(b)

(c)

a) and b) Two compositions of the same horizontals achieve different meaning. c) Upward and downward thrust of verticals unifies a wall panel. d) A church spire once thought lofty is lost in towering apartments.

Horizontal lines, usually associated with the earth, suggest stability and calm (a). They can also mean desolation or even swift relentless movement (b). It depends upon *where the contrast directs the eye.* Recurring verticals lend dignity, balance, and strength to other lines, especially when they lead upward. With contrast at the bottom they may suggest pressure, despair, or weakness (c).

Horizontals stabilize verticals, and verticals give thrust to horizontals (d). They work together better than they do separately. They are *complements.* They echo and strengthen the rectangular boundaries of a picture plane.

(a)

(b)

(c)

(d)

a) Oblique movement in these lines is controlled in direction by contrast. b) The lines above, changed in emphasis by tone, now suggest human figures. c) Lines felt within a solid form are controlled in direction by depth of cut.

When lines move obliquely, they seem to struggle, push, or climb; or they may subside, holding the eye back (a). It depends upon how fast we must move and in what direction. *Contrast makes them move.* They can mean balanced power, flight, or play. They sometimes express defeat, anger, confusion, or dread. One can easily imagine them as human figures in action, a way of thinking called *empathy* (b).

They are *dynamic.* They have no rest unless they oppose, intersect, or lean upon another. They are hard to hold within frames, on walls and floors. In sculpture they struggle inside the stone or wood (c). They thrive in plenty of space.

(a)

(b)

(c)

a) Spirals may be accented to move inward or outward. b) Spirals contained within a definite shape draw attention to its center. c) Interacting spirals support and enrich inner movement.

Lines which move spirally may seem to contract or to expand (a). It depends upon where the contrast is placed. They are *self-contained.* Placed within a regular shape, they give it life and movement (b). They help to hold attention in shapes which are too irregular. They may mean growth and energy, or an infinity of time. They may also suggest withdrawal, self-seeking, or inner confusion.

They move in a *crescendo* or *diminuendo* of space (c). A form whose axis is a spiral will climb, soar, and spin; or it will subside, constrict, or sink. Spirals never really end; they may turn within, reverse themselves, or rise to another plane.

(a)

(b)

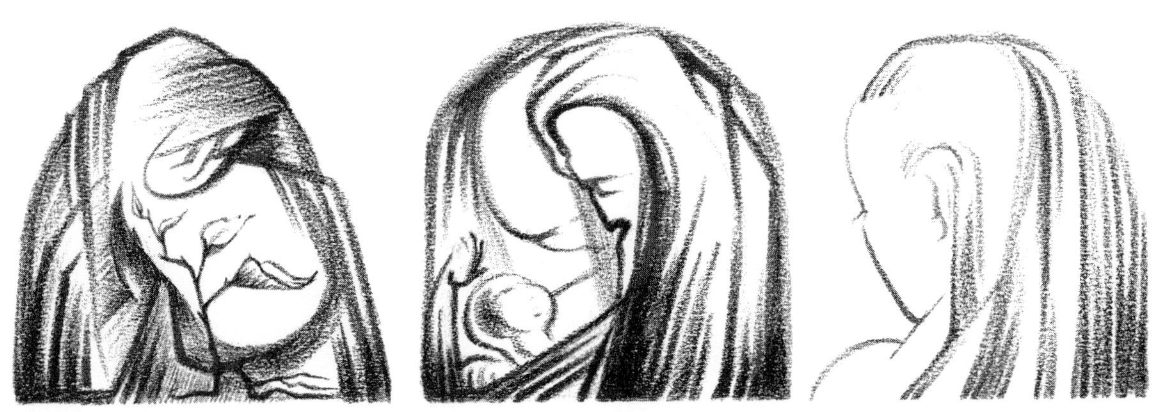

(c)

a) Stability is characteristic of the regular and geometric.
b) Some movement is implied without sacrificing unity.

The Elements of Shape and Form

The simplest shapes and forms are geometric and symmetrical (a). They are *self-contained* and easy to find with the eyes, even in confusing back grounds. They seem to stand still when their axes are horizontal or vertical; they float if their axes are oblique. They hold the eyes within, if there is good *contrast* at the center. If the outer edge is broken or overlapped by another shape, the eye will escape. Symmetrical regular forms suggest unity, safety, and inner strength, as in national and religious symbols.

Dividing a form symmetrically increases its stability (b). Regular geometric divisions of space make surfaces richer without weakening or distracting attention from structure. They are called *formal* because they are dignified and restrained.

(a)
(b)

Irregular shapes and forms are *more active.* They are seen best against a plain, orderly environment. The eye explores them, trying to find some connecting or parallel parts; for we prefer not to have them fall apart or appear pinched. The silhouette (a) may suggest many different things within (b), somewhat in the way we imagine forms in a cloud or a tree.

They seem to move in a definite direction if we can find an imaginary center or an axis. *Well-placed contrast* will strengthen this movement. Suggesting the natural and organic, their apparent freedom of movement stimulates our imagination.

Freely moving forms seem to need stable, regular ones to support them. They, in turn, set free the movement in geometric areas. The two work better together than alone.

Four irregular shapes take form with imaginative handling.

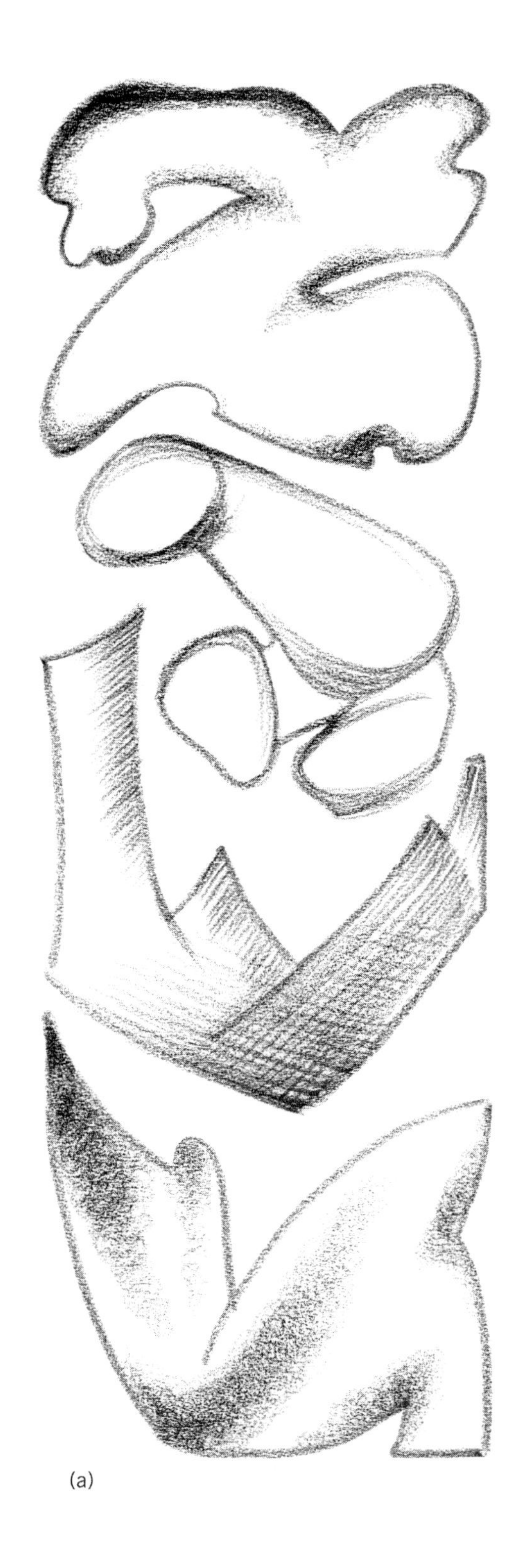

(a)

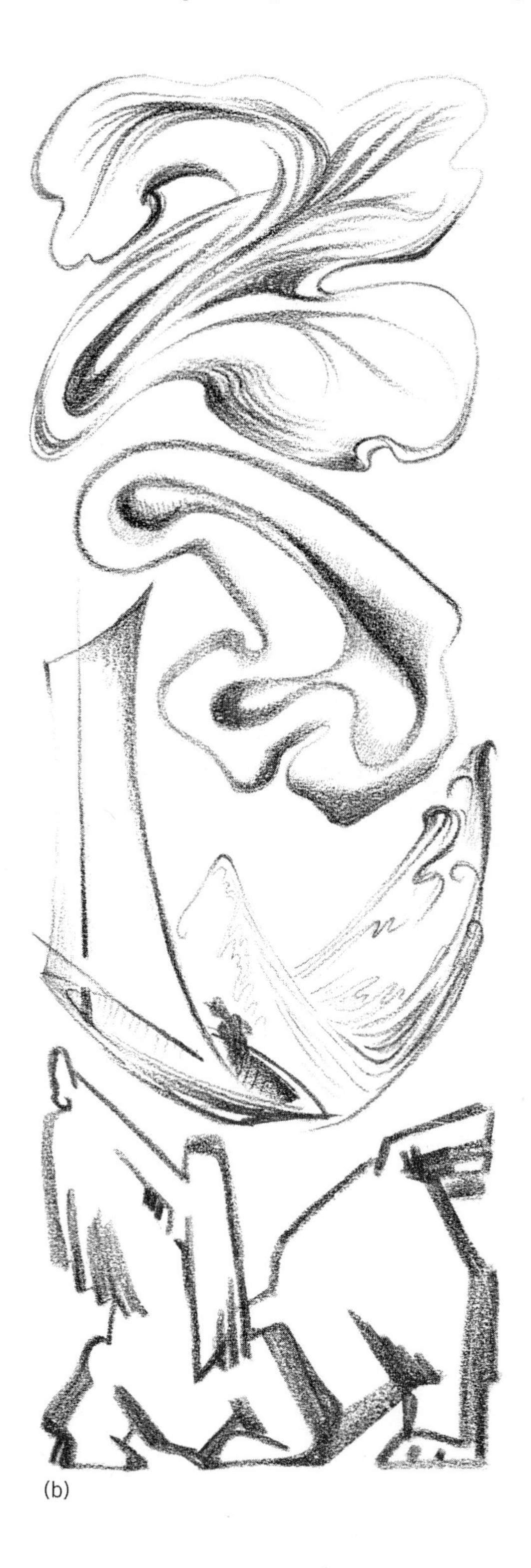

(b)

a) An orderly sequence of values creates a smooth movement. b) and c) An irregular value sequence moves toward a contrasted area. d) Triangles are identical in size. e) Value appears to change with background.

The Element of Tone

The eye can see many tones or shades between black and white. When they are placed in order, the eye travels swiftly and smoothly along them, always toward the end which contrasts the most with the background (a).

Irregular sequences of tone from dark to light also make the eye move, but not so directly. Our eyes eventually come to rest wherever the most contrast exists (b and c).

A white area on a black background will look larger than a black area of identical size on a white background, because white reflects light and seems to expand (d). A medium tone will look lighter against a dark background, but quite dark against a white background (e).

Visibility depends more on tone than on color. Contrasting an object with its background makes it easy to distinguish, but when numerous objects are equally strong in contrast, confusion and irritation result. Insufficient contrast can result in monotony or weakness.

(d)
(c)
(a)
(b)
(e)

Brush patterns with limited and full range of tones.

Tonality

We can choose to work in (a) *high key,* using only the lighter values; (b) *low key,* using only the darker tones; (c) *middle key,* using no very dark or very light tones; or (d) *full range,* using all the tones from black to white. In each case we reserve for the important center of attention the lightest we have against the darkest we have.

High key is often associated with spiritual, fanciful, or mysterious qualities. With sharp dark accents it takes on an incisive clarity.

Low key may suggest a somber mood, or luxurious depth. Light accents intensify the dark tones.

A *full range* of tones gives the greatest visibility to all forms in a composition and suggests the real rather than the imaginative. There is some danger of emphasizing all parts equally.

Choosing a tone pattern means deciding (1) how important you want each part, (2) how you want your eye to move, and (3) what tonality will express your idea best. Many painters make a tone pattern as a preliminary to using actual color. A sculptor's preliminary model serves the same purpose; he achieves different tones by depth of cut, by height of projections, and by textured surfaces.

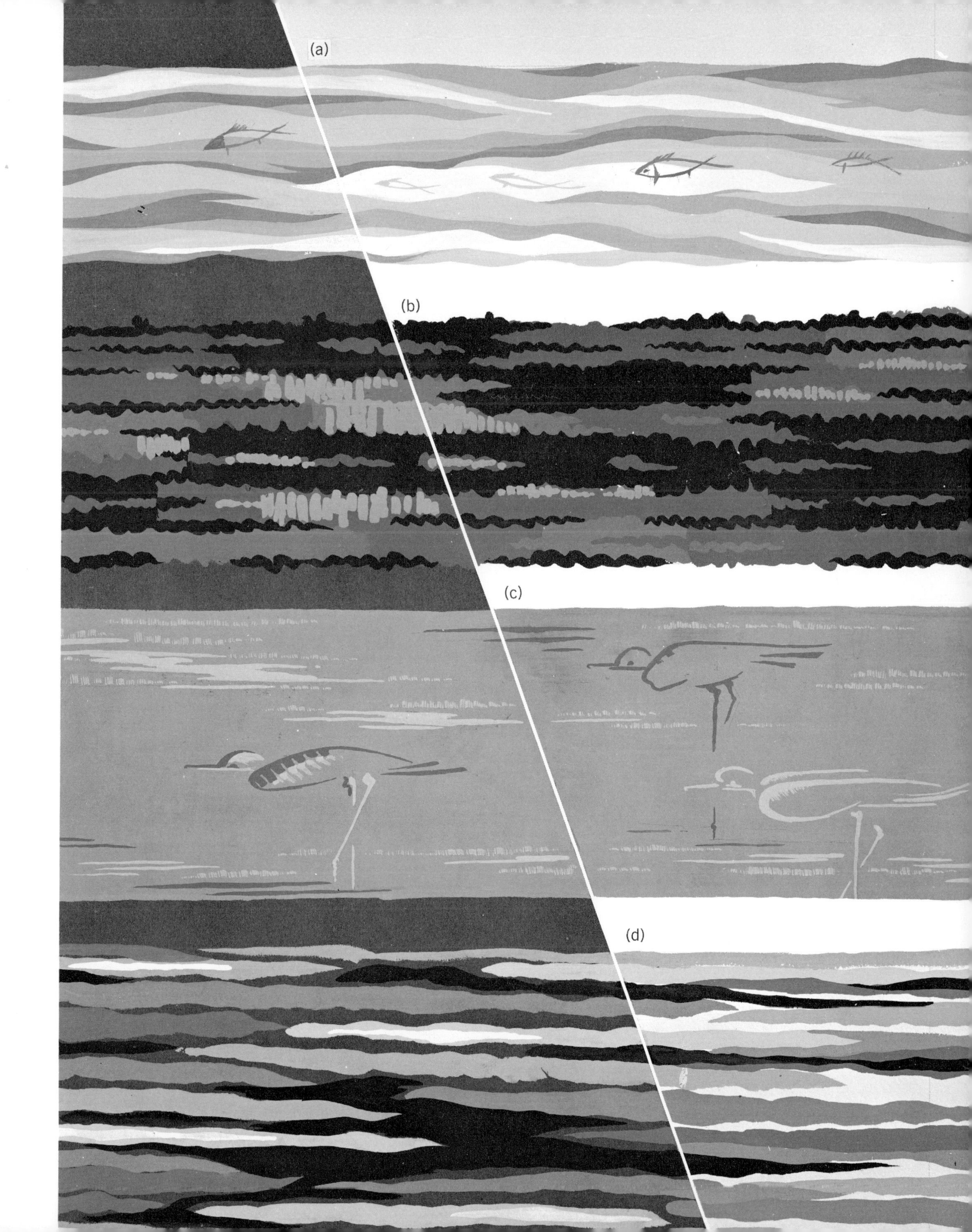
(a)
(b)
(c)
(d)

Rapid sketching with fine pen suggests a granite boulder.

The Element of Texture

Textures affect the appearance of a shape or form in essentially the same way as tones. They change the value of the area, create movement in the same way. Gradual changes make the eye move slowly; contrast of textures arrests it. Sameness of simulated or real textures help to unify a form.

Too many conflicting textures may distract the eye from an indicated path or contradict a well-lighted form. The natural complement of active textures is plainness or emptiness. Actual textures exist within the structure of the artist's materials and tools. A painter has the same responsibility as the sculptor in their use: to enhance the form. Simple forms and areas accept active textures best; for they tend to confuse the silhouette. Rough active textures suggest strength and vibrance; smooth, dull ones refinement, even softness or weakness; shiny surfaces may attract or repel: they are insistent. Symbolically, textures call forth our associations with actual touch.

Varying size and impact of pen stroke suggests depth as well as texture.

Sketch on a moving train calls for large simple forms.

Color directs eye movement and establishes form chiefly by value.

The Element of Color

Colors are distinguished from each other by their hue, their value, and their intensity. Review pages 106 to 110 of Chapter V. The eye moves through the hues most smoothly when they are arranged in value in the order found in the spectrum (a). Reversing the spectrum order (b) results in hues which are much less intense, but the eye still moves toward the end of strongest contrast with the background. In (c), keeping colors in order from light to dark, or vice versa, regardless of their hue also makes the eye move smoothly and helps to unify movement. In (d), (e), and (f), a form can be represented very simply by any succession of three to five values of a hue if the contrast is greatest at the point nearest the observer. If each major change of plane shows a corresponding difference in value, one can represent a form as in light and shadow. (g) A complete color sequence of pure hues will represent a sphere if each is used in its proper value relation to others. On a neutral ground the cool colors are reserved for the far side and the warm for the near side. Contrast of warm light against the cool dark determines that the eye will come to rest on the center of the sphere.

(a)
(c)
(d)
(b)
(e)
(f)
(g)

A design may have any desired color path, or possibly it may have several, each bringing the eye to rest by a contrast on a predetermined center of interest. Regular sequences as found in the spectrum (cool, dark, toward warm, light) guide the eye most smoothly. Irregular sequences are harder to follow but more interesting. Careful attention to the values will clarify the edges of each against the others. This is particularly important in reproduction, as in the printing of illustrations and textiles.

Natural phenomena suggest some universal reactions to color:

Orange yellow
  Sun, sand, gold, ripe grain
    Warmth, prosperity
Green yellow
  Decay, acid, slime
    Pestilence, death, fear, envy
Yellow red
  Fire, hot metal, setting sun
    Danger, violence, anger, dying
Red
  Blood, fire, fruit
    Courage, danger, manliness

Traditional associations suggest others:

Gold yellow
  Wealth, royalty, godliness
White
  Purity, youth, innocence, immortality
Black
  Death, menace, other-worldliness, authority, priestliness
Purple
  Royalty, self-sacrifice
Blue
  Truth, courage, education, health
Green
  Mystery, jealousy, medicine
Red
  Military, national banner

a) Monochromatic harmony—blue, gray, white, black. b) Analogous harmony—yellow, yellow green, yellow orange. c) Triad harmony—orange, red, purple blue, green yellow. d) A diagram of color harmonies in this illustration. e) Simple complementary harmony—blue, orange, black, gray orange. f) Split complementary harmony—blue green, orange red.

(a)
(b)
(c)
a
b
c
d
e
(d)
(e)
(f)

Triad—yellow green, red orange, blue purple.

Meanings

Certain combinations of color in the language of art have commonly accepted meanings: Monochromatic color schemes are simple, visible, and powerful if values are contrasted sufficiently. They may also express weakness, barrenness, endless waste, when values are close. If all areas are saturated intensely, they can be very irritating. Contrasting neutrals will control this.

Analogous color schemes suggest human earthy qualities if they are warm or the intellectual, spiritual, and mysterious if cool. They too can become saturated and therefore irritating. Neutrals used to relieve the saturation are usually tinged with the common color.

Triads express wholeness because they contain all three primary hues. Symbolically they are used for the Holy Trinity; for unity of body, mind, and spirit; and to express the idea of birth, death, and resurrection. Used in areas of equal intensity they mean dissension, revolution, or unreconcilable forces.

Complementary hues of equal intensity may express conflict, antagonism, or relentless opposition. They may also mean fulfillment as in male and female, poise, balance, affinity. It depends upon whether the artist reconciles them (achieves a balance or neutral dependence of the one on the other). Usually one must dominate, the other be subordinated.

Split complementary hues suggest more subtly the dominance and recessiveness of variable human relations: Aloneness, the prophetic, or the spiritual versus the earthy may be implied as well.

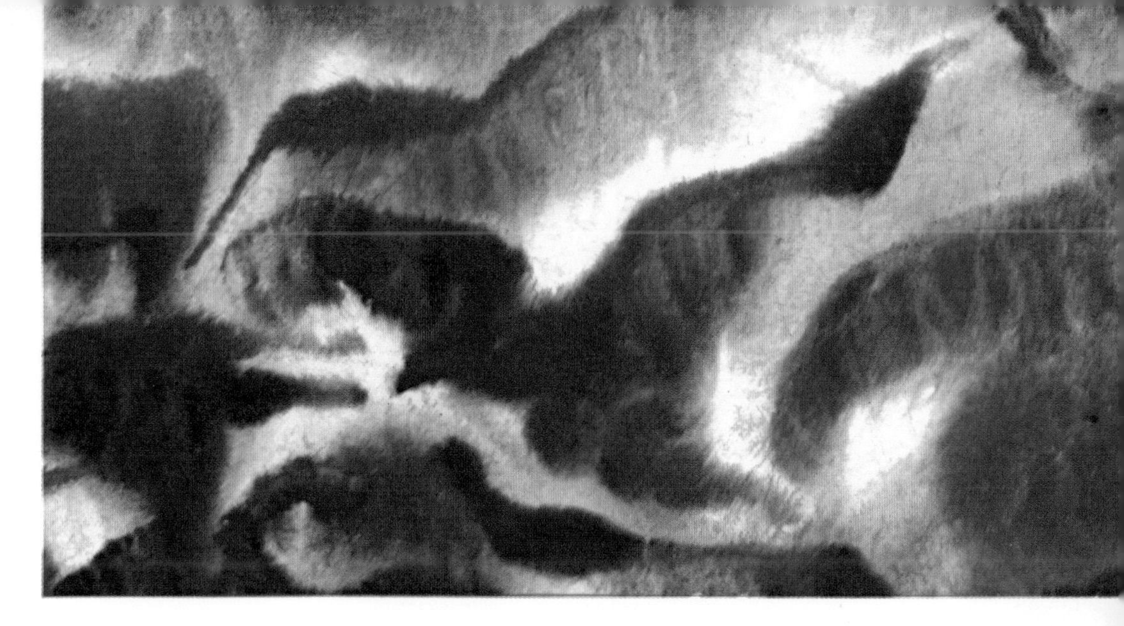

Triad—red, yellow, blue.

Split complement—red orange and red purple, blue green, yellow green.

Triple complement—orange yellow and blue purple, red and green, green yellow and purple blue.

UNITY, THE GOAL OF ART

The essential goal of all works of art is *unity,* the oneness or wholeness which we began to understand in nature. To attain unity visually in any particular thing, we must make it look, as well as be, structurally sound. We must clear away distractions. We must allow space for any real or implied movement within it to be free or to come to rest. The work may be composed of many parts or few; the same feeling of simple wholeness should be there. One might think, therefore, that the fewer the parts the more easily one would be able to attain this unity. This is not quite true. Most of our perceptions of line, shape, form, color, and texture are very complex indeed. To select a very few from so many is not a simple undertaking. Besides this, the idea we wish to convey, the materials we want to use, and the function we wish to fulfill may be composite rather than simple.

THE DESIGNER'S WORK

Let us consider one very practical example. We wish to make a chair. It must hold us comfortably, not break under our weight, withstand our sudden as well as our more studied movements, wear well, clean easily. It must be visually harmonious with our home, feel good to the touch, look well in shape, color, and texture. It must suit our own personal preferences as to style. Social and financial status will have some consideration. Still we must have just one chair. Obviously the simplest solution would be to sit on a round stool, but this does not satisfy us. The problem is to fulfill all of these other, more subtle demands we make without destroying the wholeness of the chair. This is the designer's job. For this purpose he has studied the arts of man and experimented with materials, tools, and processes.

We have discovered some of the visual characteristics of lines, shapes, forms, colors, and textures individually. Now we need to know what combinations tend to hold together visually or create unity in the final work. Some designing problems

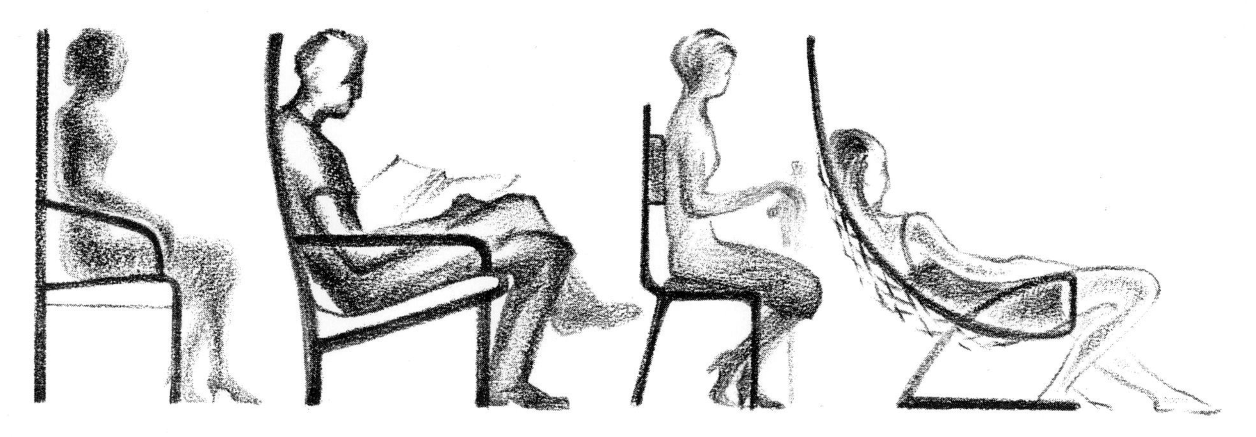

Some line considerations in designing a chair.

have certain requirements already present before we start to work. For example, in a chair the relation between seat, back, arms, and the height from the floor is dictated by the human figure. Whatever the other considerations may be, we have no choice but to follow these. In other designing problems, such as making a painting, we ourselves set all the requirements. Our subject or idea may to some extent resemble some actual thing, but regardless of this, our painting must itself be a unified whole. There is really no practical difference between designing a work of so-called fine art and making an article of the useful arts. All graphic and three-dimensional artists use the same visual elements and must combine them to produce effective work.

The diagrams which follow have an organization of their own which you need to understand before it can help you to make good choices. Read and study the diagrams. No one of these combinations is right or wrong. They are not like answers in an arithmetic book. They are only a few of the possible ways to combine things. Your answer or choice would depend upon the elements you have to use and what idea you are trying to express. Try to think of a practical example for each group of diagrams. For instances, in the line of a formal chair, the seat may be slightly slanted and the back and legs may be a continuous vertical. Between the back and legs the arms might become a transitional, more restrained curve. The upright line of leg and back would tend to dominate because of its position, length, and more rigid character. Your chair then would tend to express dignity or formality. But perhaps you want a less formal chair. You might choose a curve for the back as well as for the seat, more slant for both, and arms which give a firm horizontal-vertical area on which to balance your weight when you sit down or rise from the easy chair. In this case the curves would dominate and the stable but relatively small areas of the arms would tend to unify their movement. A chair intended for use at a desk or table would require vertical support in the lines. For lounging you might use a continuous line for the back, seat, and legs and accommodate the figure by the spring of the metal and hammock seat.

LOCATING ELEMENTS

There are four very obvious considerations about combining things which are almost as essential as the elements of line, shape, form, tone, color, and texture themselves. These are:

Position. Above or below, in front of or in back of, central or near the outer edge of our area of vision, and also the placing on a path of movement.

Size. Longer or shorter, larger or smaller than other parts or when compared with the whole, and with our area of vision.

Grouping. In contrast, overlapping or aloneness in respect to each other and in respect to the outer edge of the area of vision.

Movement. The speed or ease with which we can shift our attention from one part to another.

These are so much a part of everyone's experience of the visual world that we are almost unconscious of the effect they have on the unity of a total effect. A few simple examples should be sufficient to remind us of their usefulness.

Position

Any element (line, shape, form, tone, color, and texture) gathers strength:

1. From being placed in or near the center of our vision.
2. From being placed higher rather than lower than the geometric center of any enclosed area.
3. From being placed at the contrast end rather than at the beginning of any path of eye movement.

Size

1. In general, the longer or larger the line or area, the more attention it will claim.
2. When any line or area becomes too large to be focused upon clearly, it tends to lose importance.
3. When a line or area is nearly the size of an enclosing area, we tend to look within it rather than see its outer edge. (This can be true of a postage stamp as well as a ten-foot wall.)

Grouping

1. In general, when many things are scattered widely, we attach more importance to those which touch or overlap each other. The opposite statement is also true: when many things are touching or overlapping each other, we attach more importance to any which are free (surrounded by space).
2. The more firmly things parallel, contact, or overlap each other, the stronger their combined effect becomes.
3. The more nearly central the grouping the more importance it has.
4. When the group becomes too large to see as a whole, we tend to look within it.
5. When the group is joined to the edge of an enclosing area, it tends to become part of the foreground. We tend to see into space behind it.

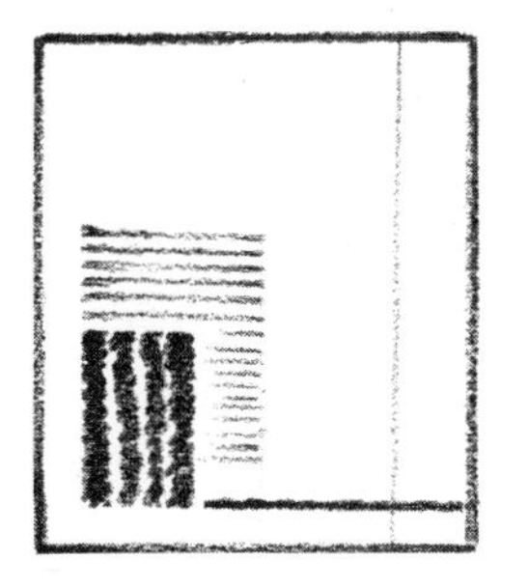
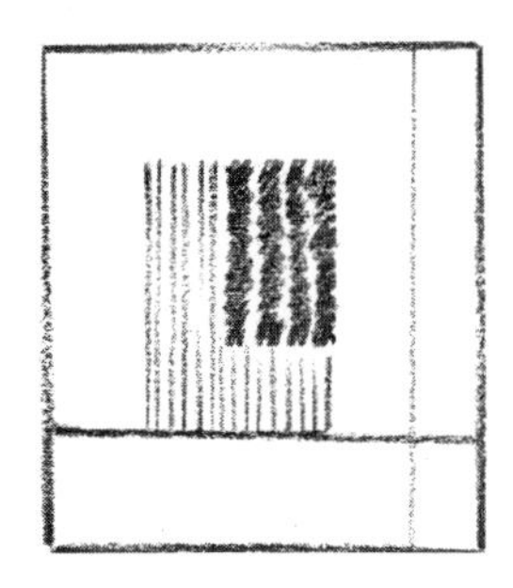

Position

Size

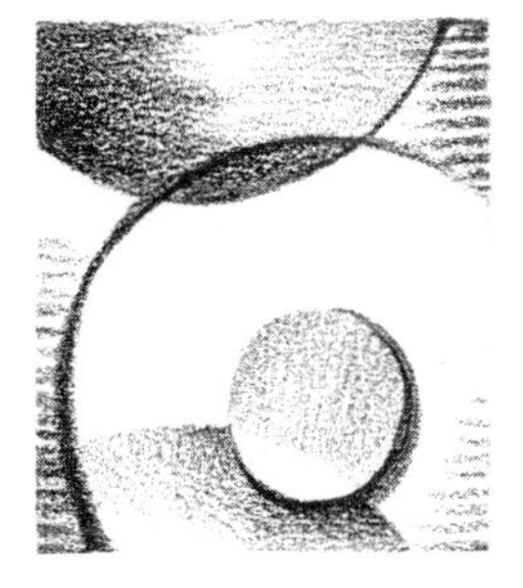

Grouping

Grouping

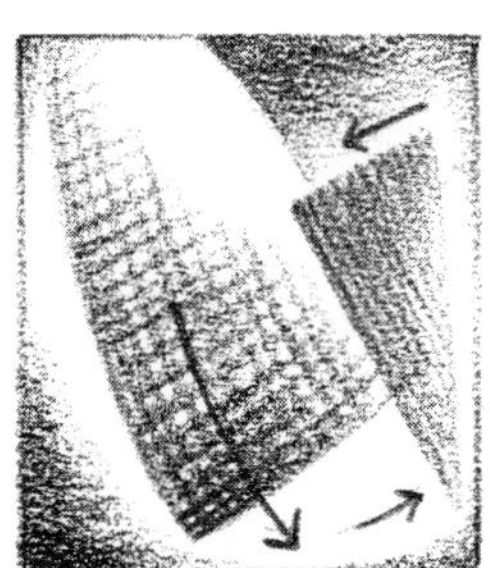

Movement

Movement

Movement

1. In general, movement excites our interest but stillness holds it. Both are necessary to see a thing whole. We must take in each of the parts by following its contours and sensing its tones and colors before we can gather the parts into a total perception.

2. The more directly we move around the silhouette and through the structural axis of a thing the more unified the thing becomes.

3. The more nearly centrally we move the stronger the whole.

4. Moving parallel to an enclosing area within it tends to unify its total effect.

5. Movements which turn within themselves or within an enclosing area tend to unify.

6. Movements which escape from an enclosing area tend to destroy unity unless the eye can easily return on the projected path or on another opposite movement.

THE MAJOR AND THE MINOR PARTS

We do not enjoy being uncertain about the real meaning of a work of art. Nor do we want to be confused about which part the artist considers first in importance. He is expecting us to catch his meaning with that as the keynote. One of the most difficult things which a designer must learn is to keep in mind the total effect while he is working intently upon some minor part. He often inadvertently makes the minor part more convincing than the really important part, thus destroying the whole effect. Then he must either tone it down, or return to his most important part and make it stronger. Of course, he could change his mind about what part he really wanted most important in the first place, but there is an unfortunate consequence to this. He has evaded the issue. He will become less and less able to do what he really wants to do. It is a "way out" but not a "way to."

It seems better to get into the habit of thinking and sketching to discover ways to combine lines, shapes, forms, colors, and textures. We can do this first of all by being very observant both of nature and of man's arts. Secondly, we must not be satisfied with our first sketches (tentative arrangements of ideas) until we have made enough trials to have a real choice between them.

COMBINING ELEMENTS

When we undertake to put together several visual elements (line, shapes, forms, tones, colors, and textures) we have only four main possibilities.

Repetition. We can use identical things.

Variation. We can use things which are basically alike but vary in some respects.

Opposition. We can use things which are entirely different from each other.

Transition. We can use some means of changing or adjusting the conflict.

HARMONY

Harmony is the product of all four of these ways. Perhaps thinking about human relations may help us to understand the relations between visual elements in a design. It is possible that the relations we sense in a work of art may also help us to understand those in life. For instance, we and the other members of our family have some characteristics which are identical and therefore help us to live as one: we are all human beings who need protection; we need food to exist; we need love and contact with others. We may even have practically identical appearance. More than likely, however, our needs and actual makeup are as varied as are our action and purposes. But they are enough alike that we can live in harmony. Our life together is by no means monotonous. The existence of the family itself came about because of the eternal principle of oppositeness, the mutual dependence of male and female, of older people and the young. The purposes of the family are harmoniously achieved by the balancing of these opposite and sometimes conflicting characteristics with each other. A great deal depends upon the "give and take", the ability of each to *change* or *adjust* to the other by conceding first importance sometimes to one, sometimes to another, depending upon the occasion. When one member insists upon first place at all times and under all circumstances, dominating the purposes of the family entirely, he is likely to find many occasions when he stands alone, and very weakly. If he is willing to accept their purposes and characteristics, they will support his own. Their existence as a unified family depends on one general purpose to which all can contribute. Somewhat in this way a work of art almost always contains some *repetitions,* some *variations,* some *oppositeness,* and some *transitions* or adjustments; but the artist makes them all work together *harmoniously* to express *one purpose.*

RHYTHM

Rhythm is also a product of the four ways of combining elements. It might be defined as harmonious movement which has a climax. We recognize it, too, in human decisions. Habits are the *repetitions.* Given the same needs and the same circumstances, we react in the same way. But habits have to be changed, for people do. We have new problems, new personal contacts, and new purposes. We vary our actions, harmoniously when we retain some old ways of thinking which still apply but change to take in the new ways. Sometimes we meet *opposition.* A drastic change must be made and we try to make this, too, help to further our main purpose. We may choose to discard the old and adopt a new direction. We may be able to compromise by accepting a *transition* between the two. Our growth, whether as a member of a family or as one person, depends upon how smoothly we make the necessary adjustments. Our own feeling of *unity or individuality* results from how completely we can use all our energies toward one dominant goal.

In a work of visual art the lines that seem to move, the tones and colors which induce our eyes to explore shape and form, and the textures which suggest material and weight all "move" us. They

Spiral movements enhance the prow and stern of a New Zealand canoe. (Courtesy of the University Museum of the University of Pennsylvania, Philadelphia, Pa.)

A rhythm, both vigorous and graceful, runs through the stripes of the Mexican's serape.

make us feel that sense of total aliveness and energy which we recognized in nature forms. A piece of sculpture may be a beautifully organized representation of a living, moving creature. It may also be an abstract form very full of fluid or sharply accented movements which do not represent anything you could call by name. It is still, but very alive. Let us consider another example, a textile design. It may be an intricately woven floral damask, of intertwined leaves, flowers, and stems which create a serpentine pattern; and yet we feel no break in the rhythmic whole. Or it may be a simple striped Mexican serape which can be thrown across the shoulders, hung from a saddle or wrapped around the whole person. The colors are so arranged that we always see it as a whole. The center has simple, bold contrast; the ends show a gradation of wide and narrow stripes which move smoothly toward the fringe. In texture the garment is made completely of native wools, some dyed, some in natural state. We find that its stripes seem to make every move of the wearer more vigorous and more graceful. Both the damask and the serape are rhythmic wholes.

We are speaking of the same rhythm as the musician uses, but in visual terms. As it is with music, rhythms may be quick, sharp, heavy, flowing, and so forth. Some are easy to follow, some more subtle. Wherever we find harmonious changes of eye movement, balanced lights and darks, colors, spaces, and forms that seem to fill space, we sense movement and wholeness at the same time. This is visual rhythm. Both harmony and rhythm are very familiar concepts to everyone.

The only reason why it is necessary to explain and define harmony and rhythm is that we shall need to concentrate upon visual means of attaining them. Like all the things which come naturally to us, we are often not conscious of them until we feel something is missing. And often when we do become self-conscious about them, they seem to desert us. Forget them, then. You have a dependable feeling for both, or you would hardly be interested in art.

RULES DISCOVERED BY AND FOR STUDENTS

Once in a while a teacher has an unsought for and unusual opportunity to give credit where it is certainly due. The pages which follow were initially composed by students. During their classroom experimenting, they seemed to feel the need of some guiding rules which would be more specific than general. They set down a few from personal experiences, discussed and reached tentative agreement on some. Others were regarded as too vague or too seldom applicable to be helpful and were therefore omitted. Some may be almost too obvious; but if so, they may serve to confirm what we all know to be true. They may give us more confidence to struggle with design problems which are not simple. Finding a valid general principle from experiences we have is called abstract thinking. It is a way of describing our own experiences in terms of everyone's. Try to make some of these experiences yours by making your own examples. Find your own rules.

a) Stripes of equal and of varying width create movement. b) Straight half-drop, and third-drop repeats; borders with reverse movements. c) The form and the function of an object determine how it is decorated. d) and e) Direct and indirect movement in a shield and a plate. f) Size and shape of a pouch call for change in repeated symbol. g) and h) Consideration of spacing will enhance a display.

Repetition of Line, Shape, and Form

Repeating identical regular lines and shapes at equal intervals tends to *unify* a surface, but we usually vary the intervals to *avoid monotony* (a). Irregular shapes when repeated create background spaces which vary the intervals sufficiently in size and shape (b).

Decorating a form by repeating its outside shape tends to *unify it* (c and f). Lines drawn directly from a center may tend to escape without a border (d). Indirect radiation usually needs no boundaries (e). Hanging a number of identically sized pictures calls for unequal spacing to avoid monotony (g). Unequally sized areas look better in groups, keeping the spaces between them equal (h). Those with greatest contrast are placed near the center or may be used to lead the eye toward a neighboring display.

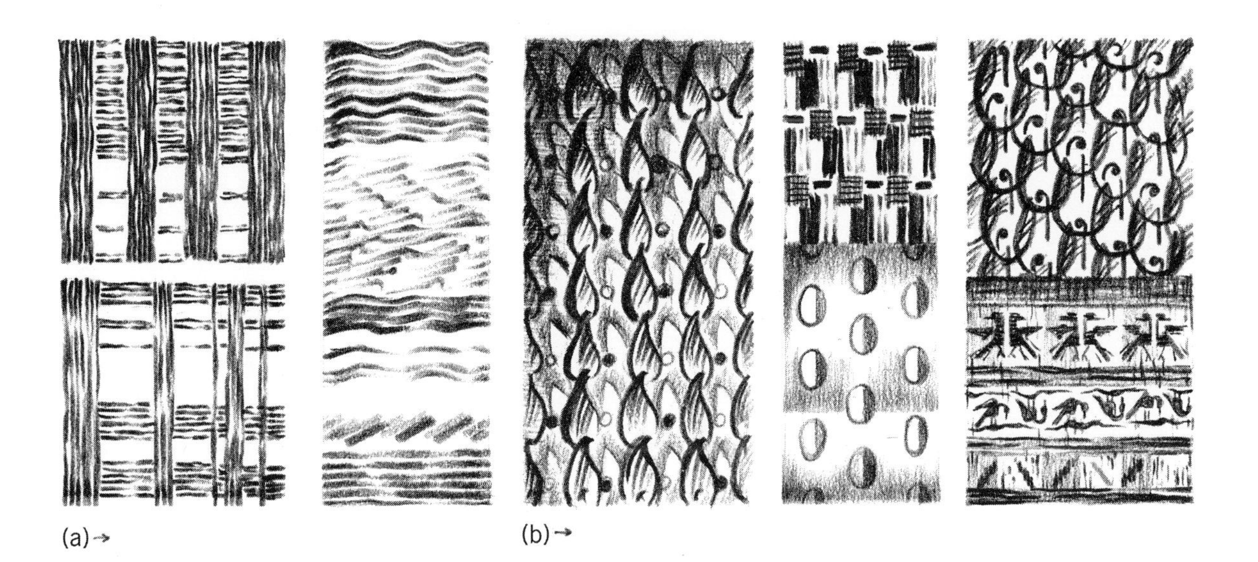
(a) →
(b) →

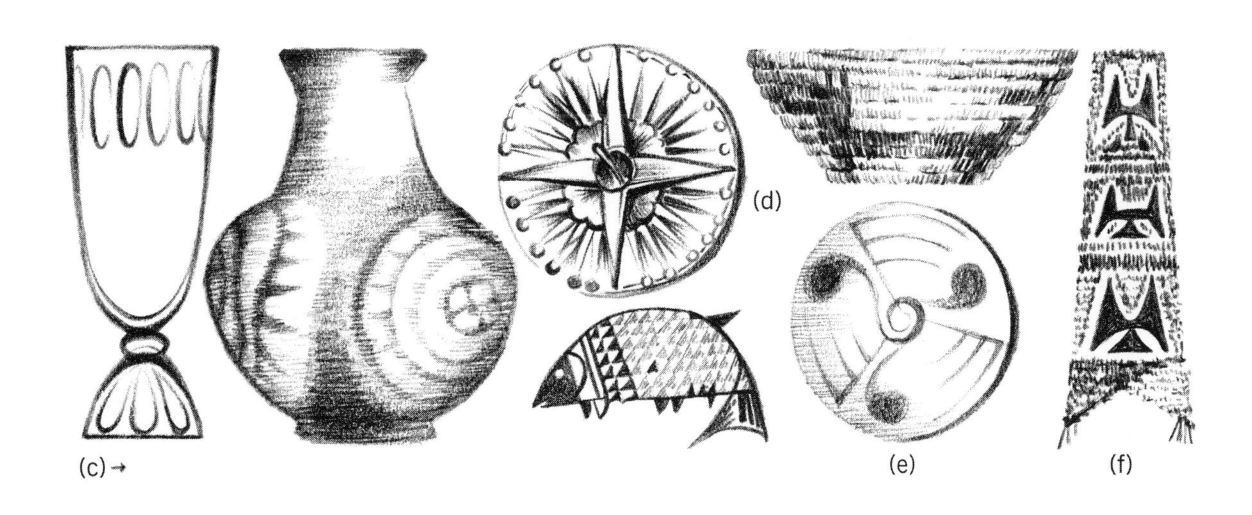
(c) →
(d)
(e)
(f)

Designs from Nature
6A
(g)

First grade's trip to the farm
(h)

Repetition of Texture

Highly decorative fences, cast in iron from molds made by master wood carvers, satisfied the love of repeated pattern still prevalent in the early industrial period. Products of the machine grad ually dominated twentieth century architecture by introducing the mechanical repetition of identical shapes, forms, and textures. The monotonous precision is beginning to be relieved by an occasional experiment with openings and closings, projections and recessions which have their origin in function as often as in visual interest. For instance, a screen of identical bricks provides effective shade for factory windows. An art gallery in which windows would interrupt display space and lighting uses large areas of unbroken texture as an effective foil for sculpture, mosaics, and paintings.

Fence and gate of cast iron, Oley, Pa.

a), b), and c) A simple experiment with similar forms. d) Company houses of different hues are unified in the morning sun. e) and f) Interior designers may "key in" paintings by judicious mounting.

Repetition of Color

Using the same hue, value, and intensity of color in regularly repeated lines, shapes, or forms makes them even more monotonous (a), but it will help to unify those which are irregularly spaced (b). Using the same value and/or intensity on adjoining areas lowers the visibility of contacting edges, even when hues are different. We tend to see the areas as one which can, therefore, strengthen the total effect (c). Using the same intervals of hue value and intensity on a path of movement tends to unify forms in light and shadow (d). Echoing the key color within a composition by repeating it in the frame or mount tends to unify and strengthen the whole (e and f).

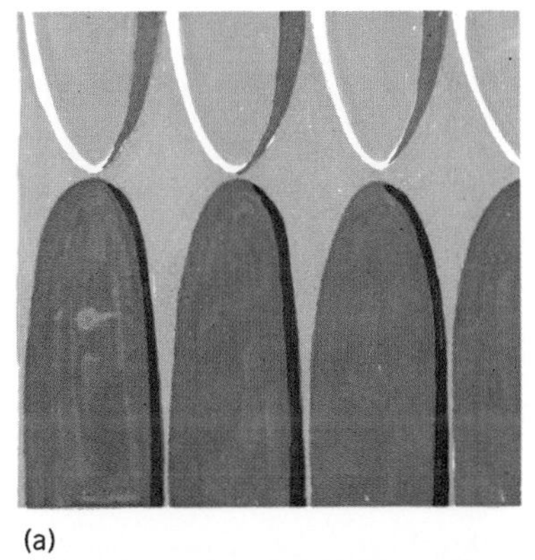
(a)

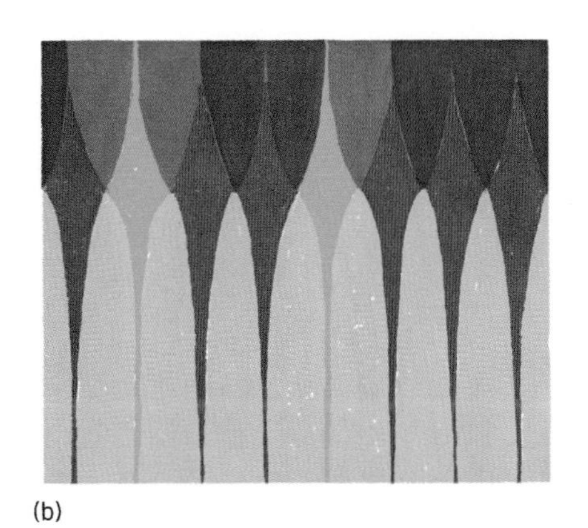
(b)

(c)

(d)

(e)

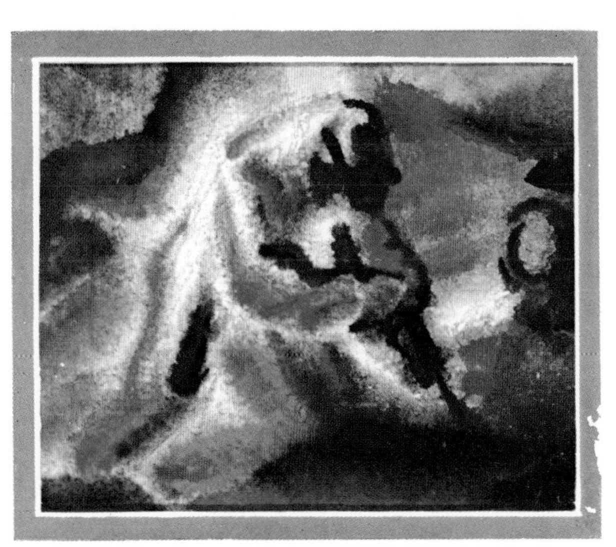
(f)

a) Similarity of character and direction harmonizes each group. b) Related shapes in nature fit together. c) Lily form varied in line and tone treatment.

Variation of Line, Shape, and Form

Lines that are of similar character, but not identical tend to hold together (a). Even at equal intervals they do not become monotonous. Keeping them nearly parallel helps to *unify their movement* in one dominant direction. Similar shapes tend to fit together better than entirely different ones (b). Connections in too many directions tend to confuse the eye.

The same form can be expressed in innumerable variations if the lines and shapes in each version are essentially the same in character (c). Keeping the axis of growth the same in all suggests the unity and growth seen in nature.

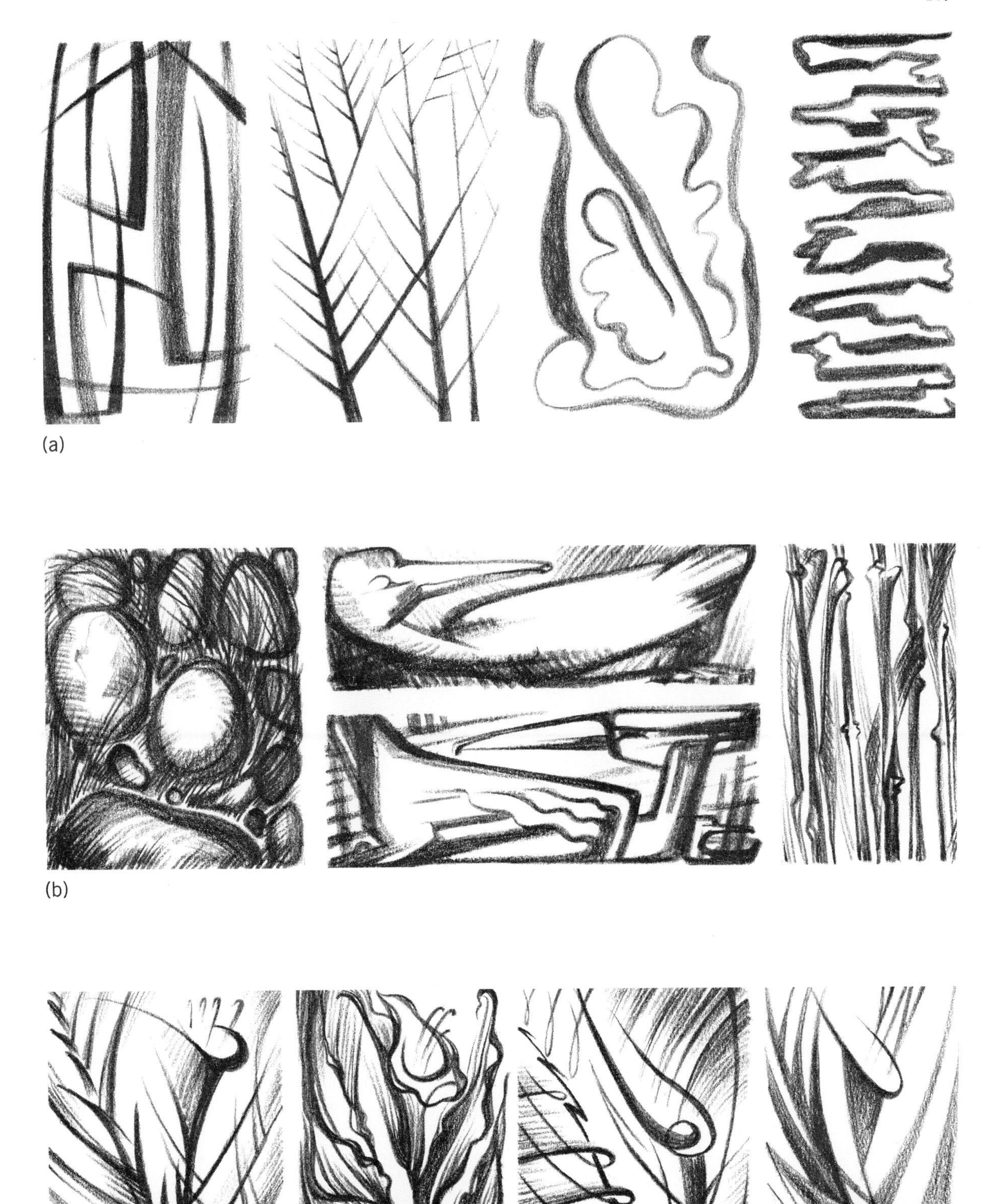

(a)

(b)

(c)

Sycamore bark peals off in successive layers as the tree matures.

Variation of Texture

Textures in nature vary with the environment and the stage of development of the living form, two good criteria for the use of textures in an art form. They may serve as a means of concealment; for changes in the surface may contradict the forms. Textural as well as color changes may serve to accent as well or to enhance a strategic part of a design in nature or man-made objects.

Live branches underlie the surf-beaten skeletons of ever-greens.

Rainwater pool on Nova Scotian granite shows the adaptation of living forms where the land and sea meet.

Sea forms suggest a wide range of hues and intensities in color.

Variation of Color

Colors which have some hue in common tend to hold together. A neutral accent will prevent the whole from looking saturated (a, c, and d). Colors which are of nearly the same value and/or the same intensity tend to hold together regardless of hue (b and e). Similar colors whose values and intensities are used in sequence follow a path of movement toward the end of strongest contrast. When similar hues get progressively warmer or cooler along a path of movement, the direction tends to be more unified, usually toward the warmer end.

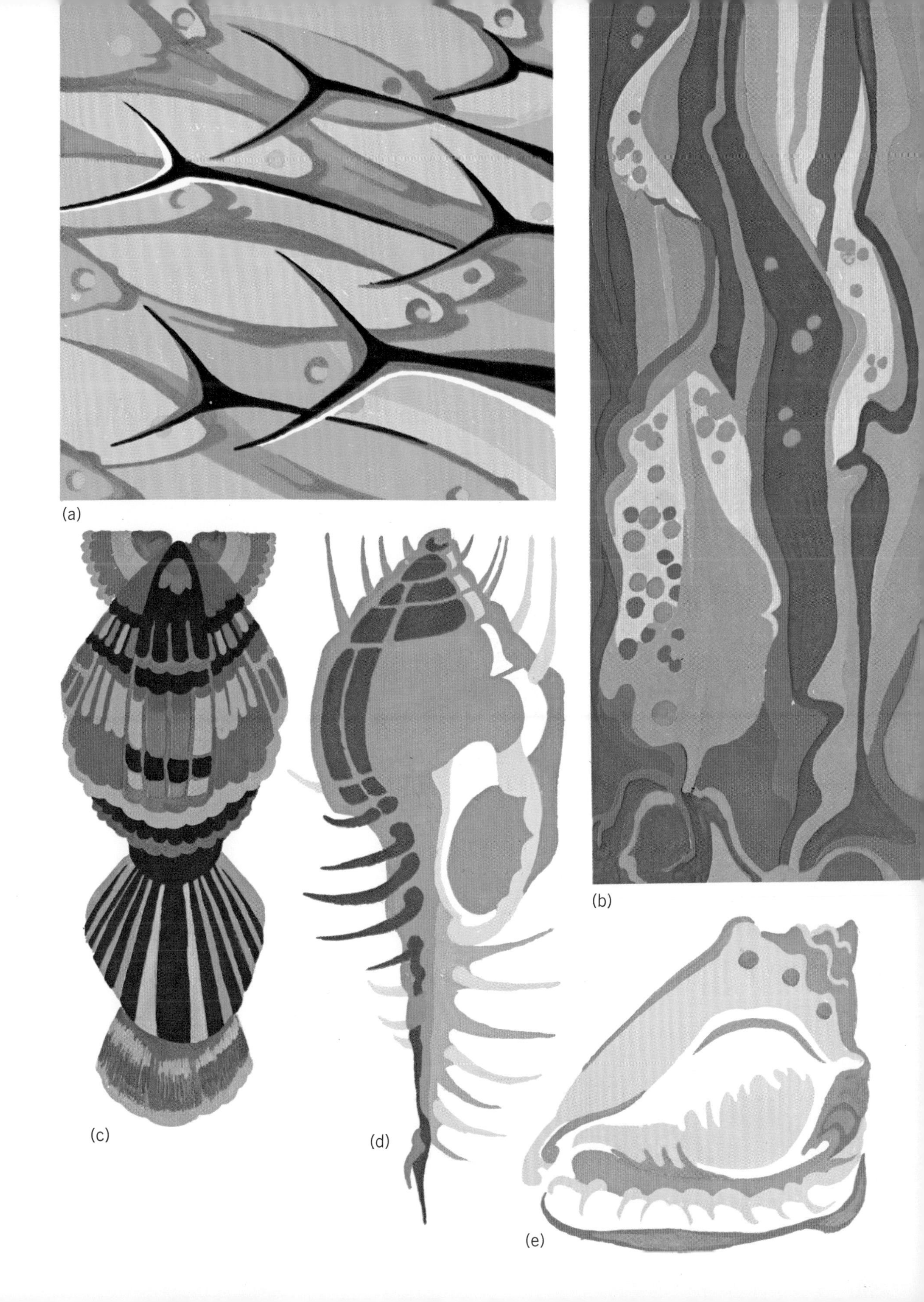
(a)
(b)
(c)
(d)
(e)

a) A vertical straight line and an active curve are reconciled.
b) Fruit shapes are held within square tiles by flowing movement, by a general tone, and by rectangular partitions.
c) Grouping and planned background areas relate the apple forms to the frame.

Opposition of Line, Area, and Form

Lines which are unlike in character create a conflict. To resolve it, *one must dominate decisively* (a). Contrasting the size and paralleling the direction of the lines will help to make one stronger. Giving one the central position and strong contrast will make it the more important. When the two intersect, the eye will escape on the line which carries the most interest.

Areas filled with conflicting shapes tend to disintegrate unless the outer edges are very strong (b). We often resort to heavy outline. If the axes of the shapes are parallel to each other or are a continuous line, they will seem better connected. Distorting the shapes to fit into sections which are like the outer shape will hold them together more firmly. In composing a group of objects, the *background shapes* (negative areas) have to be ordered also (c). We make them conform in direction both to the outer edge and to the inner forms.

(a)

(b)

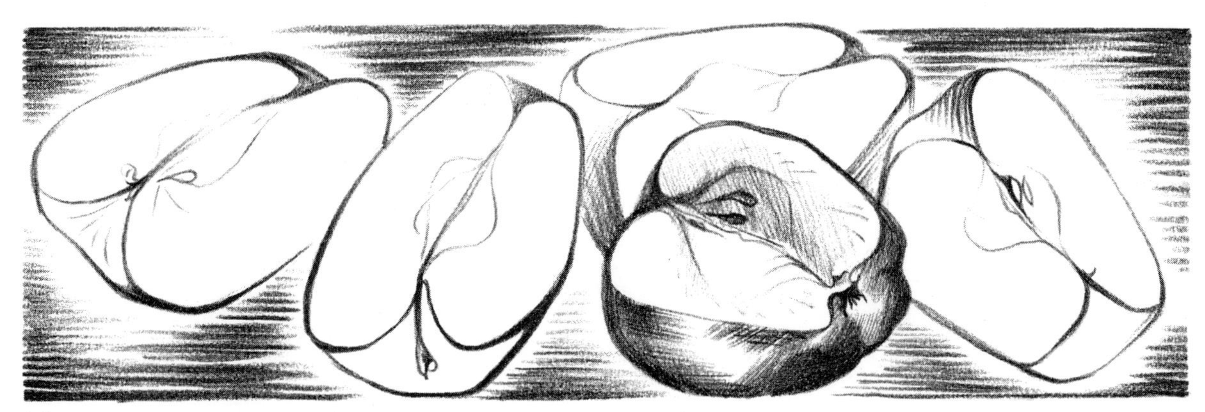

(c)

A roadside stand on the Pan American Highway in Mexico combines every available material.

Opposition of Texture

Man builds with the materials at hand and develops the skills he needs.

Contrasting textures depend for approval upon function as well as upon their beauty of light and shade, color, and tactile quality. Entirely different textures are easier to reconcile within a strong, simple form. Monotonous groupings of shapes and repetitious color combinations may be redeemed by contrasting surfaces without destroying structural wholeness.

Black, red, and buff cliffs along a Pennsylvania stream supplied the massive stones for this doorway at Virginville.

A gate in a southern colonial garden achieves a masterful pattern.

The simple needs of the Virginia pioneer were met by the superb craftsmanship of the English settlers.

Geometric symbols of unity and conflict exemplify some traditional solutions.

Opposition of Color

Complementary hues (see Prang and Munsell color wheels, Chapter V) create conflict when used in adjacent areas. One should be dominant in intensity and have the advantage of value contrast, if order is to be maintained (a). Primary triads are also oppositional in the sense that they have no common hue (d). A neutral (white, gray, or black) area or line placed between conflicting hues will make the peace (c and g). Conflicting hues may be lightened or darkened, or both made dull, to reduce their impact on each other (e and f). A large dull area of one hue near the center may be balanced by a small intense spot of the other farther away (i). When a large neutral area separates the contrasting hues, the eye will cross the intervening space (g). In (h) the intense background areas tend to project and the large neutral areas recede, a negative and positive illusion. Areas and forms which are of conflicting colors need a strong simple silhouette to keep the structure whole.

(a)
(b)
(c)
(d)
(e)
(f)
(g)
(h)
(i)

a) Tree structure suggests three ways to harmonize conflicting line directions. b) A symbol of eternity evolved from opposing tree shapes. c) Tree forms open to invite the eye within the frame. d) Upright trunks anchor the twisted trees in foreground, repeating the lines of the frame.)

Transition of Line, Shape, and Form

When two lines of equal strength intersect, we need a *bridge* between them or *some movement common to both* (a). They may be converged or made to grow from each other; eventually we must decide which should be the main stem, which the branch. We may add some lines of intermediate direction. When entirely unlike shapes must be reconciled, it helps to find a common direction, overlap them, or enclose them in a shape which is similar to both (b). The cypress and almond trees found in Persian silks were combined in this way in the Indian woven shawl and later imitated in English paisley.

Irregular objects pictured within a frame must often be reconciled to it by lines and shapes which gradually become *more nearly rectangular near the edges* (c). Usually when lines in a picture intersect the frame at sharp angles, the objects within must gradually *come to rest near the center* (d).

(a)

(b)

(c) (d)

Distinctive chairs combining walnut, cane, and silk. Modules of wood compose the wall panel. (Courtesy of John Stolz, Fleetwood, Pa.)

Transition of Texture

Large simple forms seem to need a transitional movement created by gradual changes in textural interest between the bulk and the accented part. Rougher surfaces tend to increase visual stability, suggesting rugged strength. Smoothing upper surfaces will make a heavy form seem lighter in weight. Textures which cut deeply into a surface tend to break it up; piercing mateials on an angle rather than directly allows the eye to enter on a change of plane. Combinations of unlike materials often call for a texture between them which has some of the qualities of both.

A bamboo forest suggested this experiment in translucency. (Tissue design by Jan Faust, Kutztown State College.)

Soil textures and some underground activity were the source here. (Tissue design by Mary Bleiler, Kutztown State College.)

Color in nature is seldom simple as in decorative patterns.

Transition of Color

Complementary hues often need a softening value step between them; for when they are equally strong, all movement stops (a). The eye will bridge the space between two unlike colors if one is repeated within the other with sufficient emphasis (b). The simplest transition is achieved by closely related colors used in a value sequence (c). Two hues adjacent to each of the opposing colors make the transition more smooth (d).

(a)
(b)
(c)
(d)

PERSONAL MEANINGS AND THE CHOICES YOU MAKE

When an idea comes to us, perhaps the first form in which we visualize it will not satisfy us. We tend to visualize ideas in ways which we associate, as others do, with art forms that already exist. To find our own way, we need not seek some bizarre and strange combination; rather, we need to look more deeply into what the idea means to us. Perhaps, again, an example would make clear what abstract words cannot. Let us consider for a moment that the idea we wish to express is war. Images of fighting men, flags, ammunition plants, a plane in flames, and bombs are often the first that come to mind. But suppose war to you personally means a monotonous factory job, the loss of a loved one, a glorious conquest, or a sin against humanity. How differently you might choose *your* subject matter! You might indeed use some of the usual images but in a personally meaningful way. To express your feeling that war is a monotonous and depressing business, the repetitious, heavy rhythm of dull-colored factory shapes would need to dominate over human figures. If war deprived you of one you loved, you might need intense and bitter conflict in all the visual elements you use. War as a glorious conquest would call for conflicting masses of color, shapes, and movements which are controlled by a tremendous dominance of one side over the other. But if you conceive of war as a sin against humanity, you will need some common denominator or likeness of the lines, colors, and forms of both the conquerors and the conquered, to imply that all humanity is one. You must choose the lines, shapes, forms, tones, colors, and textures to exactly express your idea. Then you will have your own expression of what war means.

RULES AND THE URGE TO CREATE

Even without studying rules and diagrams like these we could still create a really fine design. It is also possible to become skilled in combining lines, areas, forms, tones, colors, and textures in perfectly acceptable ways by rule without achieving the real purposes we had in mind. These were the basic urges, the reasons why we create in the first place: (1) to understand the nature of things, (2) to use the material world to improve and enrich our life, (3) to communicate with other human beings, (4) to belong to and (5) contribute to society, (6) to understand ourselves and to seek out the meaning of human life in relation to the divine plan. Let us not forget them.

Harmony of meanings and a crescendo of thought and of emotional power while working are even more essential than the visual harmony we attain. Indeed, the completeness of the original concept we have and the way it develops as we work almost brings to our minds the visual elements as we need them. Skills too improve while we work. Even if they did not improve, everyone recognizes complete sincerity of purpose. One would prefer a sincere, though clumsy, expression to a highly skilled performance which had no meaning and expressed no feeling.

THE STYLE OF THE ARTIST

The quality we call an artist's style is not based upon his technical mastery of his materials and tools. Nor is it his mastery of the illusion of form and perspective. It is not his recognizable subject material or his choice of nonobjective forms. His style is his personal way of stating what he alone has to say about his concept; his materials, tools, and his choices speak for him. Working in a completely concentrated way has much to do with achieving a personal style. When we feel that our idea is a valuable one, we have a genuine need for making it a reality. Nothing will interrupt or distract us.

When we choose materials and use tools which are right for our purpose, and work with love, we do not need to strain for individuality of style. It will be there. If it is really our own, it will not become a habitual mannerism; it will change and mature with us. A sincere personal and constantly maturing style is a unifying force in any kind of artwork. We feel this very strongly when we begin to recognize a certain artist's work as his, no matter where or when we see it. We seldom recognize a style as our own until we reach a high point of consistency. To learn to be consistent is by no means easy. It means that one must thoroughly understand the materials, tools, and processes with which one deals. It also means that every line, shape, form, color, and texture with which one begins a work will inevitably affect the finished whole. Consistency means that one part must never be thought of alone; that one part is as important to the other as each is to the growth of the whole, just as in nature forms we observed. For an example, let us suppose that we are illustrating a fantastic tale. We have visualized our hero and heroine in romantic and glamorous fashion, the very utmost in beauty and grace; our villain is very wicked indeed, and looks it. Shall the setting be familiarly prosaic, safe, commonplace? Of course not. Consistency in style, a sense of the rightness and appropriateness of each minor part would naturally suggest otherwise. For a different example, suppose that a painter has chosen for his theme the workers who stream through the gates of an industrial plant about five o'clock. He sees them as a mass of innumerable wedge-shaped forms not distinguishable as individual people. They are varied only by being larger, more bent in posture; some are in groups, some are alone. Of course, the buildings themselves are consistently geometric in style, but how shall he treat the faces and the landscaped trees around the office parking lot? (Treatment is an informal way of defining style.) Shall they all be geometrically simple? Or does the artist make his meaning clearer by making one or two real and poignant faces in that mass of faceless humanity? Shall he make one pathetic little shrub in full bloom or have all the shrubs painstakingly pruned? His decision will have to be consistent with what he wishes to say about industrial plants. There is, then, more to be learned than the basic properties of art elements and a few basic rules for putting the elements together. But the basic rules do help.

SUMMARY

This chapter has shown first of all that, while teaching, books, and examples of artwork are all useful, the learning takes place within the artist himself. Self-criticism and self-guidance are essential if one is to reach maturity in artwork, just as they are in other human activities. We have analyzed briefly the *elements* of line, shape, form, tone, color, and texture, and we have noted some of the meanings for them which are commonly accepted. We have suggested the word *unity* for the essential principle of art, the thing without which that peculiarly human activity would have no real reason for being. To satisfy our human urges to understand, to improve our lot, to communicate with others, to belong to and contribute to our society, to find ourselves and our place in human destiny, nothing accidental or commonplace will do. *Harmony* and *rhythm* are twin concepts of unity. We have taken time and thought for combining, harmoniously and rhythmically, the elements of visual beauty. These experiments dealt with four ways to use the elements together, by *repetition, variation, opposition,* and *transition*. We have discussed the development of an individual and personal *style* and how that in itself becomes a contributing factor in the unity of the whole. Principles and rules, however wise, are usually better when written by those who feel the need of them. They are still being written by every new generation of art-minded people. They are still being discovered by every artist for himself.

Discuss these topics with persons who do creative work and with teachers who have the ability to stimulate your imagination.

1. We have invented machines which can record, classify, and relate information of all kinds. In what way do they resemble our minds and what can we expect of our minds which machines cannot do?
2. Is it possible to plan and to execute a piece of artwork without revising or developing it as we work? Can we foresee exactly the finished product?
3. How are the exercises and experiments suggested in this chapter similar to the rules and principles of arithmetic and grammar?
4. What can systematic practice on preliminary sketches for artwork do to make the finished product more satisfying?
5. Do you find yourself more or less self-critical as your work matures? Why?
6. Why do athletes, dancers, and others who undergo systematic and rigorous physical training for their work say that it is possible to be overtrained? Does this have anything to do with imagination and the urge to win?
7. The principle of repetition seems to be as important to a musician as to a visual artist. What are his elements and how does he repeat them? How does he avoid monotony? How does he unify his compositions?
8. A novelist is writing about the same characters in various aspects of their life. What elements does he use? How does he make use of opposition to create interest in the plot?
9. How does a landscape gardener use transitional forms to make a building fit into its surroundings? What elements in his design will change over a period of years? Why does he particularly need to understand textures?
10. What evidences can you find that the essential principles of art are a necessary part of harmonious living in the political and social development of our nation?

Conclusion: A Definition of Design and the Designer's Purpose

To define art in words is as difficult as it is to explain any other perfectly natural and human act. Like having a baby, art is a thing which happens to human beings, as well as something which they do. Nevertheless, anyone who writes about art must try to say what design means to him.

To design, then, is to search for and to use the essential. The search begins in the perceptive mind of man in nature. His purpose is first to understand and then to communicate to others what he has learned of the essential character of all life; to fulfill essential human needs; and to play his own part well in the total plan. An artist is one who works with both love and skill. He will be humble in the seeking of what is essential, untiring in practice, and proud in the perfection of his work. In a lifetime devoted to art he will learn only a little of the inexhaustible design of nature, but he will discover much about himself. He will feel akin to all people; for many have searched in the same paths. The arts of man are one tangible evidence of what we know, so far, as truth.

Bibliography

From the wealth of writings on the subject of design, the author has chosen, and listed in chronological order, a few of the books which have most influenced the teaching of design not only in schools of art but also in the elementary and secondary schools of the United States. The excerpts quoted seem to express a prevailing mode of thinking, a pertinent definition, or an attitude toward the practice of design which has guided methods of art instruction since the beginning of this century.

1899 DOW, ARTHUR WESLEY. *Composition.* Garden City, N.Y.: Doubleday, Page & Company.

Composition—The "putting together" of lines, masses, and colors to make a harmony. Design, understood in its broad sense, is a better word but popular usage has restricted it to decoration.

The many different acts and processes combined in a work of art may be attacked and mastered one by one.

The approach to art through Structure is absolutely opposed to the time-honored approach through Imitation. . . . [The true relation between design and representation was lost.] Train the judgement, and the ability to draw grows naturally.

1900 CRANE, WALTER. *Line and Form.* London: George Bell & Sons.

It must never be forgotten that design is a growth which has its own stages of evolution in the mind answering to the evolution of the living forms of nature.

One cannot give any recipe for designing and no rules, principles, or methods can supply the place of imagination and fancy.

Memory, too, is an important and serviceable thing in designing . . . that selective kind of memory which, by constant and close observation, extracts and stores up the essential serviceable kind of facts for the designer: facts of form, of structure, of movement of figures, expressive lines, momentary or transitory effects of colour.

1905 JACKSON, FRANK G. *Decorative Design.* [An elementary textbook of principles and practice.] London: Chapman & Hall, Ltd.

If we disregard what has already been done, we must ever remain in artistic infancy; and again, if we close our eyes to the works of Nature, relying upon the treasures of the past, then our work will be retrogressive from the want of that vitality which the study of Nature alone can give.

1909 HATTON, RICHARD G. *The Craftsman's Plant Book.* London: Constable & Co., Ltd. New York: Dover Publications, Inc., 1960.

All design is synthesis—composition—the putting of forms together so that they conform to a demand which is made by the eye and the mind—the demand asserts itself at every turn in life's affairs. All people arrange things in orderly fashion. To do so is one of the most general of human actions. . . . Spite of the objection (by those critics who, not being producers, delight to find some paradoxical impassé to block the efforts of others) that art must be artless, one repeats what every productive artist knows, that design is conscious arrangement.

1919 KLEE, PAUL. *Paths of the Study of Nature [Wege des Naturstudiums].* Yearbook of the Staatliche Bauhaus Neimar 1919–1923. Translation by Sibyl Moholy-Nagy, *Pedagogical Sketchbook.*

For the artist communication with nature remains the most essential condition. The artist is human; himself nature; part of nature within natural space.

1934 DEWEY, JOHN. *Art as Experience.* New York: Minton, Balch & Co.

The sense of an extensive and underlying whole is the context of every experience, and it is the essence of sanity. . . . A work of art elicits and accentuates this quality of being a whole and of belonging to the larger, all-inclusive whole which is the universe in which we live . . . somehow, the work of art operates to deepen and to raise to great clarity that sense of an enveloping undefined whole that accompanies every normal experience.

To look at a work of art in order to see how well certain rules are observed and canons conformed to impoverishes perception. But to strive to note the ways in which certain conditions are fulfilled . . . sharpens esthetic perception and enriches its content.

1936 GROPIUS, WALTER. *The New Architecture and the Bauhaus.* New York: New York Museum of Modern Art. London: Faber & Faber, Ltd.

What we preached in practice was the common citizenship of all forms of creative work, and their logical interdependence on one another in the modern world. . . . The Bauhaus felt it had a double moral responsibility: to make its pupils fully conscious of the age they were living in; and to train them to turn their native intelligence and the knowledge they received, to practical account in the design of typeforms which would be the direct expression of that consciousness. . . . Our ambition was to rouse the creative artist from his other-worldliness and reintegrate him into the work-a-day world of realities and at the same time to broaden and humanize the rigid almost exclusively material mind of the business man.

1937 BEST-MAUGARD, ADOLFO. *A Method for Creative Design.* New York: Alfred A. Knopf, Inc.

Nature is necessary to the designer, but not to the design. All the arts are ways of experimenting to find the key to universal law. This new method recognizes that the development of individual artistic perception is the recapitulation of the evolving artistic perception of the race.

1940 TEAGUE, WALTER DORWIN. *Design This Day: The Technique of Order in the Machine Age.* New York: Harcourt, Brace & Company, Inc.

To separate the variables from the constants in all design and so in our own special problems . . . calls for an analysis of the art of design. The art of enforcing order on material substances for our service and satisfaction. . . . We shall begin with the first source of all form, which is also an incessant variable and this is the principle of Fitness (to Function, Materials, Techniques); the application of Laws of Relationships.

1940 VAN DOREN, HAROLD. *Industrial Design,* 1940–1954. New York: McGraw-Hill Book Company, Inc.

Design, from the strictly visual point of view, is fundamentally the art of using line, form, tone, color and texture to arouse an emotional reaction in the beholder. . . . Effective design cannot be created without emotion, and it will not be communicable to others unless it is present in the designer during the act of creation.

1941 GRAVES, MAITLAND E. *The Art of Color and Design.* New York: McGraw-Hill Book Company, Inc.

All visual design may be reduced to seven elements . . . the building blocks of art structure. When an artist organizes these elements he creates Form. . . . Art is man-made Order. . . . The Elements and the Principles of design that govern their relationship are, therefore, real and powerful forces.

1943 READ, HERBERT. *Education Through Art.* London: Faber & Faber, Ltd.

The purpose of composition is to organize all the physical elements which make up a work of art into a coherent pattern, pleasing to the senses.

1945 HONEY, WILLIAM BOWYER. *Science and the Creative Arts.* London: Faber & Faber, Ltd.

For the individual, as distinct from society, the matter [the conviction that man would not abolish the universal mutual struggle for survival] is of even greater importance. Just as an intuition of goodness is needed to justify the collective liberation of individuals from the mutually competitive and predatory struggle, so intuitions of beauty and truth give a sense of the greatest values in personal experience; they too give a sense of liberation, but a liberation of "the spirit." Education and its object, for which no better name than culture has yet been found, are concerned with the search for and establishment of these things.

[Re: Design in a building] Rational design and construction in these functional senses are not enough by themselves to produce a work of art. That sense of style in contriving

harmony and rhythm in proportions and contrast in colour and texture and in the management of lights and shadows, voids and solids—not necessarily in a traditional way, but adventurously—constitutes the art of the architect.

1946 Bradley, Charles B. *Design in the Industrial Arts.* Peoria, Ill.: Manual Arts Press.

Art is the combination of skill and taste in the production of forms of beauty and use. . . . Design is the plan originating in the mind, and consummated in the finished object produced.

Art in any utilitarian object is something inherent in its conception, design, material and construction rather than something which is applied in its final stages of finish. . . . The true approach to good design is through structure.

1946 Kandinsky, Wassily. *On the Spiritual in Art.* New York: Solomon R. Guggenheim Foundation.

Today the artist cannot progress exclusively with purely abstract forms as these forms are not sufficiently precise. Limiting oneself to the un-precise, it deprives one of possibilities, excluding the purely human and therefore weakening the power of expression. . . . For better or worse, the artist succumbs to his eye; his hands, more artistic than his soul, aim beyond photographic objectives. The genuine artist, discontented with an inventory of the material objects, definitely seeks to give the object an expression, something once called "idealization," then "stylization," and tomorrow something different.

1947 Lowenfeld, Viktor. *Creative and Mental Growth.* New York: The Macmillan Company.

The innate sense for design thus seemingly has its roots in the very same psychological urge for mastery and self-assurance that manifests itself in repetitions. . . . It is his innate space concept and his innate desire for repeating form concept (schema) that make the child an "innate designer."

In recognizing this unity of composition as the highest form of organization and economy in which nothing can be changed without doing harm to the whole, an important means of criticism is placed in the hands of the art educator. . . . In both (the visual and the haptic) realms of art, however, he will not succeed if he does not place the individual above the rules, if he does not consider unity of composition the most integrated outcome of personality and creation.

1949 Wright, Frank Lloyd. *Genius and the Mobocracy.* New York: Duell, Sloan & Pearce, Inc.

Organic building is natural building: construction proceeding harmoniously from the nature of a planned or organized inside outward to a consistent outside.

1950 Rathbone, Richard Adams. *Introduction to Functional Design.* New York: McGraw-Hill Book Company, Inc.

A work of art should have merit in three respects:
1. Conception of viewpoint which must be genuine and of sufficient worth to survive the test of time.

2. Skill in handling the means by which the idea is expressed.
3. A definite function for which the order is planned and toward which the skill is directed for a practical use.

1950 FELDSTED, C. J. *Design Fundamentals.* New York: Pitman Publishing Corporation.

Lack of design is chaos. Design is order. . . . design is that order of harmony, balance, rhythm without which there could be no art. . . . It is the basic orderly structure through which expression finds its form.

1951 NEWTON, NORMAN T. *An Approach to Design.* Reading, Mass.: Addison-Wesley Publishing Company, Inc.

Let us look for the structure of what is involved—for order and relations. A basic ingredient in design is sound evaluation. . . . This will depend in large measure if not entirely on one's own first hand experience.

A designer will benefit from sharpening his own awareness of sensory aspects of his environment. A designer needs to be oriented to change rather than to rigid fixities. . . . He works in and with the time and place confronting him. Look upon design as an active process of the human nervous system . . . a creative way in which some humans work in order to enhance the lives of other humans. Design can be good only insofar as it does good. . . . In every problem of design the most fundamental issue is some human need.

1952 MUMFORD, LEWIS. *Art and Technics.* New York: Columbia University Press.

The greatest developments to be expected of technics in future . . . will not be . . . in universalizing . . . the American system of mass production: on the contrary it will consist of using machines on a human scale, directly under human control, to fulfill with more exquisite adaptation, with a higher refinement of skill, the human needs that are to be served.

We are not prisoners of the machine, or if we are, we built the prison . . . the burden of renewal lies upon us. . . . We shall reshape our life to a new pattern, aided by all the resources that art and technics now place in our hands. . . . Our dreams will again become benign and open to rational disciples . . . our arts will recover form, structure and meaning.

1954 ARNHEIM, RUDOLF. *Art and Visual Perception: A Psychology of the Creative Eye.* Los Angeles: University of California Press.

The delicate balance of all our powers—which alone permits us to live fully and to work well . . . is upset, not only when the intellect interferes with intuition, but also when feeling dislodges reason . . . modern man must live with unprecedented self-awareness. Far from being a mechanical recording of sensory elements, vision turned out to be a truly creative grasp of reality, imaginative, inventive, shrewd, and beautiful. . . . A work of art is a statement about the nature of reality . . . the necessary and final solution of the problem of how to organize a reality pattern of given characteristics.

1956 GOMBRICK, ERNST HANS. *Art and Illustration: A Study in the Psychology of Pictorial Representation.* New York: Bollinger Foundation (Pantheon Books).

We have come to realize more and more . . . that we can never neatly separate what we see from what we know. . . . Do what we may, we shall always have to make a beginning with something like "conventional" lines or forms. The "Egyptian" in us can be suppressed, but he can never be quite defeated. . . . "The Egyptian" in us ultimately stands for the active mind, for that "effort after meaning" which cannot be defeated without our world collapsing into total ambiguity.

1957 JARRETT, JAMES L. *The Quest for Beauty.* Englewood Cliffs, N.J.: Prentice-Hall, Inc.

[Re: "form"] The psychological approach to principles of form is especially valuable in tying together qualities of the work of art and qualities of the perceptual experience. . . . Whatever else characterizes a complete aesthetic experience, the phrase unity-in-variety seems to us inescapable.

1958 DE FRANCESCO, ITALO. *Art Education, Its Means and Ends.* New York: Harper & Row, Publishers, Incorporated.

Good design is not accidental. It is founded on at least three types of activity: first, study and research; second, original and spontaneous visualization of an experimental nature in the best sense; third, a planned approach to the design for a specific purpose. These activities presuppose significant and well-understood prior experimentation with materials . . . in the transition from the idea to the product, the pupil grasps the true significance and universality of principles and elements.

1959 WOLCHONOK, LOUIS. *The Art of Three Dimensional Design.* New York: Harper & Row, Publishers, Incorporated.

Only after (the designer) is adequately prepared can he bring into play the imagination, the technical skill, the daring that each design must have in order to do justice to its creator.

1960 GUGGENHEIMER, RICHARD H. *Creative Vision for Art and Life.*

The methods of the brain do not seem best adapted to comprehending the ultimate nature of the life process. . . . Man has an insatiable yearning to overcome this handicap. . . . Every time he experiences what he calls beautiful he has a sense of growth in the direction of integration. The sense of the beautiful seems to be directly referable to the quality of wholeness or relatedness that underlies the apparently separable parts and incidents of being. Some people call it design. Some call it meaning. Some consider it the apprehension of unity out of multiplicity.

1960 KRUM, JOSEPHINE R. *Hand-Built Pottery.* Scranton, Pa.: International Textbook Company.

Design is so deeply inbedded in the forming process that it cannot and should not be considered a thing to be taught separately or prior to the actual experience with the material. . . . To set up specific problems in line, proportion, emphasis, etc. seems to defeat the main purpose of both the teacher and the student. That purpose is to make an object which is unified and consistent in its whole appearance and its construction.

1960 BALDINGER, WALLACE S. *The Visual Arts.* New York: Holt, Rinehart and Winston, Inc.

The work of art is a unity and every element it contains needs the help of other elements to bring it into being, even as nerve cells need the help of blood cells and other cells to make the body function. . . . Principles of design are not mere shortcuts to creation, rules to be memorized and applied without thinking and feeling. They codify ways of working which, artists have learned through centuries of trial and error, are more apt than other ways to succeed.

1960 OCVIRK, OTTO, ROBERT BONE, ROBERT STINSON, and PHILIP WIGG. *Art Fundamentals, Theory and Practice.* Dubuque, Iowa: William C. Brown Company, 1960, 1962.

By form we mean the totality of the work of art. Form is the organization (design) of all elements which make up the work of art . . . the use made of the visual devices available to the artist.

1961 LOWRY, BATES. *The Visual Experience.* New York: Harry N. Abrams, Inc.

What is real for us at the moment at which we see it is not what was real for the artist at the moment he painted it, and, even for the artist, the experience of seeing the finished painting is not the same as the experience that the painting records, for the painting is what the artist was at the time that he painted it.

The more the language of visual forms becomes our own, the closer we approach the point where the very idea of the artist can also be said to become our own.

1961 MCFEE, JUNE KING. *Preparation for Art.* San Francisco: Wadsworth Publishing Co., Inc.

These principles (Balance, Rhythm, Dynamic Unity and Integration) are some of the qualities of design, those qualities that give man a sense of resolution and beauty. Design is the language of the arts.

1961 BEITLER, ETHEL JANE, and BILL LOCKHART. *Design for You.* New York: John Wiley & Sons, Inc.

Design: an organization of the elements of design with two aims, order and beauty. Understanding (of design) cannot take place until there is first an awareness . . . the mechanical act of seeing in itself is not awareness. . . . Awareness results in conscious perceiving . . . including seeing and feeling but also registering the response from your total being.

1961 ANDERSON, DONALD. *Elements of Design.* New York: Holt, Rinehart and Winston.

An artist is one who, manipulating such raw materials as clay, wire, pigment data, sounds, words, numbers . . . transforms them into cohesive structures on a higher level of significance.

1961 SCHINNELLER, J. A. *Art: Search and Self-Discovery.* Scranton, Pa.: International Textbook Company.

To understand design, the terms "function," "simplicity," "directness," and "originality" must be considered; for they are prime requisites. Design is a process of building by selecting the elements of the visual arts—line, value, color and texture—and arranging them in unified two- or three-dimensional structures. It is basic to all creative activities because it relates to organizational methods in all areas of the arts.

1962 HALAS, JOHN, and ROGER MANVELL. *Design in Motion.* New York: Hastings House, Publishers, Inc.

We live physically in a world of four dimensions, three of which can be measured with a tape-measure and the fourth with a watch. The painter who wants to extend his art in time as well as in space is following a natural instinct.

Index